HOLIDAY & CELEBRATIONS

HOMEMADE FOR THE HOLIDAYS

There's no place like it: Family and friends gathered around the table, smiling and laughing—and eating delicious homemade food. The autumn and winter seasons present the perfect opportunities for not only traditional holiday meals, but also outside-the-box events like family game nights and a tropical Christmas party. But don't forget to celebrate the rest of the year, too! Whether you're interested in a spooky Halloween night, a Fourth of July barbecue or a spring garden party, there's a fresh idea for every occasion in *Taste of Home Holiday & Celebrations* cookbook. With 277 recipes, 22 events, helpful timelines, creative gift-giving ideas and simple crafts, you'll have everything you need to create your most memorable holiday yet. So, pop open the Champagne. It's time to celebrate!

© 2019 RDA Enthusiast Brands, LLC.
1610 N. 2nd St., Suite 102,
Milwaukee WI 53212-3906

All rights reserved. Taste of Home
is a registered trademark of
RDA Enthusiast Brands, LLC.

Visit us at tasteofhome.com for other
Taste of Home books and products.

**International Standard
Book Numbers:**
D 978-1-61765-903-4
U 978-1-61765-904-1

**International Standard
Serial Number:**
1535-2781

Component Numbers:
D 118000056H
U 118000058H

Executive Editor: Mark Hagen
Senior Art Director: Raeann Thompson
Editor: Amy Glander
Assistant Art Director:
Courtney Lovetere
Designer: Jazmin Delgado
Senior Copy Editor: Dulcie Shoener
Senior Food Editor:
Peggy Woodward, RDN
Editorial Intern: Daniella Peters

Cover Photography:
Photographer: Dan Roberts
Set Stylist: Stacey Genaw
Food Stylist: Josh Rink

Pictured on front cover:
Apricot-Glazed Ham, p. 136
Three-Green Salad, p. 137
Quick & Easy au Gratin Potatoes, p. 8

Pictured on back cover:
Strawberry Shortcake Pie, p. 128
Whole Wheat Dinner Rolls, p. 138
Smoked Deviled Eggs, p. 135

Printed in USA
1 3 5 7 9 10 8 6 4 2

More ways to connect with us:

SHOPTASTEOFHOME.COM

TABLE OF CONTENTS

'TIS THE SEASON

GIVING THANKS

EASTER GATHERINGS

SPECIAL CELEBRATIONS

'TIS THE SEASON

Red noses on reindeer and cold hands in mittens, carolers singing and memories waiting to be written... These may be a few of your favorite Christmas things, but it wouldn't be the holidays without an assortment of festive foods. Whether you're looking to create the perfect meal for a formal dinner party or a tasty spread of tropical delights for a more laid-back gathering, these recipes are sure to please.

HOLIDAY OPEN HOUSE

Spread joy and indulge in the flavors of the season with a casual open house where friends, family and neighbors can drop in throughout the afternoon. Guests will be eager to delight in this menu's mainstay of festive fare, perfect for all-day grazing and easy to multiply for a crowd. Just throw in a few cocktails and some jolly holiday tunes playing in the background, and you've got your best bash yet.

Quick & Easy au Gratin Potatoes (p. 8) Roasted Italian Green Beans & Tomatoes (p. 12)
Spinach Salad with Raspberries & Candied Walnuts (p. 8)

QUICK & EASY AU GRATIN POTATOES

SPINACH SALAD WITH RASPBERRIES & CANDIED WALNUTS

I created a bright spinach salad with raspberries for a big family dinner, and the festive colors were perfect for my holiday table. Even those who don't like spinach change their minds after their first bite.
—*Robert Aucelluzzo, Simi Valley, CA*

Prep: 15 min. • **Bake:** 25 min. + cooling
Makes: 8 servings

- 1 large egg white
- ¾ tsp. vanilla extract
- 2 cups walnut halves
- ½ cup sugar

DRESSING
- ¼ cup canola oil
- 2 Tbsp. cider vinegar
- 1 Tbsp. sugar
- 1½ tsp. light corn syrup
- 1 tsp. poppy seeds
- ¼ tsp. salt
- ¼ tsp. ground mustard

SALAD
- 8 oz. fresh baby spinach (about 10 cups)
- 1½ cups fresh raspberries

1. Preheat oven to 300°. In a small bowl, whisk egg white and vanilla until frothy. Stir in walnuts. Sprinkle with sugar; toss to coat evenly. Spread in a single layer in a greased 15x10x1-in. baking pan.
2. Bake nuts for 25-30 minutes or until lightly browned, stirring every 10 minutes. Spread on waxed paper to cool completely.
3. In a small bowl, whisk dressing ingredients until blended. Place spinach in a large bowl. Drizzle with dressing; toss to coat. Sprinkle with raspberries and 1 cup candied walnuts (save remaining walnuts for another use).
1½ cups: 171 cal., 13g fat (1g sat. fat), 0 chol., 100mg sod., 12g carb. (9g sugars, 3g fiber), 3g pro. **Diabetic exchanges:** 1½ fat, 1 starch, 1 vegetable.

QUICK & EASY AU GRATIN POTATOES

A friend serves these creamy, cheesy potatoes when we gather together to celebrate with friends and family.
—*Carol Blue, Barnesville, PA*

Prep: 10 min. • **Bake:** 50 min.
Makes: 12 servings

- 2 cups sour cream
- 1 can (10¾ oz.) condensed cream of chicken soup, undiluted
- ½ tsp. salt
- ¼ tsp. pepper
- 1 pkg. (30 oz.) frozen shredded hash brown potatoes, thawed
- 2 cups shredded cheddar cheese
- 1 small onion, chopped
- 2 cups crushed cornflakes
- ¼ cup butter, melted

1. Preheat oven to 350°. In a large bowl, mix sour cream, condensed soup, salt and pepper; stir in potatoes, cheese and onion. Transfer to a greased 13x9-in. baking dish.
2. In a small bowl, mix crushed cornflakes and melted butter; sprinkle over potato mixture. Bake, uncovered, 50-60 minutes or until golden brown.
¾ cup: 394 cal., 22g fat (14g sat. fat), 70mg chol., 680mg sod., 36g carb. (5g sugars, 2g fiber), 11g pro.

SPINICH SALAD
WITH RASPBERRIES &
CANDIED WALNUTS

ITALIAN HERB-CRUSTED PORK LOIN

CRANBERRY PESTO

CRANBERRY PESTO

I updated a classic Italian pesto to include cranberries and walnuts. It's so good slathered on pork loin, pasta or turkey sandwiches.
—*Aysha Schurman, Ammon, ID*

- -

Takes: 10 min. • **Makes:** 1¼ cups

- ⅔ **cup loosely packed basil leaves**
- ½ **cup dried cranberries**
- ¼ **cup chopped walnuts**
- 1 **green onion, chopped**
- 3 **garlic cloves, coarsely chopped**
- ½ **tsp. pepper**
- ¼ **tsp. salt**
- ⅔ **cup olive oil**

Place first 7 ingredients in a food processor; pulse until coarsely chopped. Continue processing while gradually adding oil in a steady stream. Store in an airtight container in the refrigerator for up to 1 week.
2 Tbsp.: 168 cal., 16g fat (2g sat. fat), 0 chol., 60mg sod., 6g carb. (4g sugars, 1g fiber), 1g pro.

HERB BUTTER

This savory butter makes a thoughtful and versatile gift at holiday time. It's great spread on French bread or chicken before baking, or tossed with hot cooked vegetables or pasta.
—*Dixie Terry, Goreville, IL*

- -

Takes: 5 min.
Makes: 2 cups

- 2 **cups butter, softened**
- ¼ **cup minced fresh parsley**
- 2 **Tbsp. minced garlic cloves**
- 4 **tsp. Italian seasoning**
- 1 **tsp. crushed red pepper flakes**

In a bowl, combine all ingredients. Beat until well blended. Cover and store in the refrigerator.
1 Tbsp.: 102 cal., 11g fat (7g sat. fat), 31mg chol., 116mg sod., 0 carb. (0 sugars, 0 fiber), 0 pro.

ITALIAN HERB-CRUSTED PORK LOIN

I switch things up during the holidays by roasting pork loin with my favorite herbs and veggies. This dazzling dish is a showpiece that never fails to impress.
—*Kim Palmer, Kingston, GA*

- -

Prep: 15 min. + chilling
Bake: 50 min. + standing • **Makes:** 8 servings

- 3 **Tbsp. olive oil**
- 5 **garlic cloves, minced**
- 1 **tsp. salt**
- 1 **tsp. each dried basil, thyme and rosemary, crushed**
- ½ **tsp. Italian seasoning**
- ½ **tsp. pepper**
- 1 **boneless pork loin roast (3 to 4 lbs.)**
- 8 **medium carrots, halved lengthwise**
- 2 **medium onions, quartered**

1. In a small bowl, mix the oil, garlic and seasonings; rub over roast. Arrange carrots and onions on the bottom of a 13x9-in. baking pan. Place roast over vegetables, fat side up. Refrigerate, covered, 1 hour.
2. Preheat oven to 475°. Roast the pork for 20 minutes.
3. Reduce oven setting to 425°. Roast until a thermometer reads 145° and vegetables are tender, 30-40 minutes longer. Remove roast from oven; tent with foil. Let stand 20 minutes before slicing.
1 serving: 295 cal., 13g fat (4g sat. fat), 85mg chol., 388mg sod., 9g carb. (4g sugars, 2g fiber), 34g pro. **Diabetic exchanges:** 5 lean meat, 1 vegetable, 1 fat.

DOVE
DINNER
ROLLS

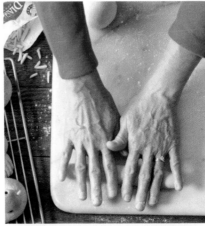

▲

DOVE DINNER ROLLS

Fluffy dinner rolls shaped like doves are a sweet nod to the holidays. They dash away faster than Santa himself.
—Frances Wirtz, West Allis, WI

- -

Prep: 50 min. + rising • **Bake:** 10 min.
Makes: 2 dozen

    2   cups whole wheat pastry flour
    ½   cup sugar
    3   pkg. (¼ oz. each) active dry yeast
    2   tsp. salt
    1   cup water
    1   cup 2% milk
    ½   cup butter, cubed
    1   large egg, room temperature
    4   to 4½ cups bread flour
ASSEMBLY
    48 dried currants
    24 slivered almonds
    1   large egg
    2   Tbsp. 2% milk

1. In a large bowl, mix pastry flour, sugar, yeast and salt. In a small saucepan, heat water, milk and butter to 120°-130°. Add to the dry ingredients; beat on medium speed 1 minute.

Add egg; beat on high 2 minutes. Stir in enough bread flour to form a soft dough (dough will be sticky).

2. Turn dough onto a floured surface; knead until smooth and elastic, 6-8 minutes. Place in a greased bowl, turning once to grease the top. Cover and let rise in a warm place until doubled, about 45 minutes.

3. Punch down dough. Let stand, covered, 15 minutes. Turn onto a lightly floured surface; divide and shape into 24 balls. Roll each into a 10-in. rope; tie into a loose knot. Bring 1 end up and tuck into center of roll to form head. Flatten opposite end; with a sharp knife, cut 4 slits to form 5 tail feathers. Press 2 currants into head for eyes and 1 almond for beak. Place rolls 2 in. apart on greased baking sheets.

4. Cover with kitchen towels; let rolls rise in a warm place until doubled, about 30 minutes. Preheat oven to 400°.

5. In a small bowl, whisk egg and milk; brush over rolls. Bake 10-12 minutes or until golden brown. Remove from pans to wire racks; serve warm.

1 roll: 177 cal., 5g fat (3g sat. fat), 27mg chol., 239mg sod., 28g carb. (5g sugars, 2g fiber), 5g pro.

How to Shape Doves

Follow these steps to create lovey-dovey rolls that are almost too pretty to eat.

1. Let dough rise, then roll. To keep the doves plump and pretty, make sure each dough rope is no longer than 10 in.

2. After tying dough in a loose knot, use the shorter end to form each dove's head.

3. Coat a sharp paring knife with nonstick cooking spray and cut slits for the tail feathers.

ROASTED ITALIAN GREEN BEANS & TOMATOES

Roasted green beans and tomatoes boast flavors that shine. The vibrant colors light up our holiday table.
—*Brittany Allyn, Mesa, AZ*

Takes: 25 min. • **Makes:** 8 servings

1½ lbs. fresh green beans,
   trimmed and halved
 1 Tbsp. olive oil
 1 tsp. Italian seasoning
 ½ tsp. salt
 2 cups grape tomatoes, halved
 ½ cup grated Parmesan cheese

1. Preheat oven to 425°. Place green beans in a 15x10x1-in. baking pan coated with cooking spray. Mix oil, Italian seasoning and salt; drizzle over beans. Toss to coat. Roast 10 minutes, stirring once.
2. Add tomatoes to pan. Roast until beans are crisp-tender and tomatoes are softened, 4-6 minutes longer. Sprinkle with cheese.
¾ cup: 70 cal., 3g fat (1g sat. fat), 4mg chol., 231mg sod., 8g carb. (3g sugars, 3g fiber), 4g pro. **Diabetic exchanges:** 1 vegetable, ½ fat.

TEST KITCHEN TIP

Buy fresh green beans with slender green pods that are free of bruises or brown spots. Store unwashed fresh green beans in a resealable plastic bag for up to 4 days. Wash just before using, removing strings and ends if necessary.

CHOCOLATE-COVERED PRALINE CHEWS

Welcome a new candymaking tradition with these caramel-like praline chews. The black and white coating gives them a modern, eye-catching twist.
—*Christina Mitchell, Haughton, LA*

- -

Prep: 40 min. • **Cook:** 45 min. + chilling
Makes: about 3 dozen

- 1 cup sugar
- 1 cup light corn syrup
  Dash salt
- ¼ cup butter, cubed
- 2 tsp. whole milk
- 2 cups pecan halves
- ½ tsp. vanilla extract
- 6 oz. white candy coating, coarsely chopped
- 6 oz. milk chocolate candy coating, coarsely chopped

1. In a large heavy saucepan, combine the sugar, corn syrup and salt. Bring to a boil over medium heat; cook until a candy thermometer reads 245° (firm-ball stage), stirring occasionally. Gradually stir in the butter, milk and pecans. Continue cooking until temperature returns to 245°. Remove from the heat; stir in vanilla. Immediately drop by tablespoonfuls onto greased baking sheets. Cool.
2. In a microwave, melt white candy coating at 70% power for 1 minute; stir. Microwave at additional 10- to 20-second intervals, stirring until smooth.
3. Dip candies halfway into coating and allow excess to drip off. Place on waxed paper-lined baking sheets; refrigerate for 15 minutes or until set.
4. In a microwave, melt milk chocolate coating at 70% power for 1 minute; stir. Microwave at additional 10- to 20-second intervals, stirring until smooth.
5. Dip other half of each candy and allow excess to drip off. Return to baking sheets; refrigerate until set.
1 piece: 149 cal., 8g fat (4g sat. fat), 3mg chol., 20mg sod., 20g carb. (20g sugars, 1g fiber), 1g pro.

We recommend that you test your candy thermometer before each use by bringing water to a boil; the thermometer should read 212°. Adjust your recipe temperature up or down based on your test.

BLACKBERRY BRANDY SLUSH

We wanted a grown-up twist on a favorite slushy, so we spiked it with blackberry brandy. The deep red color makes it perfect for a merry celebration.
—*Lindsey Spinler, Sobieski, WI*

- -

Prep: 10 min. + freezing
Makes: 28 servings (1 cup each)

- 8 cups water
- 2 cups sugar
- 3 cups blackberry brandy
- 1 can (12 oz.) frozen lemonade concentrate, thawed
- 1 can (12 oz.) frozen grape juice concentrate, thawed
- 14 cups lemon-lime soda, chilled

1. In a large bowl, stir water and sugar until sugar is dissolved. Stir in brandy and juice concentrates. Transfer to freezer containers; freeze overnight.
2. To serve, place about ½ cup brandy mixture in each glass; top with ½ cup soda.
1 cup: 235 cal., 0 fat (0 sat. fat), 0 chol., 18mg sod., 51g carb. (48g sugars, 0 fiber), 0 pro.

ROASTED ITALIAN GREEN BEANS & TOMATOES

TRIPLE GINGER COOKIES

My dad loved ginger cookies. I tinkered with the recipe my grandma handed down by using fresh, ground and crystallized ginger for more pizzazz.
—Trisha Kruse, Eagle, ID

- -

Prep: 20 min. + chilling
Bake: 15 min./batch + cooling
Makes: about 2½ dozen

- ½ cup butter, softened
- ½ cup packed brown sugar
- 1 large egg, room temperature
- 3 Tbsp. molasses
- ½ tsp. grated fresh gingerroot
- 2¼ cups all-purpose flour
- ½ tsp. baking powder
- ½ tsp. ground ginger
- ¼ tsp. salt
- ¼ tsp. baking soda

ICING
- ½ cup confectioners' sugar
- 2 to 3 tsp. water
- ¼ cup finely chopped crystallized ginger

1. Preheat oven to 350°. In a large bowl, cream butter and brown sugar until light and fluffy. Beat in egg, molasses and fresh ginger. In another bowl, whisk flour, baking powder, ground ginger, salt and baking soda; gradually beat into creamed mixture. Refrigerate the dough, covered, for 2 hours or until firm enough to handle.
2. Shape tablespoonfuls of dough into balls; place 1 in. apart on ungreased baking sheets. Flatten slightly with bottom of a glass. Bake 12-14 minutes or until cookies are set and edges begin to brown. Remove from pans to wire racks to cool completely.
3. For icing, in a small bowl, mix confectioners' sugar and enough water to reach desired consistency. Drizzle over cookies; sprinkle with crystallized ginger.
1 cookie: 97 cal., 3g fat (2g sat. fat), 15mg chol., 64mg sod., 16g carb. (7g sugars, 0 fiber), 1g pro.

PINA COLADA BUNDT CAKE

We named this cake after the tropical drink because it has the signature ingredients of coconut, pineapple and rum. It's a soothing finish at the end of a big spread.
—Debra Keil, Owasso, OK

- -

Prep: 15 min. • **Bake:** 45 min. + cooling
Makes: 12 servings

- 1 pkg. white cake mix (regular size)
- 1 pkg. (3.4 oz.) instant coconut cream pudding mix
- 1 cup canola oil
- ¾ cup water
- 2 large eggs, room temperature
- ¼ cup rum
- 1 cup drained crushed pineapple

GLAZE
- 2 cups confectioners' sugar, divided
- 2 Tbsp. unsweetened pineapple juice
- ¼ cup cream of coconut
- 1 Tbsp. rum
- ¼ cup sweetened shredded coconut

1. Preheat oven to 350°. Grease and flour a 10-in. fluted tube pan.
2. In a large bowl, combine cake mix, pudding mix, canola oil, water, eggs and rum; beat on low speed for 30 seconds. Beat on medium 2 minutes. Stir in pineapple. Transfer batter to prepared pan. Bake 45-50 minutes or until a toothpick inserted in center comes out clean. Cool in pan 15 minutes before removing to a wire rack.
3. In a small bowl, mix 1 cup confectioners' sugar and pineapple juice; brush over warm cake. Cool cake completely.
4. In another bowl, mix cream of coconut, rum and remaining confectioners' sugar; drizzle over cake. Sprinkle with coconut.
Note: This recipe was tested with Coco Lopez cream of coconut. Look for it in the liquor section. To remove cake easily, use solid shortening to grease tube pan.
1 slice: 495 cal., 25g fat (5g sat. fat), 31mg chol., 357mg sod., 64g carb. (47g sugars, 1g fiber), 3g pro.

TRIPLE GINGER COOKIES

PINA COLADA
BUNDT CAKE

A CLASSIC CHRISTMAS DINNER

Special occasions call for extraordinary food. Whether your gathering is big or small, casual or formal, here's everything you need to create a traditional crowd-pleasing feast. With mouthwatering recipes and other fun tips and ideas, these dishes will make December 25 more delicious than ever before.

Mushroom-Blue Cheese Tenderloin (p. 22)
Roasted Brussels Sprouts & Cauliflower (p. 24)

Chelsea

Christmas Day Countdown

It's the most wonderful day of the year! Many of the dishes in this menu can be prepared in advance, while others are best to make the day of. Use this timeline as your guide to get a jump on all the festivities.

A FEW WEEKS BEFORE
☐ Prepare two grocery lists—one for nonperishable items to buy now and one for perishable items to buy a few days before Christmas.

☐ Bake the Brown Sugar & Chocolate Swirl Cheesecake, but do not add whipped cream, sprinkle with walnuts or drizzle with syrup. Freeze in an airtight container.

☐ Prepare Appetizer Pinwheels but do not slice. Wrap in waxed paper and freeze in a freezer container.

☐ Bake the Garlic-Herb Braid. Wrap in heavy-duty foil and freeze.

TWO DAYS BEFORE
☐ Buy remaining grocery items.

☐ Prepare the dressing for the Cherry Brie Tossed Salad. Cover and refrigerate.

☐ Wash china, stemware and the table linens.

THE DAY BEFORE
☐ Prepare the Smoked Almond Cheese Ball. Wrap tightly and store in the refrigerator.

☐ Prepare the Creamy Red Pepper Soup. Allow to cool completely and do not add garnishes. Cover and refrigerate.

☐ Prepare Cranberry-Lemon Meringue Pie. Refrigerate until ready to serve.

☐ Remove the cheesecake from the freezer and place in the refrigerator to thaw. Remove the braid from the freezer and place on countertop to thaw.

☐ Prepare the Maple Custard, but do not add whipped cream. Refrigerate until ready to serve.

☐ Set the table.

CHRISTMAS DAY
☐ About 4 hours before dinner, tie the roast for the Mushroom-Blue Cheese Tenderloin and let it sit in the marinade in the refrigerator for 2 hours, turning occasionally.

☐ At least 3 to 4 hours before dinner, prepare the Marinated Vegetables with Olives. Refrigerate until ready to serve, stirring occasionally.

☐ About 1 hour before dinner, remove the beef tenderloin roast from the refrigerator. Prepare and bake.

☐ About 45 minutes before dinner, prepare the Roasted Brussels Sprouts & Cauliflower. Keep warm until serving.

☐ About 30 minutes before dinner, prepare the Fruit & Nut Bulgur Pilaf. Keep warm until ready to serve.

RIGHT BEFORE DINNER
☐ About 30 minutes before guests arrive, remove Appetizer Pinwheels from the freezer. Cut into slices and bake.

☐ As guests arrive, assemble the Shrimp Salad Appetizers. Remove the Smoked Almond Cheese Ball from the refrigerator and serve with crackers.

☐ Remove the salad dressing for the Cherry Brie Tossed Salad from the refrigerator and whisk. Prepare salad and toss with dressing. Sprinkle salad with sugared almonds.

☐ Prepare the mushroom-blue cheese sauce for the beef tenderloin roast.

☐ Remove red pepper soup from the refrigerator and warm it on the stovetop. Sprinkle with chives, cream and croutons just before serving.

☐ Slice braid just before serving.

☐ After dinner, remove the pie, custard and cheesecake from the refrigerator. Fold whipped cream into custard and drizzle with maple syrup. Top cheesecake with whipped cream, sprinkle with walnuts and drizzle with maple syrup. Cut and serve desserts.

MARINATED VEGETABLES WITH OLIVES

Veggies play nicely together in a healthy, easy dish that can be an appetizer or a salad.
—*Sue Hansen, Corvallis, OR*

Prep: 20 min. • **Cook:** 10 min. + chilling
Makes: 12 servings

- ⅔ cup cider vinegar
- ⅔ cup olive oil
- ¼ cup chopped onion
- 2 garlic cloves, minced
- 1 tsp. sugar
- 1 tsp. dried basil
- 1 tsp. dried oregano
- 1 lb. fresh petite carrots
- 1 can (14 oz.) water-packed quartered artichoke hearts, drained
- ½ lb. medium fresh mushrooms, halved
- 4 celery ribs, sliced diagonally
- 1 cup (6 oz.) pitted ripe olives, drained

1. In a small saucepan, combine the first 7 ingredients; bring to a boil. Simmer, uncovered, 10 minutes. Meanwhile, in a large nonreactive bowl, combine the remaining ingredients.
2. Pour hot marinade over vegetables; stir to coat. Refrigerate, covered, 3-4 hours, stirring occasionally to allow flavors to blend.
⅔ cup: 156 cal., 13g fat (2g sat. fat), 0 chol., 206mg sod., 8g carb. (3g sugars, 1g fiber), 2g pro. **Diabetic exchanges:** 2½ fat, 1 vegetable.

SMOKED ALMOND CHEESE BALL

This cheese ball makes its way to our table every year, and I often give one or more as gifts. The recipe is easily doubled or tripled.
—*Cleo Gonske, Redding, CA*

Prep: 20 min. + chilling • **Makes:** 1¾ cups

- 1 pkg. (8 oz.) cream cheese, softened
- 2 Tbsp. sweet white wine
- 2 tsp. Dijon mustard
- 1 tsp. garlic powder
- 1 to 2 drops hot pepper sauce
- 2 cups (8 oz.) finely shredded sharp cheddar cheese
- ⅔ cup chopped smoked almonds
  Assorted crackers

In a large bowl, beat the first 5 ingredients until smooth. Stir in cheddar cheese. Shape into a ball; roll in almonds. Wrap tightly and refrigerate for at least 1 hour. Serve with crackers.
2 Tbsp.: 162 cal., 14g fat (7g sat. fat), 35mg chol., 188mg sod., 3g carb. (0 sugars, 1g fiber), 6g pro.

CREAMY RED PEPPER SOUP

CREAMY RED PEPPER SOUP

Everyone loves this soup's taste, but no one guesses that pears are the secret ingredient.
—*Connie Summers, Augusta, MI*

Prep: 15 min. • **Cook:** 30 min. + cooling
Makes: 12 servings (3 qt.)

- 2 large onions, chopped
- ¼ cup butter, cubed
- 4 garlic cloves, minced
- 2 large potatoes, peeled and diced
- 2 jars (7 oz. each) roasted red peppers, drained, patted dry and chopped
- 5 cups chicken broth
- 2 cans (15 oz. each) pears in juice
- ⅛ tsp. cayenne pepper
- ⅛ tsp. black pepper
  Chopped chives, heavy cream and croutons, optional

1. In a Dutch oven, saute onions in butter until tender. Add garlic; cook 1 minute longer. Add the potatoes, red peppers and broth. Bring to a boil. Reduce heat; cover and simmer for 15-20 minutes or until vegetables are tender. Remove from the heat. Add pears; let cool.
2. Using a blender, puree soup in batches. Return to the pan. Stir in cayenne and black pepper. Cook until heated through. If desired, serve with chopped chives, heavy cream and croutons.
1 cup: 127 cal., 4g fat (2g sat. fat), 10mg chol., 494mg sod., 20g carb. (9g sugars, 2g fiber), 3g pro.

SHRIMP SALAD
APPETIZERS

SHRIMP SALAD APPETIZERS

This refreshing hors d'oeuvre has gained a big following since a friend shared her family recipe with me. To quote my younger son, the shrimp and celery are so good together.
—*Solie Kimble, Kanata, ON*

Takes: 15 min. • **Makes:** 2 dozen

- 1 lb. peeled and deveined cooked shrimp, chopped
- 1 can (6 oz.) lump crabmeat, drained
- 2 celery ribs, finely chopped
- ¼ cup Dijon-mayonnaise blend
- 24 Belgian endive leaves (3 to 4 heads) or small butterhead lettuce leaves Chopped fresh parsley, optional

In a large bowl, combine shrimp, crab and celery. Add mayonnaise blend; toss to coat. To serve, top each leaf with about 2 Tbsp. shrimp mixture. If desired, top with parsley.
1 appetizer: 31 cal., 0 fat (0 sat. fat), 35mg chol., 115mg sod., 1g carb. (0 sugars, 0 fiber), 5g pro.

CHERRY BRIE TOSSED SALAD

Draped in a light vinaigrette and sprinkled with almonds, this pretty salad is a variation of a recipe that's been passed around at school events, church functions and even birthday parties. Feel free to try other kinds of cheeses.
—*Toni Borden, Wellington, FL*

Takes: 20 min. • **Makes:** 10 servings

DRESSING
- 1 cup cider vinegar
- ½ cup sugar
- ¼ cup olive oil
- 1 tsp. ground mustard
- 1½ tsp. poppy seeds

SALAD
- 2 Tbsp. butter
- ¾ cup sliced almonds
- 3 Tbsp. sugar
- 8 cups torn romaine
- 1 round (8 oz.) Brie or Camembert cheese, rind removed and cubed
- 1 pkg. (6 oz.) dried cherries

1. In a small bowl, whisk the dressing ingredients; set aside.
2. For salad, in a heavy skillet, melt butter over medium heat. Add almonds and cook and stir until nuts are toasted, about 4 minutes. Sprinkle with sugar; cook and stir until sugar is melted, about 3 minutes. Spread on foil to cool; break apart.
3. In a large salad bowl, combine the romaine, cheese and cherries. Whisk dressing; drizzle over salad. Sprinkle with sugared almonds and toss to coat.
Note: Swiss cheese can be substituted for Brie or Camembert.
1 serving: 309 cal., 18g fat (6g sat. fat), 29mg chol., 171mg sod., 32g carb. (27g sugars, 2g fiber), 8g pro.

APPETIZER PINWHEELS

These sophisticated appetizers made of Gruyere, prosciutto and fresh sage never fail to receive compliments. They freeze well, so make a batch to have on hand for when guests drop in.
—*Shannon Koene, Blacksburg, VA*

Prep: 15 min. + chilling • **Bake:** 15 min.
Makes: about 5 dozen

- 2 cups shredded Gruyere or Swiss cheese
- 3 Tbsp. minced fresh sage
- 1 pkg. (17.3 oz.) frozen puff pastry, thawed
- 4 oz. thinly sliced prosciutto or deli ham

1. In a small bowl, mix cheese and sage. Unfold puff pastry; cut each piece in half crosswise. Top each half with prosciutto and the cheese mixture to within ½ in. of edges; roll up jelly-roll style, starting with a long side. Wrap tightly in waxed paper or plastic. Refrigerate at least 3 hours or overnight.
2. Preheat oven to 400°. Unwrap and cut each roll crosswise into sixteen ½-in. slices. Place cut side down on greased baking sheets. Bake 14-16 minutes or until golden brown.
To make ahead: Rolls can be made 2 days in advance. Wrap rolls in waxed paper and place in a container; close tightly and store in the refrigerator.
Freeze option: Freeze wrapped rolls in a resealable freezer container. To use, unwrap frozen rolls and cut into slices. Bake as directed.
1 pinwheel: 56 cal., 3g fat (1g sat. fat), 5mg chol., 85mg sod., 4g carb. (0 sugars, 1g fiber), 2g pro.

GARLIC-HERB BRAID

Savory flavors of rosemary, dill, garlic and basil blend beautifully in this homey loaf. Get ready for oohs and aahs when you bring this tender and impressive braid to the table!
—*Taste of Home Test Kitchen*

Prep: 20 min. + rising
Bake: 20 min. + cooling
Makes: 1 loaf (16 slices)

- 4 to 4½ cups all-purpose flour
- 3 Tbsp. sugar
- 2 pkg. (¼ oz. each) quick-rise yeast
- 2 tsp. dried basil
- 1¾ tsp. dill weed
- 1½ tsp. salt
- ¾ tsp. garlic powder
- ¾ tsp. dried rosemary, crushed
- ¾ cup 2% milk
- ½ cup water
- ¼ cup butter, cubed
- 1 large egg, room temperature
- 1 Tbsp. butter, melted

1. In a large bowl, combine 1½ cups flour, sugar, yeast and seasonings. In a small saucepan, heat the milk, water and cubed butter to 120°-130°. Add to dry ingredients; beat just until moistened. Add egg; beat until smooth. Stir in enough remaining flour to form a soft dough.
2. Turn onto a floured surface; knead until smooth and elastic, 4-6 minutes. Cover and let rest for 10 minutes.
3. Divide dough into thirds. Shape each into a 15-in. rope. Place ropes on a greased baking sheet, and braid; pinch ends to seal and tuck under. Cover and let rise until doubled, about 25 minutes.
4. Bake at 375° for 20-25 minutes or until golden brown. Brush with melted butter. Remove from pan to a wire rack to cool.
Freeze option: Securely wrap and freeze cooled loaf in heavy-duty foil. To use, thaw at room temperature.
1 slice: 169 cal., 5g fat (3g sat. fat), 24mg chol., 257mg sod., 27g carb. (3g sugars, 1g fiber), 4g pro. **Diabetic exchanges:** 1½ starch, 1 fat.

Use a kitchen timer and test for doneness at the minimum recommended baking time. Bread is done when it is golden brown and sounds hollow when tapped on the bottom. Or insert an instant-read thermometer in the thickest part of the loaf. The bread is done when the thermometer reads 200°.

MUSHROOM-BLUE CHEESE TENDERLOIN

Here's a simple entree that is sure to impress. I usually double the mushroom-cheese sauce because it always disappears fast. Enjoy the tenderloin!
—*Eric Schoen, Lincoln, NE*

Prep: 10 min. + marinating
Bake: 45 min. + standing
Makes: 10 servings (1½ cups sauce)

- 1 cup reduced-sodium soy sauce
- ¾ cup Worcestershire sauce
- 1 beef tenderloin roast (3½ to 4 lbs.)
- 4 garlic cloves, minced
- 1 Tbsp. coarsely ground pepper
- 1 can (10½ oz.) condensed beef broth, undiluted

SAUCE
- ½ lb. sliced fresh mushrooms
- ½ cup butter, cubed
- 2 garlic cloves, minced
- 1 cup (4 oz.) crumbled blue cheese
- 1 Tbsp. Worcestershire sauce
- ¼ tsp. caraway seeds
- 4 green onions, chopped

1. If desired, tie tenderloin with bakers twine. In a shallow dish, combine soy sauce and Worcestershire sauce; add the beef and turn to coat. Cover; refrigerate for 2 hours, turning occasionally.
2. Drain beef, discarding marinade. Rub the beef with garlic and pepper; place in a shallow roasting pan. Add broth to the pan. Bake, uncovered, at 425° for 45-55 minutes or until meat reaches desired doneness (for medium-rare, a thermometer should read 135°; medium, 140°; medium-well, 145°). Let stand for 10 minutes and remove twine before slicing.
3. Meanwhile, in a small saucepan, saute mushrooms in butter until tender. Add garlic; cook 1 minute longer. Add the cheese, Worcestershire sauce and caraway seeds; cook and stir over low heat until cheese is melted. Stir in onions; heat through. Serve sauce with beef.
1 serving: 438 cal., 29g fat (14g sat. fat), 135mg chol., 1377mg sod., 4g carb. (1g sugars, 1g fiber), 38g pro.

FRUIT & NUT BULGUR PILAF

My mother made this nutritious side dish all the time when we were growing up. I enhanced the recipe with a bigger variety of dried fruit to find an interesting balance between the sweet and salty flavors.
—*Ninette Holbrook, Orlando, FL*

Takes: 30 min. • **Makes:** 10 servings

- 1 Tbsp. canola oil
- 2 cups bulgur
- ¼ tsp. salt
- ¼ tsp. pepper
- 3 cups vegetable broth
- ½ cup slivered almonds, toasted
- ½ cup golden raisins
- ½ cup dried cranberries
- ½ cup dried apricots, chopped

1. In a large saucepan, heat oil over medium-high heat; cook and stir bulgur until toasted. Stir in salt, pepper and broth; bring to a boil. Reduce heat; simmer, covered, until tender and liquid is almost absorbed, 10-12 minutes.
2. Stir in ⅓ cup each of the almonds, raisins, cranberries and apricots. Serve with the remaining almonds and fruit.
Note: To toast nuts, bake in a shallow pan in a 350° oven for 5-10 minutes or cook in a skillet over low heat until lightly browned, stirring occasionally.
⅔ cup: 199 cal., 5g fat (0 sat. fat), 0 chol., 348mg sod., 38g carb. (13g sugars, 5g fiber), 5g pro.

MUSHROOM-
BLUE CHEESE
TENDERLOIN

ROASTED BRUSSELS SPROUTS & CAULIFLOWER

My grandkids aren't huge fans of cauliflower, but toss a little bacon on it and they can't get enough! They like it even more with golden cauliflower instead of white.
—*Patricia Hudson, Riverview, FL*

- -

Prep: 25 min. • **Cook:** 15 min.
Makes: 12 servings (½ cup each)

8	bacon strips, chopped
6	garlic cloves, minced
1	Tbsp. olive oil
1	Tbsp. butter, melted
¼	tsp. kosher salt
¼	tsp. coarsely ground pepper
4	cups Brussels sprouts, halved
4	cups fresh cauliflowerets
¼	cup grated Parmesan cheese
	Additional grated Parmesan cheese, optional

1. In a large skillet, cook bacon over medium heat until crisp, stirring occasionally. Remove with a slotted spoon; drain on paper towels. Discard drippings, reserving 1 Tbsp..
2. In a large bowl, mix the garlic, oil, butter, salt, pepper and reserved drippings. Add Brussels sprouts and cauliflower; toss to coat. Transfer to 2 greased 15x10x1-in. baking pans.
3. Bake at 425° for 15-20 minutes. Sprinkle each pan with 2 Tbsp. cheese. Bake 5 minutes longer or until vegetables are tender. Sprinkle with bacon and, if desired, additional cheese.

½ cup: 137 cal., 11g fat (4g sat. fat), 17mg chol., 221mg sod., 5g carb. (2g sugars, 2g fiber), 5g pro.

TEST KITCHEN TIP

When buying fresh cauliflower, look for a head with compact florets that are free from yellow or brown spots. The leaves should be crisp and green, not withered or discolored. Tightly wrap an unwashed head of cauliflower and refrigerate for up to 5 days. Before using, wash it, remove the leaves at the base and trim the stem.

ROASTED BRUSSELS SPROUTS
& CAULIFLOWER

CRANBERRY-LEMON MERINGUE PIE

My daughter Eliana came up with the idea for this pie one morning when she woke up early to bake. She combined the way she and I make fresh black raspberry cobbler in the summer with other recipes for cranberry sauce and lemon meringue pie. The color is absolutely beautiful, and the flavors are smooth and delicious. One of her best friends says it's the best pie she's ever had.
—Sonia Buhrer-Bowen, Carroll, OH

- -

Prep: 45 min. + chilling
Bake: 30 min. + cooling
Makes: 8 servings

Pastry for single-crust pie
3 cups fresh or frozen cranberries, thawed
1¼ cups sugar
⅓ cup water
2 Tbsp. lemon juice
3 Tbsp. quick-cooking tapioca
½ tsp. grated lemon peel
3 large eggs
2 Tbsp. butter
½ tsp. vanilla extract
MERINGUE
3 large egg whites, room temperature
½ tsp. cream of tartar
6 Tbsp. sugar
½ tsp. vanilla extract

1. Preheat oven to 450°. On a lightly floured surface, roll crust to a ⅛-in.-thick circle; transfer to a 9-in. pie plate. Trim crust to ½ in. beyond rim of plate; flute edge.
2. Line the unpricked crust with a double thickness of foil. Fill with pie weights, dried beans or uncooked rice.
3. Bake 8-10 minutes or until bottom is lightly browned. Remove foil and weights; bake until golden brown, 4-6 minutes longer. Cool on a wire rack. Reduce oven setting to 350°.
4. In a large saucepan, combine cranberries, sugar, water and lemon juice. Bring to a boil, stirring to dissolve sugar. Reduce heat to medium; cook, uncovered, 4-6 minutes or until berries pop, stirring occasionally. Stir in tapioca and lemon peel. Remove from heat; cool slightly. Process half of the cranberry mixture in a food processor until smooth. Return to pan.
5. In a small bowl, whisk a small amount of hot mixture into eggs; return all to pan, whisking constantly. Bring to a gentle boil; cook and stir 2 minutes. Remove from heat. Stir in butter and vanilla.
6. For meringue, in a large bowl, beat egg whites with cream of tartar on medium speed until foamy. Gradually add sugar, 1 Tbsp. at a time, beating on high after each addition until sugar is dissolved. Continue beating until soft glossy peaks form. Beat in vanilla.
7. Transfer hot filling to crust. Spread meringue evenly over filling, sealing to edge of crust. Bake 15-18 minutes or until meringue is golden brown. Cool 1 hour on a wire rack. Refrigerate at least 2 hours before serving.
1 piece: 421 cal., 16g fat (10g sat. fat), 117mg chol., 223mg sod., 64g carb. (43g sugars, 2g fiber), 6g pro.
Pastry for single-crust pie (9 in.): Combine 1¼ cups all-purpose flour and ¼ tsp. salt; cut in ½ cup cold butter until crumbly. Gradually add 3-5 Tbsp. ice water, tossing with a fork until dough holds together when pressed. Cover and refrigerate 1 hour.

MAPLE CUSTARD

Ring in the holidays with this rich, velvety custard. It has a light maple flavor that's a nice change from traditional chocolate and vanilla flavors.
—Sharlene Heatwole, McDowell, VA

- -

Prep: 10 min. • **Cook:** 15 min. + chilling
Makes: 12 servings

⅓ cup cornstarch
¼ cup all-purpose flour
½ tsp. salt
3¾ cups 2% milk
1 cup maple syrup
2 large eggs, beaten
1 tsp. vanilla extract
1 cup heavy whipping cream, whipped
   Sugar for rims of dishes, optional
   Additional maple syrup, optional

1. In a large saucepan, combine cornstarch, flour and salt. Gradually stir in milk and syrup until smooth. Bring to a boil; cook and stir for 2 minutes or until thickened.
2. Remove from the heat. Stir a small amount of hot milk mixture into eggs; return all to the pan, stirring constantly. Bring to a gentle boil; cook and stir for 2 minutes. Remove from the heat; stir in vanilla.
3. Transfer to a large bowl; cover and refrigerate until chilled. Just before serving, fold in whipped cream. If desired, serve in sugar-rimmed dishes and drizzle with additional syrup.
½ cup: 212 cal., 10g fat (6g sat. fat), 68mg chol., 158mg sod., 27g carb. (20g sugars, 0 fiber), 4g pro.

**BROWN SUGAR &
CHOCOLATE SWIRL
CHEESECAKE**

BROWN SUGAR &
CHOCOLATE SWIRL
CHEESECAKE

Searching for a dessert superstar? This is the one that people ask for: Maple cheesecake with fudge swirls and a buttery crust.
—*Jeanne Holt, Mendota Heights, MN*

Prep: 30 min. • **Bake:** 1 hour + chilling
Makes: 16 servings

- ¾ cup cinnamon graham cracker crumbs (about 4 whole crackers)
- ¾ cup finely chopped walnuts, divided
- 1 Tbsp. sugar
- 3 Tbsp. butter, melted

FILLING
- ¼ cup heavy whipping cream
- 1 cup (6 oz.) semisweet chocolate chips
- 4 pkg. (8 oz. each) cream cheese, softened
- ¾ cup packed brown sugar
- ½ cup sour cream
- 3 Tbsp. all-purpose flour
- 1 tsp. vanilla extract
- ¼ tsp. salt
- ¼ cup maple syrup, divided
- 3 large eggs, room temperature, lightly beaten

TOPPING
- 2 cups sweetened whipped cream

1. Preheat oven to 350°. Wrap a double thickness of heavy-duty foil (about 18 in. square) around a greased 9-in. springform pan. Combine cracker crumbs, ½ cup walnuts and the sugar; stir in butter. Press onto the bottom and 1 in. up sides of prepared pan and place on a baking sheet. Bake 10 minutes. Cool on a wire rack.

2. In a small saucepan, bring cream just to a boil. Pour over chocolate; whisk until smooth. Cool.

3. Beat cream cheese until smooth. Add next 5 ingredients and 2 Tbsp. maple syrup; beat until well blended. Add eggs; beat on low speed until combined. Pour over prepared crust. Drop spoonfuls of cooled chocolate over filling; cut through batter with a knife to swirl.

4. Place springform pan in a larger baking pan; add 1 in. of hot water to the larger pan. Bake until center is just set, 60-75 minutes. Remove springform pan from the water bath. Cool the cheesecake on a wire rack 10 minutes. Loosen sides from pan with a knife; remove foil. Cool 1 hour longer. Refrigerate overnight, covering when completely cooled.

5. Remove rim from pan. Serve with whipped cream. Sprinkle with remaining walnuts; drizzle with remaining syrup.

1 slice: 936 cal., 75g fat (40g sat. fat), 267mg chol., 613mg sod., 57g carb. (47g sugars, 2g fiber), 14g pro.

▲

Cut like a Pro

A hot knife is the secret to cutting nice tidy slices of cake and cheesecake. You'll need a sharp knife, some hot water and a towel. Dip the blade in water to heat, then wipe dry and cut. Repeat each time for pretty slices with a clean edge.

Festive Holiday Centerpiece

If your table needs a new focal point, look no further. Adorned with handmade ornaments, fruits and spices, these small packages will take center stage.

Use bleached flour to give the ornaments a whiter finish; unbleached flour will provide a warmer tone.

Dried Citrus
A dehydrator works well to make these decorative fruit slices, but if you don't have one, use this method instead:

Preheat oven to 200°. Thinly slice small oranges, lemons, limes or clementines. Place slices on a cooling rack or pizza screen in a single layer. Bake in oven until dried. To make an ornament, use a pencil or hole punch to make a hole at the top of each slice when partially dried. Thread a ribbon or string through the hole and tie a knot.

Salt-Dough Ornaments

MATERIALS
¾ to 1 cup water, room temperature
1 cup iodized salt
2 cups flour
Mixed leaves, berries or greenery
Cookie cutters
Drinking straw

1. Preheat oven to 200°. With a spoon, mix ¾ cup water, salt and flour until the dough is fairly stiff and not too wet, adding more water as needed.

2. Lightly flour a surface. Knead dough by hand, adding more flour as needed, about 5 minutes. Dough should keep an indentation when pressed with a finger.

3. Form dough into a disk; cover until ready to use.

4. Flour a sheet of waxed paper; place dough on paper. Flour the top of the dough and place a second sheet of waxed paper on top. Roll out the dough to ¼-in. thickness. Remove top sheet of waxed paper.

5. Make a pattern with leaves, berries or greenery by firmly pressing into dough. For leaves, use the underside.

6. Use cookie cutters as desired to cut shapes out of the dough, removing the excess. Make a hole at the top of each ornament by pressing a drinking straw into the dough; lift the straw out, removing the dough to form a hole.

7. Place the ornaments on a parchment-lined baking sheet. Bake until they are hard and dried out, 2-3 hours or more. (High humidity may require more baking time.) Remove to a cooling rack and allow to dry completely.

8. String a ribbon or decorative twine through the hole; knot the ribbon or twine.

MY FAVORITE THINGS PARTY

Oprah Winfrey, Ellen DeGeneres, Maria von Trapp. Like them, we all have a few favorite things—a handmade porcelain mug, comfy slippers, shiny lip gloss—that bring a small surge a joy to an otherwise ordinary day. What are yours? This year, gather your favorite gal pals for a gift swap that celebrates life's little treasures. You may find the time spent with good friends is your favorite thing of all.

Marinated Almond-Stuffed Olives (p. 33) Perfect Lemon Martini (p. 31)
Italian Sausage Bruschetta (p. 34) Walnut & Fig Goat Cheese Log (p. 31)

LITTLE PIGS IN A HAMMOCK

PERFECT LEMON MARTINI

(PICTURED ON PAGE 29)

Relax with a refreshing cocktail. This combo of tart lemon and sweet liqueur will tingle your taste buds.

—*Marilee Anker, Chatsworth, CA*

Takes: 5 min. • **Makes:** 1 serving

  1 **lemon slice**
     Sugar
     Ice cubes
  2 **oz. vodka**
1½ **oz. limoncello**
  ½ **oz. lemon juice**

Using lemon slice, moisten the rim of a chilled cocktail glass; set lemon aside. Sprinkle sugar on a plate; hold glass upside down and dip rim into sugar. Discard remaining sugar on plate. Fill a shaker three-fourths full with ice. Add vodka, limoncello and lemon juice; cover and shake until condensation forms on outside of shaker, 10-15 seconds. Strain into prepared glass. Garnish with lemon slice.

1 serving: 286 cal., 0 fat (0 sat. fat), 0 chol., 1mg sod., 18g carb. (17g sugars, 0 fiber), 0 pro.

LITTLE PIGS IN A HAMMOCK

Pigs in a blanket aren't just for kids. Dijon and Camembert transform this childhood classic into a version that's perfect for grown-ups.

—*Crystal Schlueter, Babbitt, MN*

Takes: 30 min. • **Makes:** 1½ dozen

  1 **pkg. (17.3 oz.) frozen puff pastry, thawed**
  3 **Tbsp. seedless raspberry jam**
  1 **Tbsp. Dijon mustard**
  1 **round (8 oz.) Camembert cheese**
 18 **miniature smoked sausages**
  1 **large egg**
  1 **Tbsp. water**

1. Preheat oven to 425°. Unfold puff pastry. Cut each pastry into 9 squares. Cut each square into 2 triangles. In a small bowl, mix jam and mustard; spread over triangles. Cut cheese in half crosswise; cut each half into 9 wedges.

2. Top each triangle with a cheese piece and a sausage. Fold pastry over the sausage and cheese; press to seal. Place on a parchment-lined baking sheet. In a small bowl, whisk egg with water. Brush over pastries. Bake until golden brown, 15-17 minutes.

1 appetizer: 211 cal., 13g fat (5g sat. fat), 25mg chol., 312mg sod., 18g carb. (2g sugars, 2g fiber), 6g pro.

SANTA'S ORANGE-KISSED COCKTAIL

SANTA'S ORANGE-KISSED COCKTAIL

Refreshing but not overly sweet, this drink is a festive choice for Christmas get-togethers. Serve it during cocktail hour, at dinner or even for brunch in place of mimosas.

—*Claire Beattie, Toronto, ON*

Takes: 5 min. • **Makes:** 1 serving

     Ice cubes
  ¼ **cup light rum**
  ¼ **cup unsweetened pineapple juice**
  1 **Tbsp. lime juice**
  2 **Tbsp. orange juice**
  1 **tsp. grenadine syrup**
  3 **Tbsp. lemon-lime soda**

1. Fill a shaker three-fourths full with ice. Add rum, juices and grenadine syrup.

2. Cover and shake until condensation forms on outside of shaker, 10-15 seconds. Strain into chilled glass. Top with soda.

1 serving: 209 cal., 0 fat (0 sat. fat), 0 chol., 7mg sod., 20g carb. (16g sugars, 0 fiber), 1g pro.

WALNUT & FIG GOAT CHEESE LOG

(PICTURED ON PAGE 29)

Here's a simple spread that calls for only a handful of ingredients. The tablespoon of honey is optional, but I think the little touch of sweetness nicely complements the tang of the goat cheese.

—*Ana-Marie Correll, Hollister, CA*

Prep: 10 min. + chilling • **Makes:** 1⅓ cups

  2 **logs (4 oz. each) fresh goat cheese**
  8 **dried figs, finely chopped**
  ½ **cup finely chopped walnuts, toasted, divided**
  ¾ **tsp. pepper**
  1 **Tbsp. honey, optional**
     Assorted crackers

In a small bowl, crumble cheese. Stir in figs, ¼ cup walnuts, pepper and, if desired, honey. Shape mixture into a log about 6 in. long. Roll in remaining walnuts. Refrigerate 4 hours or overnight. Serve with crackers.

2 Tbsp.: 93 cal., 7g fat (2g sat. fat), 0 chol., 92mg sod., 6g carb. (16g sugars, 1g fiber), 3g pro.

Peppermint Lip Scrub
Use leftover peppermint candy to make a festive smile smoother.

Even if you're diligent about applying lip balm in the winter, you still might end up with dry, patchy lips. Luckily, it couldn't be easier to make a DIY lip scrub. (And don't forget to make enough to gift friends or stuff in stockings!)

This peppermint lip scrub uses just three ingredients—including candy canes! The end result? A refreshing seasonal scrub that will leave your lips plump and smooth.

Place several peppermint candies or candy canes in a food processor, then pulse until finely ground. The candies should be roughly the consistency of sugar. In a bowl, add 1 Tbsp. white sugar and 1 Tbsp. coconut oil. Mix in 2 Tbsp. finely ground peppermint candy until well combined. Store in a small airtight jar. The recipe makes about 6 applications.

To use, scoop out a small amount with your finger, then gently rub the mixture over your lips, focusing on dry areas. If there's any scrub left on your lips, you can rinse them—but we won't tell if you lick the sweet mixture off.

MEXICAN SHRIMP COCKTAIL

MEXICAN SHRIMP COCKTAIL

It's up to you how to enjoy this cocktail—eat it with a spoon as a chilled soup, or use tortilla chips or crackers for scooping.
—*Erin Moreno, Arcadia, WI*

Prep: 20 min. + chilling
Makes: 12 servings (¾ cup each)

- 2 medium tomatoes, seeded and finely chopped
- 1 medium onion, finely chopped
- ½ cup chopped fresh cilantro
- 1 Tbsp. grated lime zest
- ½ tsp. salt
- 1 bottle (12½ oz.) mandarin natural flavor soda
- 1½ cups Clamato juice
- ¼ cup lime juice
- ¼ cup ketchup
- 1½ lbs. peeled and deveined cooked shrimp (100-150 per lb.)
- 2 avocados, finely chopped
  Tortilla chips

1. In a large bowl, combine first 5 ingredients. Stir in soda, Clamato juice, lime juice and ketchup. Add shrimp. Refrigerate, covered, at least 2 hours.
2. Just before serving, add avocados. Serve with a slotted spoon and tortilla chips.
¾ cup: 142 cal., 5g fat (0 sat. fat), 122mg chol., 826mg sod., 11g carb. (3g sugars, 2g fiber), 14g pro.

ROASTED RED PEPPER TAPENADE

When entertaining, I often rely on my pepper tapenade recipe because it takes only 15 minutes to whip up and pop in the fridge. You can use walnuts or pecans intead of almonds.
—*Donna Magliaro, Denville, NJ*

Prep: 15 min. + chilling • **Makes:** 2 cups

- 3 garlic cloves, peeled
- 2 cups roasted sweet red peppers, drained
- ½ cup blanched almonds
- ⅓ cup tomato paste
- 2 Tbsp. olive oil
- ¼ tsp. salt
- ¼ tsp. pepper
  Minced fresh basil
  Toasted French bread baguette slices or water crackers

1. In a small saucepan, bring 2 cups water to a boil. Add garlic; cook, uncovered, just until tender, 6-8 minutes. Drain and pat dry. Place red peppers, almonds, tomato paste, olive oil, garlic, salt and pepper in a small food processor; process until blended. Transfer mixture to a small bowl. Refrigerate at least 4 hours to allow flavors to blend.
2. Sprinkle tapenade with basil. Serve with baguette slices.
2 Tbsp. spread: 58 cal., 4g fat (0 sat. fat), 0 chol., 152mg sod., 3g carb. (2g sugars, 1g fiber), 1g pro. **Diabetic exchanges:** 1 fat.

MARINATED ALMOND-STUFFED OLIVES

(PICTURED ON PAGE 29)
Marinated stuffed olives go over so well with company that I try to keep a batch of them in the fridge at all times.
—*Larissa Delk, Columbia, TN*

Prep: 15 min. + marinating • **Makes:** 8 cups

- 1 cup blanched almonds, toasted
- 3 cans (6 oz. each) pitted ripe olives, drained
- 3 jars (7 oz. each) pimiento-stuffed olives, undrained
- ½ cup white balsamic vinegar
- ½ cup dry red wine
- ½ cup canola oil
- 1 medium garlic clove, minced
- ½ tsp. sugar
- 1 tsp. dried oregano
- 1 tsp. pepper
- ½ tsp. dill weed
- ½ tsp. dried basil
- ½ tsp. dried parsley flakes

Insert an almond into each ripe olive; place in a large bowl. Add pimiento-stuffed olives with olive juice. In a small bowl, whisk vinegar, wine, oil, garlic, sugar and seasonings. Pour mixture over olives. Refrigerate, covered, 8 hours or overnight, stirring occasionally. Transfer to a serving bowl.
¼ cup: 78 cal., 7g fat (0 sat. fat), 0 chol., 455mg sod., 3g carb. (0 sugars, 1g fiber), 1g pro.

CHILI-LIME ROASTED CHICKPEAS

Looking for a lighter snack that's still a crowd-pleaser? You've found it! These zesty, crunchy chickpeas will have everyone happily munching.
—*Julie Ruble, Charlotte, NC*

Prep: 10 min. • **Bake:** 40 min. + cooling
Makes: 2 cups

- 2 cans (15 oz. each) chickpeas or garbanzo beans, rinsed, drained and patted dry
- 2 Tbsp. extra virgin olive oil
- 1 Tbsp. chili powder
- 2 tsp. ground cumin
- 1 tsp. grated lime zest
- 1 Tbsp. lime juice
- ¾ tsp. sea salt

1. Preheat oven to 400°. Line a 15x10x1-in. baking sheet with foil. Spread chickpeas in a single layer over foil, removing any loose skins. Bake until very crunchy, 40-45 minutes, stirring every 15 minutes.

2. Meanwhile, whisk remaining ingredients. Remove chickpeas from oven; let cool for 5 minutes. Drizzle with oil mixture; shake pan to coat. Cool completely. Store chickpeas in an airtight container.

Note: Drying chickpeas before roasting helps make them as crisp as possible; just rub them with a paper or kitchen towel. Chickpeas are tossed with the spice mixture after baking because spices can become bitter if they burn.

⅓ cup: 178 cal., 8g fat (1g sat. fat), 0mg chol., 463mg sod., 23g carb. (3g sugars, 6g fiber), 6g pro.

Rosemary-Sea Salt variation: Prepare chickpeas according to step 1 in the recipe above. Toss beans with 2 Tbsp. extra virgin olive oil, 1 Tbsp. minced fresh rosemary and ½ tsp. sea salt.

Orange Curry variation: Prepare chickpeas according to step 1 in the recipe above. Whisk 2 Tbsp. extra virgin olive oil, 1 tsp. grated orange zest and 1 Tbsp. curry powder. Toss beans with oil mixture. Cool completely.

Lemon-Pepper variation: Prepare chickpeas according to step 1 in the recipe above. Whisk 2 Tbsp. extra virgin olive oil, 1 tsp. grated lemon zest and 2 tsp. freshly ground pepper. Toss beans with oil mixture. Cool completely.

ITALIAN SAUSAGE BRUSCHETTA

ITALIAN SAUSAGE BRUSCHETTA

Sometimes I garnish each slice of this bruschetta with a sprig of fresh basil.
—*Teresa Ralston, New Albany, OH*

Takes: 20 min. • **Makes:** 2 dozen

- 1 lb. bulk Italian sausage
- 8 oz. mascarpone cheese, softened
- 3 Tbsp. prepared pesto
- 24 slices French bread baguette (½ in. thick)
- 3 Tbsp. olive oil
- ¾ cup finely chopped seeded plum tomatoes
- 3 Tbsp. chopped fresh parsley
- 3 Tbsp. shredded Parmesan cheese

1. In a large skillet, cook sausage over medium heat for 6-8 minutes or until no longer pink, breaking into crumbles; drain. In a small bowl, combine mascarpone cheese and pesto.

2. Preheat broiler. Place bread on ungreased baking sheets. Brush bread slices on 1 side with oil. Broil 3-4 in. from heat 30-45 seconds on each side or until golden brown. Spread with mascarpone mixture. Top each with sausage, tomatoes, parsley and Parmesan cheese. Serve warm.

1 appetizer: 131 cal., 11g fat (4g sat. fat), 22mg chol., 202mg sod., 5g carb. (0 sugars, 0 fiber), 4g pro.

TEST KITCHEN TIP

Mascarpone is a soft fresh cheese made from whole cream and citric or tartaric acid. It's rich, buttery and has a slightly sweet flavor. It has a smooth, thick texture and a creamy white color. Mascarpone can be added to a variety of sweet and savory dishes. It's delicious paired with berries, shortbread or figs.

PICKLED GREEN BEANS WITH SMOKED SALMON DIP

I came up with this appetizer for my son, who's big on healthy food that's delicious. The lighter beans-and-dip combo has won over even finicky eaters.
—*Dinah Halterman, Harmony, NC*

Prep: 30 min. + marinating
Makes: 12 servings (2⅓ cups dip)

- 1½ lbs. fresh green beans, trimmed
- 2 Tbsp. dill seed
- 3 garlic cloves, coarsely chopped
- 4 cups water
- 1¼ cups white wine vinegar
- 2 Tbsp. sea salt

DIP
- 1 pkg. (8 oz.) reduced-fat cream cheese or non-dairy imitation cream cheese
- ¾ cup plain yogurt
- 2 Tbsp. chopped fresh parsley
- 1 Tbsp. minced chives
- 1 tsp. horseradish
- ½ tsp. grated lemon zest
- ½ tsp. lemon juice
- ½ tsp. dill weed
- ¼ tsp. sea salt
- 1½ cups flaked smoked salmon fillets
  Fresh dill sprig, optional
  Assorted crackers, optional

1. Place beans in a 13x9-in dish. Add dill seed and garlic. In a large saucepan, combine the water, vinegar and salt. Bring to a boil; cook and stir until salt is dissolved. Pour hot brine over beans. Cool completely. Refrigerate, covered, 2 days.
2. For dip, in a small bowl, beat cream cheese and yogurt until smooth. Stir in parsley, chives, horseradish, lemon zest and juice, dill weed and salt. Stir in salmon. Refrigerate, covered, 1 hour to allow flavors to blend.
3. To serve, drain green beans; arrange on a platter. If desired, top dip with dill sprig. Serve dip with beans and, if desired, crackers.
1 serving: 99 cal., 5g fat (3g sat. fat), 19mg chol., 274mg sod., 7g carb. (3g sugars, 2g fiber), 7g pro.

PICKLED GREEN BEANS
WITH SMOKED
SALMON DIP

How to Host a My Favorite Things Party

If you've ever participated in a white elephant gift exchange, you know how much fun they are. Here's a similar gift swap, but with a twist. First, a my favorite things party is typically a ladies-only affair (sorry, guys). Second, it's way more fun than a white elephant party because there are fewer rules and the gifts are items any woman would love to receive (versus hilarious, but impractical, gag gifts).

You can get creative with any party variations of your choosing, but here's a rundown of the most widely accepted way to play:

- Each guest brings three of her favorite things to exchange during the party. Guests can bring three different favorite items or three of the same. For example, a coffee lover might bring three mugs, or a fashion lover might bring three scarves. Before the party, the host will designate a price limit per gift.

- Upon arrival, each guest drops off her individually wrapped gifts and writes her name on three slips of paper, which get tossed into a hat or bowl.

- When it's time to exchange gifts, each guests draws a number. These numbers determine the order of the presentation of gifts.

- Once every guest has a number, Guest No. 1 presents her gifts by explaining what they are, where she purchased them and why they are among her favorite things.

- She then selects three names out of the bowl. Those three ladies receive Guest No. 1's gift. If she draws her own name or selects the same name twice, those names are put back into the bowl.

- The exchange continues until all guests have presented their gifts and everyone has received three gifts. Unlike a white elephant exchange, there is no stealing or swapping.

- Guests may also bring a sweet treat or bottle of wine to share. And don't forget to take a group photo at the end of the night!

SPICED CRANBERRY GLOGG

Years ago, a friend of mine shared her easy recipe for glogg. Simmered on the stove, it'll warm up everyone from head to toe on a cold, blustery day.
—June Lindquist, Hammond, WI

Takes: 30 min. • **Makes:** 8 servings

- 6 whole cloves
- 2 cinnamon sticks (3 in.)
- 4 cardamom pods, crushed
- 4 cups cranberry juice, divided
- 1 cup raisins
- ¼ cup sugar
- 2 cups ruby port wine
  Additional raisins, optional

1. Place cloves, cinnamon and cardamom on a double thickness of cheesecloth. Gather corners of cloth to enclose seasonings; tie securely with string. Place in a large saucepan. Add 2 cups cranberry juice, raisins and sugar. Bring mixture to a simmer; cook, uncovered, 10 minutes.
2. Discard spice bag. Add wine and remaining cranberry juice; bring just to a simmer (do not boil). Serve warm in mugs with additional raisins if desired.
¾ cup: 231 cal., 0 fat (0 sat. fat), 0 chol., 10mg sod., 44g carb. (37g sugars, 1g fiber), 1g pro.

AUNT GRACE'S EGGNOG

When I was growing up, I could never get enough of the nonalcoholic eggnog my aunt always prepared for us kids. Now I enjoy the adult version.
—Susan Hein, Burlington, WI

Prep: 15 min. • **Cook:** 15 min. + chilling
Makes: 20 servings

- 8 cups 2% milk, divided
- 6 large eggs
- 1 cup plus 2 Tbsp. sugar, divided
- ½ cup rum
- ½ cup brandy
- ½ tsp. ground nutmeg
- 3 cups heavy whipping cream
  Cinnamon sticks and additional ground nutmeg, optional

1. In a large saucepan, heat 4 cups milk until bubbles form around sides of pan. Meanwhile, in a large bowl, whisk eggs and 1 cup sugar until blended. Slowly stir in hot milk; return all to saucepan.
2. Cook over medium-low heat until slightly thickened and a thermometer reads at least 160°, 6-8 minutes, stirring constantly (do not allow to boil). Immediately transfer to a large bowl.
3. Stir in rum, brandy, nutmeg and remaining milk. Refrigerate, covered, several hours or until cold.
4. In a large bowl, beat cream until it begins to thicken. Add remaining sugar; beat until soft peaks form. Fold into egg mixture. (Mixture may separate; stir before serving.) If desired, serve with cinnamon sticks and additional grated nutmeg.
¾ cup: 263 cal., 16g fat (10g sat. fat), 104mg chol., 77mg sod., 17g carb. (17g sugars, 0 fiber), 6g pro.

SWEET & SPICY CURRIED NUTS

The bowl is soon empty after I set out this zippy mix. You may want to make extra!
—Ginny Carmen, Pearl River, NY

Prep: 15 min. • **Bake:** 1½ hours • **Makes:** 8 cups

- 1 large egg white
- 2 cups pecan halves
- 2 cups salted cashews
- 2 cups salted roasted almonds
- ¾ cup packed dark brown sugar
- 2 Tbsp. mild curry powder
- 2 tsp. garlic salt
- 1 tsp. dried rosemary, crushed
- ½ to 1 tsp. cayenne pepper
- ½ tsp. ground cinnamon

Preheat oven to 250°. In a large bowl, whisk egg white until frothy. Add nuts; stir gently to coat. In a small bowl, combine brown sugar and seasonings. Sprinkle over nut mixture and toss to coat. Spread into a greased 15x10x1-in. baking pan. Bake 1½-2 hours or until dry and crisp, stirring every 15 minutes. Cool completely. Store in an airtight container.
⅓ cup: 226 cal., 18g fat (2g sat. fat), 0 chol., 276mg sod., 14g carb. (9g sugars, 3g fiber), 5g pro.

CRANBERRY BRIE PIE

Now you don't have to wait for dessert to have a slice of pie. Give everyone a thin slice of this extra special appetizer that joins tart cranberries with rich Brie.

—*Marie Parker, Milwaukee, WI*

Prep: 30 min. • **Bake:** 30 min. + cooling
Makes: 12 servings

- 3 cups fresh or frozen cranberries
- 1 cup packed brown sugar
- 1 cup orange juice
- ⅓ cup all-purpose flour
- 1 tsp. balsamic vinegar
- 1 sheet refrigerated pie crust
- 4 oz. Brie cheese, finely chopped
- 1 tsp. vanilla extract
- 2 Tbsp. butter

TOPPING
- ½ cup all-purpose flour
- ¼ cup packed brown sugar
- ¼ cup cold butter, cubed

1. Preheat oven to 450°. In a small saucepan, combine cranberries, brown sugar, orange juice, flour and vinegar. Cook over medium heat until berries pop, about 15 minutes.
2. Meanwhile, unroll crust into a 9-in. metal pie plate; flute edges. Sprinkle with cheese; bake 8 minutes or until cheese begins to melt. Reduce oven setting to 350°.
3. Remove cranberry mixture from heat; stir in vanilla. Pour into crust. Dot with butter.
4. For topping, in a small bowl, combine flour and brown sugar; cut in butter until crumbly. Sprinkle over filling.
5. Bake 30-35 minutes or until crust is golden brown and filling is bubbly (cover edges with foil during the last 20 minutes to prevent overbrowning if necessary). Serve warm or at room temperature. Refrigerate leftovers.
1 piece: 297 cal., 13g fat (7g sat. fat), 28mg chol., 179mg sod., 42g carb. (26g sugars, 1g fiber), 4g pro.

CRANBERRY
BRIE PIE

GAME NIGHT BEFORE CHRISTMAS

The merriest month of the year is also the busiest. Amid the hubbub of holiday preparations, it's easy to lose sight of what matters most. This year, start a new tradition with a family game night. Turn off the TV, put down the phones and bring out the games! Enjoy some of these snacks and treats while creating lasting memories with those you love most.

Game Night Domino Brownies (p. 48)

PINEAPPLE SMOKIES

With a tangy-sweet sauce, these sausages are an excellent starter for holiday parties or any occasion. Plus, the recipe takes only 15 minutes to prepare.
—*Dorothy Anderson, Ottawa, KS*

Takes: 15 min. • **Makes:** about 8 dozen

- 1 cup packed brown sugar
- 3 Tbsp. all-purpose flour
- 2 tsp. ground mustard
- 1 cup pineapple juice
- ½ cup white vinegar
- 1½ tsp. reduced-sodium soy sauce
- 2 lbs. miniature smoked sausages

In a large saucepan, combine the sugar, flour and mustard. Gradually stir in the pineapple juice, white vinegar and soy sauce. Bring to a boil over medium heat; cook and stir until thickened, about 2 minutes. Add sausages; stir to coat. Cook, uncovered, until heated through, about 5 minutes longer. Serve warm.

1 sausage: 40 cal., 3g fat (1g sat. fat), 6mg chol., 100mg sod., 3g carb. (3g sugars, 0 fiber), 1g pro.

CRANBERRY-CHILI CHEESE SPREAD

Appetizers just don't get much easier than this ritzy-looking cheese spread with its refreshing hint of lime. I turn to this recipe whenever unexpected guests drop in.
—*Laurie LaClair, North Richland Hills, TX*

Takes: 10 min. • **Makes:** 14 servings

- 2 pkg. (8 oz. each) cream cheese, softened
- 1 can (14 oz.) whole-berry cranberry sauce
- 1 can (4 oz.) chopped green chiles, drained
- 1 green onion, sliced
- 1 Tbsp. lime juice
- ½ tsp. garlic salt
- ½ tsp. cayenne pepper
- ½ tsp. chili powder
  Assorted crackers

Place cream cheese on a serving plate. In a small bowl, combine the cranberry sauce, chopped green chiles, onion, lime juice and spices. Spoon over cream cheese. Serve with assorted crackers.

¼ cup: 157 cal., 11g fat (7g sat. fat), 36mg chol., 200mg sod., 12g carb. (7g sugars, 1g fiber), 3g pro.

APPETIZER WREATH

I have lots of fun with this festive appetizer wreath. I often place a bowl of stuffed olives in the center.
—*Shirley Privratsky, Dickinson, ND*

Prep: 20 min. • **Bake:** 15 min. + cooling
Makes: 16 servings

- 2 tubes (8 oz. each) refrigerated crescent rolls
- 1 pkg. (8 oz.) cream cheese, softened
- ½ cup sour cream
- 1 tsp. dill weed
- ⅛ tsp. garlic powder
- 1½ cups chopped fresh broccoli florets
- 1 cup finely chopped celery
- ½ cup finely chopped sweet red pepper
  Celery leaves

1. Remove crescent dough from packaging (do not unroll). Cut each tube into 8 slices. Arrange in an 11-in. circle on an ungreased 14-in. pizza pan.
2. Bake at 375° for 15-20 minutes or until golden brown. Cool for 5 minutes before carefully removing the wreath to a serving platter; cool completely.
3. In a small bowl, beat the cream cheese, sour cream, dill and garlic powder until smooth. Spread on wreath; top with the broccoli, celery and red pepper. Form a bow garnish with celery leaves.

1 slice: 125 cal., 9g fat (5g sat. fat), 21mg chol., 166mg sod., 7g carb. (2g sugars, 0 fiber), 3g pro.

APPETIZER WREATH

DECADENT SPINACH-STUFFED
SHELLS

DECADENT SPINACH-STUFFED SHELLS

I created this comforting dish to serve on Christmas Eve, but it's so good we enjoy it all year long. It can easily be assembled and frozen to bake at a later date. If you have any leftover cheese mixture, it can be served as a dip either cold or spooned into ramekins and baked until brown. If you don't like roasted red peppers, feel free to substitute chopped sun-dried tomatoes in the filling and any other pasta sauce.

—*Crystal Schlueter, Babbitt, MN*

Prep: 25 min. • **Cook:** 30 min.
Makes: 12 servings

- 1 pkg. (12 oz.) jumbo pasta shells
- 1 jar (24 oz.) roasted red pepper and garlic pasta sauce, divided
- 2 pkg. (8 oz. each) cream cheese, softened
- 1 cup roasted garlic Alfredo sauce
  Dash salt
  Dash pepper
  Dash crushed red pepper flakes, optional
- 2 cups shredded Italian cheese blend
- ½ cup grated Parmesan cheese
- 1 pkg. (10 oz.) frozen chopped spinach, thawed and squeezed dry
- ½ cup finely chopped water-packed artichoke hearts
- ¼ cup finely chopped roasted sweet red pepper
  Additional Parmesan cheese, optional

1. Preheat oven to 350°. Cook pasta shells according to the package directions for al dente. Drain.

2. Spread 1 cup pasta sauce into a greased 13x9-in. baking dish. In a large bowl, beat the cream cheese, Alfredo sauce and seasonings until blended. Stir in cheeses and vegetables. Spoon into the shells. Arrange in prepared baking dish.

3. Pour remaining sauce over top. Bake, covered, 20 minutes. If desired, sprinkle with additional Parmesan cheese. Bake, uncovered, 10-15 minutes longer or until cheese is melted.

3 stuffed pasta shells: 389 cal., 22g fat (13g sat. fat), 70mg chol., 707mg sod., 33g carb. (7g sugars, 3g fiber), 14g pro.

Here's the Scoop
Use an ice cream scoop to easily fill the cooked pasta shells.

PEPPERY VEGETABLE SALAD

I'm always looking for great recipes to use all the harvest our large garden produces every year, and this colorful combination is one of my favorites. It's loaded with crunch and well-seasoned flavor.

—*Andrea Sheatz, Knox, PA*

Prep: 20 min. + chilling • **Makes:** 12 servings

- 15 poblano and/or banana peppers, seeded and coarsely chopped (about 7 cups)
- 1½ cups fresh cauliflowerets, cut into bite-size pieces
- 3 small carrots, coarsely chopped
- 1 large sweet red pepper, coarsely chopped
- 1 cup pitted ripe olives
- 3 garlic cloves, minced
- 1 cup water
- 1 cup white vinegar
- ¾ cup olive oil
- 4 tsp. dried oregano
- 1 tsp. salt

In a large bowl, combine poblano peppers, cauliflowerets, carrots, red pepper, olives and garlic. In a large bowl, whisk remaining ingredients. Pour over vegetable mixture and toss to coat. Cover and refrigerate overnight. Serve with a slotted spoon.

Note: Wear disposable gloves when cutting hot peppers; the oils can burn skin. Avoid touching your face.

¾ cup: 175 cal., 15g fat (2g sat. fat), 0 chol., 297mg sod., 11g carb. (5g sugars, 4g fiber), 2g pro. **Diabetic exchanges:** 3 fat, 2 vegetable.

Poblano peppers have thick walls and a mild, earthy flavor. They're generally sold fresh, young and dark green, but once ripened and dried, they're called ancho peppers and hold much more heat.

SOFT ONION BREADSTICKS

These breadsticks bake up golden and chewy. They make the perfect complement to your favorite pasta dish.

—Maryellen Hays, Wolcottville, IN

Prep: 30 min. + rising • **Bake:** 20 min.
Makes: 2 dozen

- ¾ cup chopped onion
- 1 Tbsp. canola oil
- 1 pkg. (¼ oz.) active dry yeast
- ½ cup warm water (110° to 115°)
- ½ cup warm whole milk (110° to 115°)
- ¼ cup butter, softened
- 2 large eggs, room temperature, divided use
- 1 Tbsp. sugar
- 1½ tsp. salt
- 3½ to 4 cups all-purpose flour
- 2 Tbsp. cold water
- 2 Tbsp. sesame seeds
- 1 Tbsp. poppy seeds

1. In a small skillet, saute onion in oil until tender; cool. In a large bowl, dissolve yeast in warm water. Add the milk, butter, 1 egg, sugar, salt and 1 cup flour. Beat on medium speed for 2 minutes. Stir in onion and enough remaining flour to form a soft dough.

2. Turn onto a floured surface; knead until smooth and elastic, 6-8 minutes. Place in a greased bowl, turning once to grease top. Cover and let rise in a warm place until doubled, about 1 hour.

3. Punch dough down. Let dough stand for 10 minutes. Turn onto a lightly floured surface; divide into 32 pieces. Shape each piece into an 8-in. rope. Place 2 in. apart on greased baking sheets. Cover and let rise for 15 minutes.

4. Beat cold water and remaining egg; brush over breadsticks. Sprinkle half with sesame seeds and half with poppy seeds. Bake at 350° for 16-22 minutes or until golden brown. Remove to wire racks.

1 breadstick: 82 cal., 3g fat (1g sat. fat), 16mg chol., 129mg sod., 12g carb. (1g sugars, 1g fiber), 2g pro.

SOFT ONION
BREADSTICKS

ITALIAN SAUSAGE & FENNEL SOUP

Many years ago I watched chef and TV personality Mario Batali make an Italian soup that had fennel, garlic and bread as the base. I have dietary restrictions that don't allow me to eat bread, so I made my own version by omitting the bread and adding sausage for protein. It's hearty and irresistible on a cold night. It can feed a crowd or provide plenty of leftovers. If you find yourself missing the bread, serve it on the side to perfectly round out your meal.
—*Suzanne Clark, Fort Dodge, IA*

Prep: 20 min. • **Cook:** 30 min.
Makes: 12 servings (3 qt.)

- 2 Tbsp. olive oil, divided
- 1 pkg. (12 oz.) fully cooked Italian or spicy chicken sausage links, halved lengthwise and sliced ¾-in. thick
- 1 medium fennel bulb, cut into ¾-in. pieces (2 cups)
- 3 medium carrots, cut into ½-in. slices
- 1 medium onion, coarsely chopped
- 3 garlic cloves, thinly sliced
- ¾ lb. red potatoes (about 3 medium), cut into ¾-in. cubes
- 1 can (15 oz.) cannellini beans, rinsed and drained
- 1 carton (32 oz.) chicken broth
- 4 cups water
- 1 can (14½ oz.) diced tomatoes, drained
- ½ tsp. salt
- ½ tsp. pepper

1. In a 6-qt. stockpot, heat 1 Tbsp. oil over medium-high heat; saute sausage until lightly browned, 2-3 minutes. Remove sausage, reserving drippings in pot.
2. In same pot, heat the remaining oil over medium heat; saute fennel, carrots and onion 8 minutes. Add garlic; cook and stir 1 minute. Add potatoes, beans, broth and water; bring to a boil. Reduce heat; simmer, covered, for 10 minutes.
3. Stir in tomatoes, salt, pepper and sausage; return to a boil. Reduce the heat; simmer, uncovered, until vegetables are tender, about 5 minutes.
1 cup: 140 cal., 5g fat (1g sat. fat), 23mg chol., 707mg sod., 16g carb. (4g sugars, 4g fiber), 8g pro. **Diabetic exchanges:** 1 starch, 1 lean meat, ½ fat.

ORANGE GINGERBREAD TASSIES

I make big Christmas cookie plates every year and it's fun to have something with a different shape to include. These have a delicious flavor with the gingerbread and orange, and they are really easy! This is also yummy with lemon zest if you prefer that over the orange. You can also decorate with some candied orange peel if you have it.
—*Elisabeth Larsen, Pleasant Grove, UT*

Prep: 20 min. + chilling
Bake: 15 min. + cooling • **Makes:** 2 dozen

- ½ cup butter, softened
- 4 oz. cream cheese, softened
- ¼ cup molasses
- 1 tsp. ground ginger
- ½ tsp. ground cinnamon
- ½ tsp. ground allspice
- ¼ tsp. ground cloves
- 1 cup all-purpose flour
- ½ cup white baking chips
- ¼ cup heavy whipping cream
- 2 Tbsp. butter
- 4 tsp. grated orange zest

1. Beat first 7 ingredients until light and fluffy. Gradually beat in flour. Refrigerate, covered, until firm enough to shape, about 1 hour.
2. Preheat oven to 350°. Shape dough into 1-in. balls; press evenly onto bottom and up sides of ungreased mini-muffin cups. Bake until golden brown, 15-18 minutes. Press centers with the handle of a wooden spoon to reshape as necessary. Cool completely in pan before removing to wire rack.
3. In a microwave-safe bowl, heat the baking chips, cream and butter until blended, stirring occasionally. Stir in orange zest; cool mixture completely. Spoon into crusts.
1 cookie: 91 cal., 6g fat (4g sat. fat), 13mg chol., 43mg sod., 9g carb. (5g sugars, 0 fiber), 1g pro.

COCONUT
SNOWMAN

COCONUT SNOWMAN

My mom made her basic coconut candy recipe for years, but I took it a step further and created jolly snowman heads. These cute little characters are worth the extra effort because they're always a big hit!
—*Donell Mayfield, Rio Rancho, MN*

Prep: 4 hours + chilling • **Makes:** 4 dozen

- 4 cups sweetened shredded coconut, coarsely chopped
- 3¾ cups confectioners' sugar
- ⅔ cup sweetened condensed milk
- ¼ cup butter, softened
- 1½ cups vanilla or white chips
- 2 pkg. (11½ oz. each) milk chocolate chips
- 1 pkg. (10 oz.) large marshmallows
  Black, orange and red decorator icing
  Green leaf-shaped decorator candies

1. In a large bowl, combine the coconut, confectioners' sugar, milk and butter. Shape into 1¼-in. balls; place on waxed paper-lined baking sheets. Loosely cover and chill for 1¼ hours or until firm.
2. In a microwave, melt the vanilla chips at 70% power for 1 minute; stir. Microwave in additional 10- to 20-second intervals, stirring until smooth.
3. Dip balls in melted chips; place on waxed paper-lined baking sheets. Chill until firm, about 15 minutes. Set aside remaining melted vanilla chips.
4. In a microwave, melt semisweet chips on high for about 1 minute; stir. Microwave in additional 10- to 20-second intervals, stirring until smooth.
5. For hats, dip each marshmallow in chocolate; place on a waxed paper-lined baking sheet, allowing excess to drip down. Swirl the marshmallows in chocolate on waxed paper to create hat brims. Chill until firm, about 15 minutes.
6. Level the top of coated coconut balls. Attach marshmallows hats, using reserved melted vanilla chips. With black icing, add eyes and a mouth to each face; with orange icing, add a nose. Use red icing and leaf candies for holly on hats. Store in an airtight container.
1 snowman: 181 cal., 8g fat (6g sat. fat), 7mg chol., 49mg sod., 28g carb. (21g sugars, 1g fiber), 1g pro.

CHRISTMAS POPCORN

Keep this fun, munchable snack on hand for carolers, neighbors and other drop-in visitors. You'll be glad you did!
—*Karen Eiben, La Salle, IL*

Takes: 15 min. • **Makes:** 8 cups

- 1 pkg. (3.3 oz.) butter-flavored microwave popcorn
- 1 cup white baking chips
- 1 cup red and green milk chocolate M&M's
- 8 miniature candy canes, coarsely crushed
- ½ cup salted peanuts

1. Microwave popcorn according to package directions. Transfer to a large bowl. In a microwave, melt white baking chips; stir until smooth. Pour over the popcorn and stir until coated. Add the M&M's, crushed candy canes and peanuts.
2. Immediately spread onto waxed paper; let stand until set. Store in an airtight container.
1 cup: 376 cal., 21g fat (9g sat. fat), 7mg chol., 183mg sod., 44g carb. (33g sugars, 2g fiber), 6g pro.

WHITE HOT CHOCOLATE

This is a favorite at my house. The creamy drink is smooth and soothing with a hint of seasonal spice.
—*Debbi Smith, Crossett, AR*

Takes: 15 min. • **Makes:** 4 servings (1 qt.)

- 3 cups half-and-half cream, divided
- ⅔ cup white baking chips
- 1 cinnamon stick (3 in.)
- ⅛ tsp. ground nutmeg
- 1 tsp. vanilla extract
- ¼ tsp. almond extract
  Ground cinnamon, optional

In a large saucepan, combine ¼ cup cream, white chips, cinnamon stick and nutmeg. Stir over low heat until chips are melted; discard cinnamon. Add remaining cream; stir until heated through. Remove from the heat; add extracts. Sprinkle each serving with ground cinnamon if desired.
1 cup: 397 cal., 27g fat (18g sat. fat), 96mg chol., 116mg sod., 23g carb. (6g sugars, 0 fiber), 8g pro.

GAME NIGHT
DOMINO BROWNIES

Around the Clock

Upcycle an old set of dominoes into the numbers on a clever homemade timepiece. The clock will come in handy the next time you host game night, and it's sure to be a conversation starter. Who needs a stopwatch when you have this beauty hanging on the wall?

WHAT YOU'LL NEED
Dominoes numbered 1-12
11-in. round craft plaque or round
    piece of wood
Clock mechanism kit and batteries
4-in.-long wood block, slightly wider
    than clock mechanism
Iron gear or other decorative element,
    optional
Picture hook
Wood glue
Paint
Paintbrush
Drill

DIRECTIONS
1. In the center of the wooden plaque, drill a hole large enough to accommodate the clock mechanism.

2. Paint wood with 2-3 coats of paint, allowing to dry between coats. Paint the dots on the dominoes, if desired.

3. After the paint has thoroughly dried, adhere an iron gear or other decorative piece onto center of circle, if desired, using wood glue. Press down firmly and allow glue to set.

4. With wood glue, attach dominoes to gear, if using, or to the wooden plaque. There are clock templates online to help with proper alignment. Place the 12 o'clock piece first, then the 6 o'clock, then 3, then 9 and so on until the face is filled in.

5. Attach picture hook to the block of wood. Using wood glue, adhere wooden block to back of plaque in top center. Make sure to align block with 12 o'clock position.

6. Insert clock mechanism through center hole of plaque. Attach clock hands and washers provided in kit. Insert batteries, set the clock and hang on a wall.

Note: Clock hands come in a variety of colors, most often black or gold. They can be spray-painted in any color.

GAME NIGHT DOMINO BROWNIES

Brownies are the perfect handheld treat, and they're even more fun when decorated like dominoes. Chocolate lovers, rejoice!
—*Barbara Birk, St. George, UT*

- -

Prep: 15 min. • **Bake:** 25 min. + cooling
Makes: 32 servings

    1   cup butter, softened
    2   cups sugar
    4   large eggs, room temperature
    2   tsp. vanilla extract
    1¾ cups all-purpose flour
    6   Tbsp. baking cocoa
    1   tsp. baking powder
    ¼   tsp. salt
    ½   cup vanilla frosting

1. In a large bowl, cream butter and sugar. Add 1 egg at a time, beating well after each addition. Beat in vanilla. Combine the flour, cocoa, baking powder and salt; gradually add to creamed mixture and mix well.
2. Spread into a greased 13x9-in. baking pan. Bake at 350° for 25-30 minutes or until a toothpick inserted in the center comes out clean. Cool on a wire rack.
3. Cut into 32 bars. Use frosting to decorate like dominoes.
1 brownie: 104 cal., 1g fat (1g sat. fat), 23mg chol., 51mg sod., 21g carb. (15g sugars, 0 fiber), 2g pro.

TROPICAL CHRISTMAS PARTY

Dreaming of a warmer climate? This year, say goodbye to chilly weather and aloha to a fun and festive beach bash. With this island-inspired menu, floral leis strung throughout the house and Bing Crosby crooning "Mele Kalikimaka" in the background, tropical bliss is just a step away—even if you still have to shovel snow!

Tropical Cooler (p. 54) **Broiled Papaya-Shrimp Kabobs** (p. 58)

PINEAPPLE
& CURRY DIP

PINEAPPLE & CURRY DIP

The flavors of pineapple, mustard and curry blend deliciously in this appetizing dip. It's also terrific with an assortment of vegetables or your favorite fancy crackers.
—*Barb Meninga, Kalamazoo, MI*

Takes: 15 min. • **Makes:** 1¼ cups dip

- 1 fresh pineapple
- 1 pkg. (8 oz.) cream cheese, softened
- ⅓ cup plus 1 Tbsp. chutney
- ½ to ¾ tsp. curry powder
- ¼ tsp. ground mustard
- ¼ cup slivered almonds, toasted
  Assorted crackers, optional

1. Cut pineapple in half vertically, leaving the top attached. Remove fruit from 1 half, leaving a ¾-in. shell. Remove fruit and discard outer peel from remaining half; cut pineapple into bite-sized pieces. Set aside.

2. In a small bowl, beat the cream cheese, chutney, curry and mustard until smooth. Spoon into the pineapple shell and top with almonds. Serve immediately or refrigerate for up to 4 hours (remove from the refrigerator 30 minutes before serving). Serve with cut pineapple and, if desired, crackers.

2 Tbsp. dip and 3 pineapple pieces: 179 cal., 9g fat (5g sat. fat), 23mg chol., 180mg sod., 23g carb. (16g sugars, 2g fiber), 2g pro.

NUTTY HAWAIIAN

I came up with this tropical-tasting cocktail on a whim one day. Later, when my husband and I went to Key West, Florida, I asked the bartender at an open bar to make it. He loved it so much he asked if he could use it, and of course I said yes!
—*Tracy Davidheiser, Reading, PA*

Takes: 5 min. • **Makes:** 2 servings

-   Ice cubes
- 2 oz. Southern Comfort
- 2 oz. coconut rum
- 1½ oz. amaretto
- 2 cans (6 oz. each) unsweetened pineapple juice
    Maraschino cherries

Fill a shaker three-fourths full with ice. Add Southern Comfort, rum, amaretto and juice. Cover and shake for 10-15 seconds or until condensation forms on outside of shaker. Strain into chilled glasses filled with ice. Top with cherries.

1 cup: 299 cal., 0 fat (0 sat. fat), 0 chol., 6mg sod., 30g carb. (25g sugars, 0 fiber), 1g pro.

▲
How to Make a Pineapple Bowl

Pineapples add a sweet touch to any party. Here's how to create a fun serving bowl using this tropical fruit.

1. Using a large knife, cut the pineapple in half lengthwise.

2. Using a small serrated knife, cut around the edge of the pineapple, leaving about a ¾-in. shell.

3. Next, remove the center core by cutting down both sides of the core at a slight angle.

4. Remove the center core of the pineapple. Place dip inside bowl of pineapple. Slice removed pineapple and serve alongside dip.

BANANA-NUT GREEN SALAD

Ripe sliced bananas and crunchy ginger-roasted walnuts create a yummy combo in this fresh tossed salad. Try swapping in Gorgonzola cheese for extra flavor.
—*Betty Jean Nichols, Eugene, OR*

Prep: 15 min. • **Bake:** 20 min.
Makes: 10 servings

- 1 Tbsp. vegetable oil
- 1 tsp. soy sauce
- ¼ tsp. salt
- ¼ tsp. ground ginger
- ⅛ tsp. onion powder
- 1 cup walnut halves

DRESSING

- ⅓ cup orange juice
- ¼ cup lime juice
- ¼ cup vegetable oil
- ½ tsp. salt
- ⅛ tsp. white pepper

SALAD

- 12 cups torn leaf lettuce
- 4 medium firm bananas, cut into ½-in. slices
- ⅔ cup crumbled blue cheese

1. Preheat oven to 300°. In a bowl, combine the oil, soy sauce, salt, ginger and onion powder. Add walnuts; toss to coat. Transfer to an ungreased baking sheet. Bake until the nuts are lightly browned and evenly coated, 18-20 minutes, stirring every 5 minutes. Set aside.
2. In a small bowl, whisk the dressing ingredients. In a large bowl, combine the lettuce and bananas. Drizzle with dressing; toss to coat. Sprinkle with cheese and toasted walnuts. Serve immediately.
1 cup: 219 cal., 16g fat (3g sat. fat), 7mg chol., 340mg sod., 16g carb. (11g sugars, 3g fiber), 5g pro.

TROPICAL COOLER

With only four simple ingredients, this refreshing punch is easy to stir up in just 10 minutes. I served it at a party for my son, and everyone liked the slightly tart flavor.
—*Robin Werner, Brush Prairie, WA*

Takes: 10 min.
Makes: 12 servings (¾ cup each)

- 1 bottle (32 oz.) cranberry juice, chilled
- 1 liter ginger ale, chilled
- 1 cup chilled tropical fruit punch
- 1 cup chilled orange juice
  Assorted fresh fruit or edible flowers, optional

Just before serving, combine the first 4 ingredients in a punch bowl. If desired, garnish with fruit or edible flowers.
¾ cup: 87 cal., 0 fat (0 sat. fat), 0 chol., 10mg sod., 23g carb. (22g sugars, 0 fiber), 0 pro.

CALYPSO SNACK MIX

Get your party on with this tempting snack mix. While it's a definite treat for the kids, it's also the perfect afternoon pick-me-up for adults.
—*Beth Royals, Richmond, VA*

Takes: 25 min. • **Makes:** 2 qt.

- 1 cup Corn Chex
- 1 cup Rice Chex
- 5 Tbsp. flaked coconut, divided
- 3 oz. white baking chocolate, chopped
- 2 tsp. shortening
- 2 cups Golden Grahams
- 1½ cups miniature pretzels
- 1 pkg. (7 oz.) dried tropical fruit
- 1 jar (3 oz.) macadamia nuts

1. In a large bowl, combine the Chex cereals and 2 Tbsp. coconut; set aside.
2. In a microwave, melt chocolate and shortening; stir until smooth. Pour over Chex mixture and toss to coat. Immediately spread onto a waxed paper-lined baking sheet; refrigerate until set, about 5 minutes.
3. In another large bowl, combine Golden Grahams, pretzels, fruit, nuts, Chex mixture and the remaining coconut. Store in an airtight container.
¾ cup: 273 cal., 12g fat (4g sat. fat), 2mg chol., 277mg sod., 40g carb. (24g sugars, 2g fiber), 3g pro.

TROPICAL
COOLER

SWEET & SMOKY BBQ HAM STEAKS

My husband and I enjoy grilling our meals during the summer months and never tire of experimenting with new recipes. This past summer, he suggested pairing my homemade barbecue sauce with grilled ham steaks—and the results were mouthwatering! The sauce can be made several days ahead of time, if necessary; refrigerate until ready to use.
—*Sue Gronholz, Beaver Dam, WI*

Prep: 30 min. + marinating • **Grill:** 10 min.
Makes: 10 servings

- 1 Tbsp. olive oil
- 1 cup chopped onions
- 1 garlic clove, minced
- ⅔ cup pineapple spreadable fruit
- 1 can (15 oz.) tomato sauce
- ½ cup packed brown sugar
- ¼ cup cider vinegar
- 2 Tbsp. soy sauce
- 1 Tbsp. lemon juice
- 1½ tsp. molasses
- 1 tsp. ground mustard
- ½ tsp. liquid smoke, optional
- ¼ tsp. pepper
- ¼ tsp. celery seed
- 3 fully cooked bone-in ham steaks (1 lb. each and ⅜ in. thick)

1. In a large saucepan, heat olive oil over medium heat. Add onions; saute until softened and lightly browned, 5-6 minutes. Add garlic; cook 1 minute more. Pulse onions, garlic and pineapple preserves in a food processor or blender until smooth. Return to pan. Add next 10 ingredients. Bring to a boil over medium heat; cook, stirring constantly, until sauce reaches desired consistency, 10-15 minutes. Remove from heat and cool slightly.
2. Reserve ½ cup sauce; spread remaining sauce generously over both sides of ham steaks. Refrigerate, covered, 1-2 hours.
3. Grill ham steaks, covered, on a greased grill rack over medium direct heat, turning and brushing frequently with reserved sauce, until heated through, 10-15 minutes.
3 oz. ham: 250 cal., 8g fat (2g sat. fat), 52mg chol., 1369mg sod., 28g carb. (24g sugars, 1g fiber), 18g pro.

ISLAND
CHICKEN
WINGS

ISLAND CHICKEN WINGS

This recipe brings a tasty twist to a regular chicken wing. The orange flavor changes the game and has you coming back for seconds!
—*Caren Berry, Lancaster, CA*

Prep: 35 min. • **Bake:** 40 min. • **Makes:** 3 dozen

- 18 chicken wings (about 3½ lbs.)
- 1 can (12 oz.) frozen orange juice concentrate, thawed
- 3 cups flaked coconut
- 3 cups panko (Japanese) bread crumbs
- 3 Tbsp. grated orange zest
- 1 Tbsp. minced fresh gingerroot
- 1 tsp. curry powder
- ½ tsp. salt
- ¼ tsp. pepper
- 1 cup orange marmalade
- 3 Tbsp. hot water
- ¼ to ½ tsp. crushed red pepper flakes

1. Preheat oven to 350°. Line a 15x10x1-in. baking pan with foil and coat with cooking spray; set aside.
2. Cut wings into 3 sections; discard wing tip sections. Place orange juice concentrate in a shallow bowl. In a separate shallow bowl, combine the coconut, bread crumbs, orange zest, ginger, curry powder, salt and pepper. Dip chicken wings in orange juice concentrate then coat with coconut mixture.
3. Place on prepared baking sheet. Bake until juices run clear, 40-50 minutes. Meanwhile, in a small bowl, combine the marmalade, hot water and pepper flakes. Serve with wings.

1 piece: 128 cal., 6g fat (3g sat. fat), 14mg chol., 81mg sod., 14g carb. (10g sugars, 1g fiber), 5g pro.

⬆

Uncooked chicken wing sections (wingettes) may be substituted for whole chicken wings.

FRUIT & NUT SWEET POTATO CASSEROLE

Here's a naturally sweet and comforting twist on a classic holiday dish. Fruit, cinnamon, ginger and chopped nuts make it something guests won't soon forget!
—*Athena Russell, Greenville, SC*

Prep: 35 min. • **Bake:** 40 min.
Makes: 14 servings (¾ cup each)

- 4 lbs. sweet potatoes, peeled and cubed
- 1½ cups unsweetened apple juice
- ¼ cup lemon juice
- 4 small bananas, peeled and chopped
- 2 large apples, peeled and chopped
- 2 Tbsp. butter
- 1 Tbsp. minced fresh gingerroot
- 1 tsp. salt
- ½ tsp. ground cinnamon
- ½ tsp. ground allspice
- ½ cup chopped dried apricots
- 1 cup chopped pecans

1. Place sweet potatoes in a large saucepan or Dutch oven; cover with water. Bring to a boil. Reduce heat; cover and cook just until tender, 10-15 minutes. Drain. In a large bowl, mash potatoes with apple juice and lemon juice.
2. Meanwhile, in a large skillet, saute bananas and apples in butter until tender. Stir in the ginger, salt, cinnamon and allspice; cook and stir 5 minutes longer. Cool slightly.
3. Place banana mixture in a food processor; cover and process until smooth. Stir the banana mixture and apricots into mashed potato mixture. Transfer to a 13x9-in. baking dish coated with cooking spray; sprinkle with pecans.
4. Bake, uncovered, at 350° until edges are golden brown, 40-50 minutes.

¾ cup: 219 cal., 8g fat (2g sat. fat), 4mg chol., 192mg sod., 37g carb. (20g sugars, 5g fiber), 3g pro.

CURRIED RICE WITH ALMONDS

In this rice dish, green onions and sweet red pepper give holiday color, raisins bring a touch of sweetness and almonds add crunch. I think you'll agree that the mild curry flavor pleases all palates.
—*Janice Christofferson, Eagle River, WI*

Prep: 10 min. • **Cook:** 35 min.
Makes: 10 servings

- ½ cup thinly sliced green onions
- ⅓ cup chopped sweet red pepper
- 3 Tbsp. butter, divided
- 1½ cups uncooked long grain rice
- 1 tsp. minced fresh gingerroot
- 3 cups hot water
- ¼ cup golden raisins
- 2 Tbsp. lime juice
- 2 Tbsp. soy sauce
- 2 tsp. chicken bouillon granules
- 1 to 2 tsp. curry powder
- 1 tsp. grated lime zest
- 1 can (8 oz.) pineapple chunks, drained and cut into thirds
- ⅓ cup slivered almonds, toasted

1. In a large saucepan, saute the onions and red pepper in 1 Tbsp. butter until tender; set aside.
2. In the same saucepan, saute rice and ginger in the remaining butter until golden brown, 4-5 minutes. Stir in the water, raisins, lime juice, soy sauce, bouillon, curry and lime zest. Bring to a boil. Reduce heat; cover and simmer until rice is tender, 16-20 minutes. Stir in pineapple and the red pepper mixture. Garnish with almonds.

¾ cup: 195 cal., 6g fat (2g sat. fat), 9mg chol., 382mg sod., 33g carb. (6g sugars, 2g fiber), 4g pro. **Diabetic exchanges:** 2 starch, 1 fat.

BROILED PAPAYA-SHRIMP KABOBS

Any gathering will be special when you serve flavorful and juicy kabobs. They're easy to assemble and broil to perfection.
—*Anthony Glazik, Peotone, IL*

- -

Prep: 30 min. + marinating • **Cook:** 10 min.
Makes: 10 servings

1	cup chutney
⅓	cup minced fresh cilantro
2	Tbsp. lime juice
4	tsp. olive oil
2	tsp. hot pepper sauce
4	garlic cloves, minced
10	bacon strips
1½	lbs. uncooked shrimp (31-40 per lb.), peeled and deveined
2	medium papayas, peeled and cut into 1-in. cubes
30	pineapple chunks
30	cherry tomatoes
8	green onions or shallots

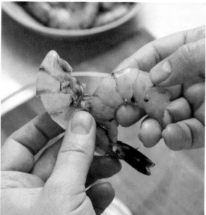

1. In a small bowl, combine the chutney, cilantro, lime juice, oil, pepper sauce and garlic. Cover and refrigerate.
2. Cut bacon strips in half lengthwise and widthwise. In a skillet, partially cook the bacon for 2 minutes on each side; drain. Wrap a piece of bacon around each shrimp.
3. On 10 metal or soaked wooden skewers, alternately thread the shrimp, papaya, pineapple, tomatoes and green onions. Brush with half the chutney mixture. Turn and brush with remaining chutney mixture. Cover and refrigerate for at least 30 minutes.
4. Broil 4-5 in. from the heat for 5 minutes. Turn and broil until the shrimp turn pink, 5-7 minutes.

1 kabob: 343 cal., 6g fat (1g sat. fat), 91mg chol., 523mg sod., 58g carb. (41g sugars, 3g fiber), 15g pro.

▲

Peeling & Deveining Shrimp

1. Start on the underside at the head area to remove shell from shrimp. Pull legs and first section of shell to 1 side. Continue pulling shell up around the top and to the other side. Pull off shell by tail if desired.

2. Remove the black vein running down the back of the shrimp by making a shallow slit with a paring knife along the back from the head area to the tail.

3. Rinse shrimp under cold water to remove the vein.

BROILED
PAPAYA-SHRIMP
KABOBS

KEY LIME BLONDIES WITH
GRAHAM STREUSEL

KEY LIME BLONDIES WITH GRAHAM STREUSEL

Here's my tropical take on a classic treat. It combines the taste of Key lime pie in a blondie form with a pie crust bottom and cream cheese frosting. You can make a thicker crust if desired.
—Kristin LaBoon, Austin, TX

- -

Prep: 35 min. + chilling
Bake: 25 min. + cooling • **Makes:** 16 servings

- 1⅓ cups graham cracker crumbs, divided
- ⅓ cup plus 2 Tbsp. melted butter, divided
- 3 Tbsp. plus ¼ cup packed brown sugar, divided
- ⅔ cup butter, softened
- 1 cup plus 1 Tbsp. sugar, divided
- 2 large eggs, room temperature
- 1 large egg white, room temperature
- 3 Tbsp. Key lime juice
- 4½ tsp. grated Key lime zest
- 1 cup all-purpose flour
- ½ tsp. plus ⅛ tsp. salt, divided
- 1 tsp. vanilla extract
- ⅛ tsp. ground cinnamon
- FROSTING
- ¼ cup butter, softened
- ¼ cup cream cheese, softened
- 4 cups confectioners' sugar
- 2 Tbsp. 2% milk
- 1 tsp. vanilla extract
- Key lime slices, optional

1. Preheat oven to 350°. Line a 9-in. square baking pan with parchment, letting ends extend up sides. Combine 1 cup cracker crumbs, ⅓ cup melted butter and 3 Tbsp. brown sugar; press onto bottom of prepared pan. Bake 10 minutes. Cool on a wire rack.
2. For blondie layer: In a large bowl, cream softened butter and 1 cup sugar until light and fluffy. Beat in eggs, egg white, lime juice and zest. In a small bowl, mix flour and ½ tsp. salt; gradually add to the creamed mixture, mixing well.
3. Spread over crust. Bake until a toothpick inserted in center comes out clean, 25-30 minutes (do not overbake). Cool completely in pan on a wire rack.
4. For streusel, combine the remaining ⅓ cup cracker crumbs, 2 Tbsp. melted butter, ¼ cup brown sugar, 1 Tbsp. sugar and ⅛ tsp. salt, along with the vanilla and cinnamon, until crumbly. Reserve ½ cup for topping.
5. In a large bowl, combine all frosting ingredients; beat until smooth. Stir in the remaining ½ cup streusel. Spread over bars. Sprinkle with reserved topping. Refrigerate at least 4 hours before cutting. Lifting with parchment, remove from pan. Cut into bars. Store in an airtight container in refrigerator. If desired, garnish with sliced Key limes.
1 blondie: 422 cal., 19g fat (11g sat. fat), 69mg chol., 283mg sod., 62g carb. (51g sugars, 1g fiber), 3g pro.

MANDARIN CUSTARD TARTS

This simple dessert recipe is packed with a lot of flavor. Although easy to prepare, the tarts make a striking impression when served.
—Mary Ann Lee, Clifton Park, NY

- -

Prep: 15 min. + chilling
Bake: 15 min. + cooling
Makes: 2½ dozen

- 1 Tbsp. cornstarch
- 1 Tbsp. confectioners' sugar
- 1 cup sour cream
- ¼ cup thawed orange juice concentrate
- 1 large egg yolk
- 1 tsp. vanilla extract
- 2 pkg. (1.9 oz. each) frozen miniature phyllo tart shells
- 1 cup dark chocolate chips
- ½ tsp. shortening
- 1 can (15 oz.) mandarin oranges, drained and patted dry

1. Preheat oven to 350°. In a small bowl, combine cornstarch, confectioners' sugar, sour cream, orange juice concentrate, egg yolk and vanilla until smooth. Spoon into tart shells. Place on a baking sheet.
2. Bake until filling is set, 15-18 minutes. Cool on wire racks. Refrigerate, covered, for 30 minutes.
3. Meanwhile, in a microwave, melt chocolate chips and shortening; stir until smooth. Dip each mandarin orange segment halfway, allowing excess to drip off. Place on waxed paper; chill until set.
4. Just before serving, garnish each tart with a chocolate-coated mandarin segment. Refrigerate leftovers.
1 tart: 87 cal., 5g fat (3g sat. fat), 8mg chol., 15mg sod., 10g carb. (7g sugars, 1g fiber), 1g pro.

GOLDEN MACADAMIA NUT PIE

If you love all things Hawaiian, you'll love this pie filled with one of the island's most abundant crops—macadamia nuts. It makes a luscious ending to any meal.
—Cathy Evans, Madison, MO

- -

Prep: 20 min. + cooling • **Bake:** 35 min.
Makes: 8 servings

- Pastry for single-crust pie (9 in.)
- ½ cup packed brown sugar
- 3 Tbsp. all-purpose flour
- ¼ tsp. salt
- 1 cup light corn syrup
- 3 Tbsp. butter
- 3 large eggs, lightly beaten
- ½ tsp. vanilla extract
- 1½ cups roasted macadamia nuts (about 8 oz.), coarsely chopped

1. Preheat oven to 350°. On a lightly floured surface, roll dough to a ⅛-in.-thick circle; transfer to a 9-in. pie plate. Trim crust to ½ in. beyond rim of plate; flute edge.
2. In a large saucepan, mix brown sugar, flour and salt; stir in corn syrup until smooth. Add butter; bring to a boil, stirring constantly. Remove from heat; cool 10 minutes. Stir in eggs and vanilla. Stir in macadamia nuts; pour into crust.
3. Bake on a lower oven rack until a knife inserted near the center comes out clean, 35-40 minutes. Cool on a wire rack. Refrigerate leftovers.
1 piece: 605 cal., 37g fat (14g sat. fat), 111mg chol., 409mg sod., 68g carb. (49g sugars, 3g fiber), 7g pro.
Pastry for single-crust pie (9 in.): Combine 1¼ cups all-purpose flour and ¼ tsp. salt; cut in ½ cup cold butter until crumbly. Gradually add 3-5 Tbsp. ice water, tossing with a fork until dough holds together when pressed. Wrap and refrigerate 1 hour.

TEST KITCHEN TIP

Like peanuts, macadamia nuts are available roasted, raw and flavored. Look for dry roasted nuts.

EASY CHRISTMAS COOKIES

What's Christmas without the cookies?
But if time's not on your side this season,
breathe easy. These stress-free merry morsels
are super simple to whip up for last-minute
gifts or get-togethers. And most are easy
enough for little ones to get in on the mixing
and decorating fun. Let the cookie parade begin!

Frosted Red Velvet Cookies (p. 67) Italian Horn Cookies (p. 65)
Easy Gingerbread Cutouts (p. 69) Colorful Candy Bar Cookies (p. 71)
Chocolate Almond Wafers (p. 66)

ITALIAN
HORN
COOKIES

ITALIAN HORN COOKIES

My family has been making these delicate fruit-filled cookies for generations. They're light and flaky and have the look of an elegant old-world pastry.
—*Gloria Siddiqui, Houston, TX*

- -

Prep: 30 min. + chilling • **Bake:** 10 min./batch
Makes: about 5 dozen

- 1 cup cold butter, cubed
- 4 cups all-purpose flour
- 2 cups vanilla ice cream, softened
- 1 can (12 oz.) cherry cake and pastry filling
  Sugar
  Confectioners' sugar, optional

1. In a large bowl, cut butter into flour until mixture resembles coarse crumbs. Stir in ice cream. Divide dough into 4 portions. Cover and refrigerate for 2 hours.
2. On a lightly floured surface, roll each portion to ⅛-in. thickness. With a fluted pastry cutter, cut into 2-in. squares. Place about ½ tsp. filling in the center of each square. Overlap 2 opposite corners of dough over filling and seal. Sprinkle lightly with sugar.
3. Place on ungreased baking sheets. Bake at 350° for 10-12 minutes or until bottoms are light brown. Cool on wire racks. If desired, dust with confectioners' sugar before serving.
Note: This recipe was tested with Solo brand cake and pastry filling. Look for it in the baking aisle of your grocery store.
1 cookie: 79 cal., 4g fat (2g sat. fat), 10mg chol., 32mg sod., 10g carb. (3g sugars, 0 fiber), 1g pro.

TEST KITCHEN TIP

To soften ice cream in the refrigerator, transfer from the freezer to the refrigerator 20-30 minutes before using. Or let it stand at room temperature for 10-15 minutes. Hard ice cream can also be softened in the microwave at 30% power for about 30 seconds.

Hardworking Lazy Susans

Use a lazy Susan for your next cookie-decorating extravaganza. It's a handy way to keep icings, sugars and sprinkles within reach. It keeps the mess at bay, too.

QUICK COCONUT MACAROONS

Here is the recipe for the best macaroon cookies I've ever tasted. The short list of ingredients makes them especially appealing to busy cooks like me!
—*Nancy Tafoya, Fort Collins, CO*

- -

Prep: 10 min. • **Bake:** 15 min./batch
Makes: 1½ dozen

- 2½ cups sweetened shredded coconut
- ⅓ cup all-purpose flour
- ⅛ tsp. salt
- ⅔ cup sweetened condensed milk
- 1 tsp. vanilla extract

1. In a large bowl, combine the coconut, flour and salt. Add milk and vanilla; mix well (batter will be stiff).
2. Drop by tablespoonfuls 1 in. apart onto a greased baking sheet. Bake at 350° until golden brown, 15-20 minutes. Remove to wire racks.
1 cookie: 110 cal., 6g fat (5g sat. fat), 4mg chol., 65mg sod., 14g carb. (12g sugars, 1g fiber), 2g pro.

BUTTER MINT COOKIES

These buttery cookies with a hint of mint were a big hit when I made them for a work party. Feel free to use other colors of sugar for extra pop on your cookie tray.
—*Anita Epitropou, Zion, IL*

- -

Prep: 15 min. • **Bake:** 10 min./batch
Makes: 3 dozen

- 1 cup butter, softened
- ½ cup confectioners' sugar
- 1½ tsp. peppermint extract
- 1¾ cups all-purpose flour
  Green colored sugar

1. In a large bowl, cream softened butter and confectioners' sugar until light and fluffy. Beat in extract. Gradually add flour and mix well.
2. Roll tablespoonfuls of dough into balls. Place 1 in. apart on ungreased baking sheets; flatten with a glass dipped in colored sugar. Bake at 350° for 10-12 minutes or until firm. Remove to wire racks to cool.
1 cookie: 74 cal., 5g fat (3g sat. fat), 14mg chol., 41mg sod., 6g carb. (2g sugars, 0 fiber), 1g pro.

CHOCOLATE ALMOND WAFERS

When my children were younger, we'd make dozens of cookies and candies each season. Then we'd pack up an assortment and deliver them to our friends and family. These wafers were always a favorite.
—*Phyl Broich-Wessling, Garner, IA*

- -

Prep: 20 min. + chilling • **Bake:** 10 min./batch
Makes: about 4½ dozen

- ¾ cup butter, softened
- ¾ cup sugar
- 1 large egg, room temperature
- 1 tsp. vanilla extract
- 1¼ cups all-purpose flour
- ⅔ cup baking cocoa
- 1 tsp. baking powder
- ¾ cup sliced almonds
- ⅔ cup ground almonds

1. In a large bowl, cream butter and sugar until light and fluffy. Beat in egg and vanilla. Combine the flour, cocoa and baking powder; gradually add to creamed mixture and mix well. Stir in sliced almonds.
2. Shape the dough into a 14-in. log. Roll in ground almonds. Wrap in plastic. Refrigerate for 2 hours or until firm.
3. Unwrap and cut into ¼-in. slices. Place 1 in. apart on ungreased baking sheets. Bake at 375° for 9-11 minutes or until set. Remove to wire racks.
1 cookie: 60 cal., 4g fat (2g sat. fat), 10mg chol., 26mg sod., 6g carb. (3g sugars, 1g fiber), 1g pro.

CATHEDRAL COOKIES

The colorful marshmallows in these festive confections look like stained-glass windows when sliced. The chopped nuts and shredded coconut add a nice texture.
—*Carol Shaffer, Cape Girardeau, MO*

- -

Prep: 10 min. + freezing
Cook: 10 min. + chilling
Makes: about 5 dozen

- 1 cup (6 oz.) semisweet chocolate chips
- 2 Tbsp. butter
- 1 large egg, room temperature, lightly beaten
- 3 cups pastel miniature marshmallows
- ½ cup chopped pecans or walnuts
- 1 cup sweetened shredded coconut

1. In a heavy saucepan, melt chocolate chips and butter over low heat, stirring occasionally. Stir a small amount into the egg, then return all to pan. Cook and stir mixture over low heat for 2 minutes. Pour into a bowl; let cool for 15 minutes. Gently stir in marshmallows and nuts. Chill for 30 minutes.
2. On a sheet of waxed paper, shape mixture into a 1½-in.-diameter log. Place coconut on another sheet of waxed paper. Gently roll log over coconut to coat sides. Wrap up tightly, twisting ends to seal.
3. Freeze for 4 hours or overnight. Remove waxed paper. Cut into ¼-in. slices. Store in an airtight container in the refrigerator.
1 cookie: 40 cal., 3g fat (1g sat. fat), 4mg chol., 11mg sod., 5g carb. (4g sugars, 0 fiber), 0 pro.

TEST KITCHEN TIP

Even Cuts Every Time

Here's a fast and easy way to get evenly sized slice-and-bake cookies. Begin by neatly rolling up the dough into a log inside parchment. Position the ruler next to the roll and use a pencil or food-safe marker to mark even slices. With a knife, lightly score the dough at each mark. Unwrap the dough and slice along the score marks.

FROSTED RED VELVET COOKIES

FROSTED RED VELVET COOKIES

My student job in college was in the bakery. These dreamy morsels take me back to that special place and time. Red velvet cake lovers will appreciate this fun riff.

—Christina Petri, Alexandria, MN

Prep: 20 min. • **Bake:** 10 min./batch + cooling
Makes: 5 dozen

- 2 oz. unsweetened chocolate, chopped
- ½ cup butter, softened
- ⅔ cup packed brown sugar
- ⅓ cup sugar
- 1 large egg, room temperature
- 1 Tbsp. red food coloring
- 1 tsp. vanilla extract
- 2 cups all-purpose flour
- ½ tsp. baking soda
- ½ tsp. salt
- 1 cup sour cream
- 1 cup (6 oz.) semisweet chocolate chips
- 1 can (16 oz.) cream cheese frosting
  Sprinkles, optional

1. In a microwave, melt unsweetened chocolate; stir until smooth. Cool.
2. In a large bowl, cream butter and sugars until light and fluffy. Beat in the egg, food coloring and vanilla. Add cooled chocolate; beat until blended. In another bowl, mix the flour, baking soda and salt; add to creamed mixture alternately with sour cream, beating well after each addition. Stir in semisweet chocolate chips.
3. Drop by tablespoonfuls 2 in. apart onto parchment-lined baking sheets. Bake at 375° for 6-9 minutes or until set. Remove to wire racks to cool completely. Spread with frosting. If desired, decorate with sprinkles.
1 cookie: 103 cal., 5g fat (3g sat. fat), 8mg chol., 62mg sod., 14g carb. (10g sugars, 0 fiber), 1g pro.

EASY GINGERBREAD
CUTOUTS

EASY GINGERBREAD CUTOUTS

I rely on this clever recipe during the holidays. The cream cheese icing complements the cookies' gingery flavor and sets up nicely for easy packaging and stacking.
—*Sandy McKenzie, Braham, MN*

- -

Prep: 20 min. + chilling
Bake: 10 min./batch + cooling
Makes: 2½ dozen

- 1 pkg. spice cake mix (regular size)
- ¾ cup all-purpose flour
- 2 large eggs, room temperature
- ⅓ cup canola oil
- ⅓ cup molasses
- 2 tsp. ground ginger
- ¾ cup canned cream cheese frosting, slightly warmed
  Red Hots

1. In a bowl, combine the cake mix, flour, eggs, oil, molasses and ginger until well blended. Refrigerate for 30 minutes or until easy to handle.
2. On a floured surface, roll out dough to ⅛-in. thickness. Cut with lightly floured 5-in. cookie cutters. Place 3 in. apart on ungreased baking sheets.
3. Bake at 375° for 7-10 minutes or until the edges are firm and bottom is lightly browned. Remove to wire racks to cool. Decorate the cookies with cream cheese frosting and Red Hots as desired.
1 cookie: 141 cal., 4g fat (1g sat. fat), 12mg chol., 148mg sod., 24g carb. (14g sugars, 0 fiber), 2g pro.

BETTER-THAN-FRUITCAKE COOKIES

These chewy treats studded with fruit and nut clusters make excellent gifts, freeze well and can be shipped easily. Most importantly, they live up to their name. Even fruitcake lovers agree!
—*Lillian Charves, New Bern, NC*

- -

Prep: 15 min. + standing • **Bake:** 15 min./batch
Makes: 3 dozen

- 2 cups raisins
- ¼ cup bourbon or unsweetened apple juice
- 2 Tbsp. butter, softened
- ¼ cup packed brown sugar
- 1 large egg, room temperature
- ¾ cup all-purpose flour
- 1 tsp. ground cinnamon
- ¾ tsp. baking soda
- ¼ tsp. ground nutmeg
- ¼ tsp. ground cloves
- 1 cup pecan halves

- ¾ cup red candied cherries, halved
- ¾ cup green candied cherries, halved

1. In a small bowl, combine the raisins and bourbon. Cover and let stand for 30 minutes.
2. In a large bowl, cream butter and brown sugar until blended. Beat in egg. Combine the flour, cinnamon, baking soda, nutmeg and cloves; gradually beat into creamed mixture. Stir in the pecans, cherries and raisin mixture.
3. Drop by tablespoonfuls onto baking sheets coated with cooking spray. Bake at 325° for 12-15 minutes or until firm. Cool for 2 minutes before removing to wire racks to cool completely. Store in an airtight container.
1 cookie: 93 cal., 3g fat (1g sat. fat), 8mg chol., 40mg sod., 16g carb. (11g sugars, 1g fiber), 1g pro. **Diabetic exchanges:** 1 starch, ½ fat.

WHITE CHOCOLATE CRANBERRY COOKIES

These sweet cookies feature white chocolate and cranberries for a delightful taste. And the red and white coloring add a great holiday feel to any cookie tray.
—*Donna Beck, Scottdale, PA*

- -

Prep: 20 min. • **Bake:** 10 min./batch
Makes: 2 dozen

- ⅓ cup butter, softened
- ½ cup packed brown sugar
- ⅓ cup sugar
- 1 large egg, room temperature
- 1 tsp. vanilla extract
- 1½ cups all-purpose flour
- ½ tsp. salt
- ½ tsp. baking soda
- ¾ cup dried cranberries
- ½ cup white baking chips

1. In a large bowl, beat the butter and sugars until crumbly, about 2 minutes. Beat in egg and vanilla. Combine the flour, salt and baking soda; gradually add to butter mixture and mix well. Stir in cranberries and chips.
2. Drop by heaping tablespoonfuls 2 in. apart onto baking sheets coated with cooking spray. Bake at 375° for 8-10 minutes or until lightly browned. Cool for 1 minute before removing to wire racks.
1 cookie: 113 cal., 4g fat (2g sat. fat), 16mg chol., 109mg sod., 18g carb. (10g sugars, 0 fiber), 1g pro.

Storing Cookies

Before storing, allow cookies to cool completely and allow icing on cookies to dry completely.

- To keep cookies and other baked goods soft and moist when storing, add a slice of white bread to the container. The cookies will absorb the moisture from the bread so you don't have treats that are too hard and crunchy to eat.

- Store soft cookies and crisp cookies in separate airtight containers. If stored together, the moisture from the soft cookies will soften the crisp cookies.

- Flavors can blend in storage; don't store strong-flavored cookies in the same container as treats that have a more delicate flavor.

- Store cookies with waxed paper between layers.

- Store unfrosted cookies in a cool, dry place in airtight containers for about 3 days. Cookies that are topped with cream cheese frosting should be stored in the refrigerator.

- For longer storage, wrap unfrosted cookies in plastic wrap, stack them in an airtight container, seal and freeze up to 3 months. Thaw wrapped cookies at room temperature before frosting and serving.

- If crisp cookies become soft during storage, crisp them up by heating in a 300° oven for 5 minutes.

CANDY COOKIE CUPS

Take classic macadamia nut cookies to the next level with these cute cups. With only three ingredients, they couldn't be easier. And everyone goes crazy for the peanut butter cup in the center.
—*Sarah Vasques, Milford, NH*

Prep: 15 min. • **Bake:** 15 min. + cooling
Makes: 2 dozen

- ½ cup finely chopped macadamia nuts
- 1 pkg. (16 oz.) individually portioned refrigerated white chip macadamia nut cookie dough
- 24 miniature peanut butter cups

1. Sprinkle macadamia nuts into 24 greased miniature muffin cups, 1 tsp. in each. Cut each portion of cookie dough in half; place each half in a muffin cup.
2. Bake at 325° for 11-13 minutes or until golden brown. Immediately place a peanut butter cup in each cookie; press down gently. Cool completely before removing from pans to wire racks.

1 cookie cup: 154 cal., 9g fat (3g sat. fat), 3mg chol., 104mg sod., 17g carb. (12g sugars, 0 fiber), 2g pro.

SWEETHEART COOKIES

These rounds filled with fruit preserves were blue-ribbon winners at the county fair two years running. A family favorite, they never last beyond Christmas!
—*Pamela Esposito, Smithville, NJ*

Prep: 25 min. • **Bake:** 15 min./batch
Makes: 2 dozen

- ¾ cup butter, softened
- ½ cup sugar
- 1 large egg yolk, room temperature
- 1½ cups all-purpose flour
- 2 Tbsp. raspberry or strawberry preserves
  Confectioners' sugar, optional

1. In a bowl, cream butter and sugar. Add egg yolk; mix well. Stir in the flour by hand. On a lightly floured surface, gently knead dough for 2-3 minutes or until thoroughly combined.
2. Roll into 1-in. balls. Place 2 in. apart on greased baking sheets. Using the end of a wooden spoon handle, make an indention in the center of each. Fill each with ¼ tsp. raspberry preserves.
3. Bake at 350° for 13-15 minutes or until edges are lightly browned. Remove to wire racks. Dust warm cookies with confectioners' sugar if desired. Cool.

1 cookie: 102 cal., 6g fat (4g sat. fat), 23mg chol., 46mg sod., 11g carb. (5g sugars, 0 fiber), 1g pro.

Ironing Board = Cooling Rack

Remove the cover from an ironing board to use it as a cooling rack when you're doing a lot of baking. The air circulation from both top and bottom helps baked goods cool evenly. An added advantage is that it frees up counter space in the kitchen. Just be sure to use pans, paper liners, parchment or some other barrier between baked goods and the rack.

COLORFUL CANDY BAR COOKIES

No one will guess these sweet treats with the candy bar center start with store-bought dough. Roll them in colored sugar or just dip the tops for even faster assembly. Instead of using miniature candy bars, you can also slice regular size Snickers candy bars into 1-inch pieces for the centers.
—Taste of Home *Test Kitchen*

- -

Prep: 35 min. • **Bake:** 10 min./batch
Makes: about 3 dozen

1 tube (16½ oz.) refrigerated sugar cookie dough, softened
⅔ cup all-purpose flour
40 miniature Snickers candy bars
Red and green colored sugar

1. Preheat oven to 350°. Using an electric mixer, beat cookie dough and flour until combined. Shape 2 teaspoonfuls of dough around each candy bar. Roll in colored sugar.
2. Place 2 in. apart on parchment-lined baking sheets. Bake until set, 9-11 minutes. Cool on pans 1 minute. Remove to wire racks to cool.
1 cookie: 93 cal., 4g fat (1g sat. fat), 4mg chol., 65mg sod., 13g carb. (7g sugars, 0 fiber), 1g pro.

COLORFUL
CANDY BAR COOKIES

GIVING THANKS

Even before you carve the Thanksgiving turkey, there are endless ways to ward off the chill in the autumn air with warm, savory dishes and sweet treats. After digging into slow-cooked seasonal staples and fresh adaptations of the harvest fair foods you love most, the only thing better than indulging in a delectable dessert is sharing the fun with family and friends. So why not pay the flavor forward?

TRADITIONAL TURKEY DINNER

Thanksgiving is one of the most anticipated days of the year. What's better than gathering with family and friends to count blessings and celebrate with a bountiful feast? The treasured home holiday deserves an array of down-home delicious foods. From a top-notch turkey to legendary side dishes and luscious desserts, let our lineup of memorable mainstays be your inspiration for creating the perfect menu.

Apple-Sage Roasted Turkey (p. 82) **Sourdough Dressing** (p. 78)
Cranberry Sauce with Walnuts (p. 77)

Thanksgiving Day Countdown

It's among the most joyous holidays of the year, but Thanksgiving is also one of the busiest. Refer to this timeline to help plan the big feast. Many of the dishes in this menu can be prepared in advance, while others are best to make the day of. From turkey to trimmings, we have you covered.

A FEW WEEKS BEFORE

☐ Prepare two grocery lists—one for nonperishable items to buy now and one for perishable items to buy a few days before Thanksgiving.

☐ Bake the Parker House Rolls. Place in an airtight container and store in the freezer.

TWO DAYS BEFORE

☐ Buy remaining grocery items.

☐ Bake the Cranberry Nutella Sandwich Cookies. Store in an airtight container.

☐ Wash china, stemware and table linens.

THE DAY BEFORE

☐ Bake the Crispy Cheese Sticks. Store in an airtight container until ready to serve.

☐ Bake the cake layers for the Ganache-Topped Pumpkin Layer Cake, but do not assemble. Store in an airtight container.

☐ Bake the Browned Butter Chess Pie. Refrigerate overnight.

☐ Set the table.

THANKSGIVING DAY

☐ In the morning, remove the Parker House Rolls from the freezer.

☐ About 5½ hours before dinner, bake bread cubes for the Sourdough Dressing.

☐ About 5 hours before dinner, roast eggplants for Rustic Eggplant Dip. When roasting is finished, blend dip ingredients. Place dip in refrigerator.

☐ While the eggplants bake, prepare the Apple-Sage Roasted Turkey. When eggplants are done, lower oven setting and put the turkey in.

☐ About 2 hours before dinner, make pumpkin cake filling and spread between prebaked cake layers. Make ganache and spread over top. Cover and refrigerate.

☐ About 1½ hours before dinner, continue preparations for the Sourdough Dressing using toasted bread cubes; bake as directed.

☐ About 1 hour before dinner, prepare the Mashed Red Potatoes. Keep warm.

☐ About 40 to 50 minutes before dinner, prepare the Cranberry Sauce with Walnuts, but do not stir in nuts. Cool it or keep it warm, as you prefer.

☐ About 30 to 40 minutes before dinner, prepare the Herb-Stuffed Mushrooms and Dijon Green Beans. After removing turkey from oven, put mushrooms in; keep green beans warm as needed.

☐ About 20 minutes before dinner, prepare the Roquefort Pear Salad and toss with mustard vinaigrette.

☐ Just before dinner, carve turkey. Stir walnuts into the cranberry sauce.

CRANBERRY SAUCE
WITH WALNUTS

ROQUEFORT PEAR SALAD

Guests at a barbecue we hosted one summer brought this cool, refreshing salad. Now it's a mainstay at many of our gatherings all year round. The mingling of zesty tastes and textures instantly wakes up the taste buds!
—Sherry Duval, Baltimore, MD

- -

Takes: 20 min. • **Makes:** 10 servings

10　cups torn salad greens
　3　large ripe pears, sliced
　½　cup thinly sliced green onions
　4　oz. crumbled blue cheese
　¼　cup slivered almonds, toasted
MUSTARD VINAIGRETTE
　⅓　cup olive oil
　3　Tbsp. cider vinegar
1½　tsp. sugar
1½　tsp. Dijon mustard
　1　garlic clove, minced
　½　tsp. salt
　　　Pepper to taste

In a large bowl, combine the salad greens, pears, onions, cheese and almonds. In a jar with a tight-fitting lid, combine the vinaigrette ingredients; shake well. Pour over salad; toss to coat.

1¼ cups: 171 cal., 12g fat (3g sat. fat), 9mg chol., 303mg sod., 14g carb. (8g sugars, 4g fiber), 4g pro. **Diabetic exchanges:** 2½ fat, 1 vegetable, ½ fruit.

CRANBERRY SAUCE WITH WALNUTS

Traditional cranberry sauce is nice, but this jazzed-up version is several steps above. It travels well, and all the women in my family serve it. The apricot preserves, lemon and toasted walnuts make it different.
—Dee Buckley, Salado, TX

- -

Prep: 5 min. • **Cook:** 35 min. • **Makes:** 3½ cups

　2　cups sugar
　1　cup water
　1　pkg. (12 oz.) fresh or
　　　frozen cranberries
　½　cup apricot preserves
　¼　cup lemon juice
　½　cup chopped walnuts, toasted

1. In a large saucepan over medium heat, bring sugar and water to a boil. Simmer, uncovered, for 10 minutes. Stir in the cranberries. Cook until berries pop, about 15 minutes.

2. Remove from the heat. Stir in preserves and lemon juice. Transfer to a bowl. Serve warm, at room temperature or chilled. Stir in walnuts just before serving.

¼ cup: 178 cal., 3g fat (0 sat. fat), 0 chol., 5mg sod., 40g carb. (37g sugars, 1g fiber), 1g pro.

TEST KITCHEN TIP

Add Booze to Boost Flavor

A splash of your favorite tipple can go a long way in adding richness to cranberry sauce. Our Test Kitchen recommends trying a tablespoon of orange liqueur or spiced rum to add some traditional holiday flavor. In this recipe, you can add a splash of port or wine (white or red). Add the liquor or wine at the same time as the water, sugar and cranberries. The cooking process will burn away any harsh alcohol taste (and the alcohol itself), leaving only the extra layer of intriguing flavor.

DIJON GREEN BEANS

This recipe combines the freshness of garden green beans with a warm and tangy dressing. It's a wonderful, quick and easy side.
—*Jannine Fisk, Malden, MA*

- -

Takes: 20 min. • **Makes:** 10 servings

1½ lbs. fresh green beans, trimmed
2   Tbsp. red wine vinegar
2   Tbsp. olive oil
2   tsp. Dijon mustard
½   tsp. salt
¼   tsp. pepper
1   cup grape tomatoes, halved
½   small red onion, sliced
2   Tbsp. grated Parmesan cheese

1. Place beans in a large saucepan and cover with water. Bring to a boil. Cook, covered, for 10-15 minutes or until crisp-tender.
2. Meanwhile, whisk the vinegar, oil, mustard, salt and pepper in a small bowl. Drain beans; place in a large bowl. Add the tomatoes and onion. Drizzle with dressing and toss to coat. Sprinkle with cheese.
¾ cup: 54 cal., 3g fat (1g sat. fat), 1mg chol., 167mg sod., 6g carb. (2g sugars, 2g fiber), 2g pro. **Diabetic exchanges:** 1 vegetable, ½ fat.

TEST KITCHEN TIP

To trim fresh green beans quickly, simply line up the ends of the beans; then, using a chef's knife, slice several at a time.

PARKER HOUSE ROLLS

My mom is especially well known for her baked goods, like these tender golden rolls. When that basket comes around the table, we all automatically take two because one is never enough.
—*Sandra Melnychenko, Grandview, MB*

- -

Prep: 30 min. + rising • **Bake:** 10 min.
Makes: 2½ dozen

2   pkg. (¼ oz. each) active dry yeast
1   tsp. plus 6 Tbsp. sugar, divided
1   cup warm water (110° to 115°), divided
1   cup warm 2% milk (110° to 115°)
2   tsp. salt
1   large egg, room temperature
2   Tbsp. plus 2 tsp. canola oil
5½ to 6 cups all-purpose flour
3   Tbsp. butter, melted, optional

1. In a large bowl, dissolve yeast and 1 tsp. sugar in ½ cup warm water; let stand for 5 minutes. Add milk, salt, egg, oil, 2 cups flour and the remaining water and sugar. Beat on medium speed until smooth. Stir in enough remaining flour to form a soft dough.
2. Turn dough onto a floured surface; knead until smooth and elastic, 6-8 minutes. Place in a greased bowl, turning once to grease the top. Cover and let rise in a warm place until doubled, about 45 minutes.
3. Punch dough down. Turn onto a lightly floured surface; divide into 2 portions. Roll each portion to ½-in. thickness. Cut with a floured 2½-in. biscuit cutter. If desired, brush with butter.
4. Using the dull edge of a knife, crease each slightly off-center. Fold at the crease. Press edges together lightly. Place 2 in. apart on greased baking sheets. Cover with a kitchen towel; let rise in a warm place until doubled, about 30 minutes. Preheat oven to 375°.
5. Bake 10-15 minutes or until golden brown. Remove from pans to wire racks to cool.
1 roll: 113 cal., 2g fat (0 sat. fat), 7mg chol., 164mg sod., 21g carb. (3g sugars, 1g fiber), 3g pro.

SOURDOUGH DRESSING

While we love our traditional Thanksgiving recipes, sometimes we want to change things up. This dressing is a fun twist on an old favorite. Whenever we make it after the big feast, we like to add a cup or more of cubed leftover turkey.
—*Pat Dazis, Charlotte, NC*

- -

Prep: 45 min. • **Bake:** 1 hour
Makes: 16 servings

16 cups cubed sourdough bread
¼   cup olive oil, divided
4   garlic cloves, minced, divided
2   medium red onions, chopped
¾   cup chopped roasted sweet red peppers
1   tsp. dried oregano
1   carton (32 oz.) reduced-sodium chicken broth
2   large eggs, lightly beaten
1   cup cubed cooked turkey, optional
4   oz. Asiago cheese, cut into ½-in. cubes
4   green onions, chopped
2   Tbsp. butter

1. Preheat oven to 350°. Place bread cubes in a large bowl. Drizzle with 2 Tbsp. oil; toss lightly. Sprinkle with half the garlic; toss to combine. Transfer to 2 ungreased 15x10x1-in. baking pans. Bake until lightly browned, 20-25 minutes, turning occasionally. Let cool.
2. Meanwhile, in a large skillet, heat remaining 2 Tbsp. oil over medium-high heat. Add red onions; cook and stir 5-7 minutes or until softened. Add the red peppers, oregano and remaining garlic; cook 1 minute longer. Stir in broth; bring to a boil. Remove from heat.
3. Set oven to 325°. Place toasted bread in large bowl. Stir in broth mixture, eggs, turkey if desired, cheese and green onions. Transfer to a greased 13x9-in. baking dish; dot with butter. Cover and bake 35 minutes. Uncover; bake until golden brown, 25-35 minutes longer.
¾ cup without optional turkey: 207 cal., 8g fat (3g sat. fat), 34mg chol., 475mg sod., 24g carb. (4g sugars, 1g fiber), 8g pro. **Diabetic exchanges:** 1½ starch, 1½ fat, 1 lean meat.

SOURDOUGH
DRESSING

HERB-STUFFED
MUSHROOMS

MASHED RED POTATOES

These chunky mashed potatoes are rich enough to stand on their own. But if you like, take them over the top by adding your choice of cheese, bacon and/or sour cream.
—Taste of Home *Test Kitchen*

- -

Takes: 30 min. • **Makes:** 12 servings

- 4½ lbs. red potatoes, cut into 1-in. pieces
- 6 Tbsp. butter, cubed
- 1½ tsp. salt
- ¾ tsp. pepper
- 1 to 1⅓ cups heavy whipping cream, warmed

1. Place potatoes in a large saucepan or Dutch oven and cover with water. Bring to a boil. Reduce heat; cover and cook for 10-15 minutes or until tender. Drain.
2. In a large bowl, mash the potatoes with butter, salt, pepper and enough cream to achieve desired consistency.
¾ cup: 242 cal., 13g fat (8g sat. fat), 38mg chol., 356mg sod., 28g carb. (2g sugars, 3g fiber), 4g pro.

HERB-STUFFED MUSHROOMS

You'll love the freshness from the parsley and thyme in these little bites. Our family loves the cheesiness!
—Rachel Reed, Gainesville, GA

- -

Takes: 30 min. • **Makes:** 16 appetizers

- 16 large fresh mushrooms
- 1 pkg. (8 oz.) cream cheese, softened
- 1 cup grated Parmesan cheese, divided
- 1 Tbsp. minced fresh parsley
- 2 tsp. minced fresh rosemary
- 2 tsp. minced fresh thyme
- 1 tsp. Worcestershire sauce
  Pinch ground nutmeg
- ⅛ tsp. pepper

1. Remove stems from mushrooms and set caps aside (discard stems or save them for another use).
2. In a bowl, beat the cream cheese, ¾ cup Parmesan cheese, herbs, Worcestershire sauce, nutmeg and pepper. Spoon into the mushroom caps. Place on a foil-lined baking sheet. Sprinkle with the remaining Parmesan cheese.
3. Bake at 425° for 8-10 minutes or until mushrooms are tender. If desired, sprinkle with additional parsley.
1 stuffed mushroom: 77 cal., 6g fat (4 g sat. fat), 20mg chol., 123mg sod., 2g carb. (0 fiber), 4g pro.

Preparing Mushrooms for Stuffing
Hold mushroom cap in one hand and grab the stem with the other hand. Twist to snap off the stem. Proceed as recipe directs.

RUSTIC EGGPLANT DIP

One summer I came up with this recipe after I harvested loads of eggplants, tomatoes and herbs from my garden. You can also grill the eggplants for extra flavor.
—Debra Keil, Owasso, OK

- -

Prep: 20 min. • **Bake:** 30 min. + chilling
Makes: 2 cups

- 2 small eggplants
- 1 medium sweet red pepper, halved and seeds removed
- 3 Tbsp. olive oil, divided
- ½ cup chopped seeded plum tomatoes
- 3 Tbsp. finely chopped onion
- 1 Tbsp. minced fresh parsley
- 1 tsp. lemon juice
- 1 tsp. red wine vinegar
- 1 tsp. each minced fresh oregano, thyme and basil
- 2 mint leaves, coarsely chopped
- 1 tsp. salt
- ½ tsp. pepper
  Baked pita chips or pita wedges

1. Cut stems from eggplants; pierce several times with a fork. Place eggplants and red pepper on a foil-lined 15x10x1-in. baking pan. Rub 2 Tbsp. oil over vegetables.
2. Bake at 400° for 30-35 minutes or until tender, turning occasionally. Cool slightly. Peel and coarsely chop eggplants; coarsely chop red pepper.
3. In a food processor, combine tomatoes, onion, parsley, lemon juice, red wine vinegar, herbs, salt, pepper, eggplants, red pepper and the remaining oil. Cover and process until blended.
4. Cover and refrigerate for at least 3 hours. Serve with pita chips.
¼ cup: 77 cal., 5g fat (1g sat. fat), 0 chol., 299mg sod., 7g carb. (4g sugars, 3g fiber), 1g pro. **Diabetic exchanges:** 1 vegetable, 1 fat.

CRISPY CHEESE STICKS

For cheesy appetizers, I use sharp cheddar in the dough, bake them as twists and finish with a sprinkle of Parmesan.
—*Jane Uphoff, Cunningham, KS*

Prep: 20 min. • **Bake:** 10 min./batch
Makes: about 5 dozen

1¼ cups all-purpose flour
½ cup yellow cornmeal
1 tsp. salt
1 jar (5 oz.) sharp cheddar
    cheese spread
¼ cup butter, softened
¼ cup water
    Grated Parmesan cheese

1. Preheat oven to 400°. Mix flour, cornmeal and salt. Cut in the cheese and butter until crumbly. Stir in water; mix well.
2. Divide dough in half; cover half. On a lightly floured surface, roll 1 portion into a 14x8-in. rectangle. Cut into 7x½-in. strips; place on a baking sheet. Grasp strips at each end and twist in opposite directions, pressing ends onto sheet to help them hold their shape. Repeat with remaining dough.
3. Bake until lightly browned, 8-10 minutes; immediately sprinkle with Parmesan cheese. Remove sticks from baking sheet; cool on a wire rack.

1 cheese stick: 26 cal., 1g fat (1g sat. fat), 4mg chol., 79mg sod., 3g carb. (0 sugars, 0 fiber), 1g pro.

Cornmeal can be white, yellow or blue, depending on which strain of corn is used. Traditionally, white cornmeal is more popular in the South and yellow is preferred in the North. Blue cornmeal can be found in specialty stores. All three types can be used interchangeably in recipes.

APPLE-SAGE ROASTED TURKEY

A hint of apple flavor gives a slightly sweet spin to the dinner's main event. The lovely aroma wafting from your kitchen as this turkey cooks will have everybody talking.
—*Suzy Horvath, Milwaukie, OR*

Prep: 20 min. • **Bake:** 3½ hours + standing
Makes: 14 servings

½ cup apple cider or juice
½ cup apple jelly
⅓ cup butter, cubed
TURKEY
⅓ cup minced fresh sage
¼ cup butter, softened
1 turkey (14 to 16 lbs.)
2 Tbsp. apple cider or juice
1½ tsp. salt
1½ tsp. pepper
2 large apples, cut into wedges
1 large onion, cut into wedges
8 fresh sage leaves

1. Preheat oven to 325°. In a small saucepan, combine apple cider, jelly and butter. Cook and stir until butter is melted. Remove from heat and set aside.
2. In a small bowl, combine minced sage and butter. With fingers, carefully loosen skin from the turkey breast; rub butter mixture under the skin. Brush turkey with apple cider. Sprinkle salt and pepper over turkey and inside cavity.
3. Place apples, onion and sage leaves inside the cavity. Tuck wings under turkey; tie the drumsticks together. Place breast side up on a rack in a roasting pan.
4. Bake, uncovered, 3½-4 hours or until a thermometer inserted in thickest part of thigh reads 170°-175°, basting occasionally with cider mixture. Cover loosely with foil if turkey browns too quickly. Cover and let stand for 20 minutes before slicing.

Freeze option: Place sliced turkey in freezer containers; top with any cooking juices. Cool and freeze. To use, partially thaw in the refrigerator overnight. Heat through in a covered saucepan, gently stirring and adding a little broth or water if necessary.

9 oz. cooked turkey: 506 cal., 19g fat (9g sat. fat), 191mg chol., 466mg sod., 14g carb. (12g sugars, 1g fiber), 66g pro.

APPLE-SAGE
ROASTED TURKEY

BROWNED BUTTER CHESS PIE

This simple pie is so smooth and velvety, it will warm everyone's heart. It's a timeless recipe with southern roots, but I recommend trying it no matter where you live!
—*Michael Cohen, Los Angeles, CA*

Prep: 20 min. • **Bake:** 40 min.
Makes: 8 servings

½   cup butter, cubed
    Pastry for single-crust pie
3   large eggs
1½ cups packed dark brown sugar
¼   cup whole milk
4   tsp. white vinegar
1   Tbsp. cornmeal
1¼ tsp. vanilla extract
½   tsp. ground cinnamon
    Vanilla ice cream, optional

1. In a small heavy saucepan, cook and stir butter over medium heat for 5-7 minutes or until golden brown; remove from the heat.
2. Roll out crust to fit a 9-in. pie plate. Transfer crust to pie plate; trim to ½ in. beyond edge of plate. Flute edges. Line unpricked crust with a double thickness of heavy-duty foil. Fill crust with dried beans, uncooked rice or pie weights.
3. Bake at 400° for 8 minutes. Remove foil and weights; bake 5 minutes longer. Cool on a wire rack.
4. In a large bowl, beat eggs for 3 minutes. Gradually add the brown sugar; beat for 2 minutes or until mixture becomes thick. Beat in milk, vinegar, cornmeal, vanilla, cinnamon and the browned butter. Pour into crust. Cover edges with foil.
5. Bake at 350° for 40-45 minutes or until a knife inserted near the center comes out clean. Cool on a wire rack. Refrigerate, covered, for 3 hours or until cold. Serve with ice cream if desired. Refrigerate leftovers.
1 piece: 469 cal., 25g fat (15g sat. fat), 131mg chol., 288mg sod., 57g carb. (41g sugars, 1g fiber), 5g pro.

GANACHE-TOPPED
PUMPKIN LAYER CAKE

GANACHE-TOPPED PUMPKIN LAYER CAKE

My dreamy pumpkin cake with cream cheese filling and rich chocolate ganache is perfect for any autumnal gathering.
—*Michelle Sorensen, Bountiful, UT*

Prep: 1 hour • **Bake:** 15 min. + cooling
Makes: 12 slices

- 3 large eggs, room temperature
- 1 cup sugar
- ¾ cup canned pumpkin
- ¾ cup all-purpose flour
- 1½ tsp. pumpkin pie spice
- 1 tsp. baking powder
- ¼ tsp. salt

FILLING
- ½ cup heavy whipping cream
- 4 oz. cream cheese, softened
- ½ cup confectioners' sugar

GANACHE
- 1 cup dark chocolate chips
- ½ cup heavy whipping cream

1. Preheat oven to 375°. Line bottoms of 2 greased 8-in. round baking pans with parchment; grease paper.
2. In a large bowl, beat eggs on high speed 3 minutes. Gradually add sugar, beating until thick and lemon-colored. Beat in pumpkin. In another bowl, whisk flour, pie spice, baking powder and salt; fold into the egg mixture. Transfer to prepared pans, spreading evenly.
3. Bake until a toothpick inserted in center comes out clean, 15-20 minutes. Cool in pans 10 minutes before removing to a wire rack; remove paper. Cool completely.
4. For filling, in a large bowl, beat cream until stiff peaks form. In another large bowl, beat cream cheese and confectioners' sugar until blended; fold in whipped cream. Spread between cake layers. Refrigerate at least 1 hour.
5. Place chocolate in a small bowl. In a small saucepan, bring cream just to a boil. Pour over chocolate; let stand 5 minutes. Stir with a whisk until smooth; cool slightly. Press plastic wrap onto surface of ganache; cool to room temperature. Spread over cake. Refrigerate until serving.
1 slice: 331 cal., 18g fat (11g sat. fat), 79mg chol., 150mg sod., 42g carb. (34g sugars, 2g fiber), 5g pro.

CRANBERRY NUTELLA SANDWICH COOKIES

I created these cookies for my family after I realized that we had been without Nutella for far too long! Tart dried cranberries are a natural pairing to the hazelnut flavor. We can't get enough of these sweet cookies!
—*Nancy Mock, Colchester, VT*

Prep: 25 min. + chilling
Bake: 20 min./batch + cooling
Makes: 16 sandwich cookies

- 1 cup unsalted butter, softened
- 1 cup confectioners' sugar
- 3 tsp. vanilla extract
- 2¼ cups all-purpose flour
- ¼ tsp. salt
- ½ cup dried cranberries, finely chopped
- ¼ cup 2% milk
- ¾ cup Nutella

1. In a bowl, cream butter and confectioners' sugar until light and fluffy. Beat in vanilla. In another bowl, whisk flour and salt; gradually beat into creamed mixture. Stir in cranberries. Divide dough in half. Shape each half into a disk. Wrap and refrigerate for 30 minutes or until firm enough to roll.
2. Preheat oven to 325°. On a lightly floured surface, roll each portion of dough to ¼-in. thickness. Cut with a floured 2-in. diamond-shaped cookie cutter. Place 2 in. apart on parchment paper-lined baking sheets. Brush with milk.
3. Bake until the edges begin to brown, 18-20 minutes. Remove from pans to wire racks to cool completely. Spread Nutella over bottoms of half of the cookies; top with the remaining cookies. Store in an airtight container.
1 sandwich cookie: 284 cal., 16g fat (8g sat. fat), 31mg chol., 47mg sod., 34g carb. (19g sugars, 1g fiber), 3g pro.

SLOW-COOKER THANKSGIVING

Thanksgiving is that special day we look forward to all year. But when you're the host, it can bring equal parts joy and chaos. This year, make meal prep a little easier by relying on the magic of your slow cooker. From cozy appetizers and savory sides to hearty main dishes and comforting sweets, these slowly simmered dishes are sure to please. Some recipes also include instructions for prepping the dish in an electric pressure cooker.

Brown Rice & Vegetables (p. 90) Cheesy Southwest Spoon Bread (p. 89)
Butter & Herb Turkey (p. 92)

CHEESY SOUTHWEST
SPOON BREAD

CHEESY SOUTHWEST SPOON BREAD

I love this casserole because it's creamy with a little southwestern flavor kick. It's comfort food at its finest and a vivid way to add a unique dish to the usual Thanksgiving Day lineup. Sometimes we scoop chili on top.
—*Barbara Miller, Oakdale, MN*

- -

Prep: 20 min. • **Cook:** 4 hours
Makes: 8 servings

- 2 cups shredded cheddar cheese
- 1 can (15¼ oz.) whole kernel corn, drained
- 1 can (14½ oz.) diced tomatoes, drained
- 1 cup sour cream
- ⅔ cup all-purpose flour
- ½ cup yellow cornmeal
- ½ cup butter, melted
- 3 Tbsp. sugar
- 2 Tbsp. taco seasoning
- 2½ tsp. baking powder
- ½ tsp. salt
  Optional toppings: chopped green onions and minced fresh cilantro

Combine the first 11 ingredients in a greased 3-qt. slow cooker. Cook, covered, on low until a toothpick inserted in the center comes out clean, 4-5 hours. If desired, top with green onions and cilantro.
1 serving: 412 cal., 28g fat (16g sat. fat), 66mg chol., 1028mg sod., 31g carb. (11g sugars, 3g fiber), 11g pro.

SLOW-COOKED VEGETABLES WITH CHEESE SAUCE

Who can pass up veggies smothered in cheese? No one I know! This is an inviting recipe to serve kids who normally shy away from vegetables.
—*Teresa Flowers, Sacramento, CA*

- -

Prep: 5 min. • **Cook:** 3 hours
Makes: 6 servings

- 1 pkg. (16 oz.) frozen Italian vegetables, thawed
- 3 cups frozen broccoli florets, thawed
- 1 pkg. (8 oz.) process cheese (Velveeta), cubed
- 1½ cups frozen cut kale, thawed and squeezed dry
- ⅓ cup chicken broth
- 1 Tbsp. butter
- ¼ tsp. salt
- ¼ tsp. pepper

Place all ingredients in a 3- or 4-qt. slow cooker. Cook, covered, on low until cheese is melted, 3-4 hours. Stir before serving.
¾ cup: 209 cal., 16g fat (7g sat. fat), 42mg chol., 704mg sod., 14g carb. (6g sugars, 4g fiber), 10g pro.
Pressure cooker: Increase broth to 1 cup; place in a 6-qt. electric pressure cooker. Add Italian vegetables, broccoli, kale, butter, salt and pepper. Lock lid; close pressure-release valve. Adjust to pressure-cook on high for 3 minutes. Quick-release pressure. Press cancel. Drain vegetables and return to pressure cooker. Select saute setting; adjust for low heat. Add cheese; cook and stir until melted, 1-2 minutes.

SLOW-COOKER CITRUS CARROTS

These carrots are yummy and so simple. The recipe is from my mom, who tweaked it a bit to suit her tastes. You can make this dish a day in advance and refrigerate until needed. Then just reheat it in the slow cooker right before the party.
—*Julie Puderbaugh, Berwick, PA*

- -

Prep: 10 min. • **Cook:** 4¼ hours
Makes: 12 servings

- 12 cups frozen sliced carrots (about 48 oz.), thawed
- 1¾ cups orange juice
- ½ cup sugar
- 3 Tbsp. butter, cubed
- ½ tsp. salt
- 3 Tbsp. cornstarch
- ¼ cup cold water

1. In a 3- or 4-qt. slow cooker, combine the first 5 ingredients. Cook, covered, on low for 4-5 hours or until carrots are tender.
2. In a small bowl, mix cornstarch and water until smooth; gradually stir into slow cooker. Cook, covered, on high until the sauce is thickened, 15-30 minutes.
¾ cup: 136 cal., 4g fat (2g sat. fat), 8mg chol., 208mg sod., 25g carb. (18g sugars, 5g fiber), 1g pro.
Pressure cooker: In a 6-qt. electric pressure cooker, combine the first 5 ingredients. Lock lid; close pressure-release valve. Adjust to pressure-cook on high for 2 minutes. Quick-release pressure. Press cancel. In a small bowl, mix cornstarch and water until smooth; stir into pressure cooker. Select saute setting and adjust for low heat. Simmer, stirring constantly, until thickened, 1-2 minutes.

BROWN RICE & VEGETABLES

This nutritious rice dish, full of big chunks of butternut squash and sweet potatoes, is a standout combination of sweet and savory flavors. It's a winner every Thanksgiving.
—Taste of Home *Test Kitchen*

Prep: 20 min. • **Cook:** 5 hours
Makes: 12 servings

- 1 cup uncooked brown rice
- 1 medium butternut squash (about 3 lbs.), cubed
- 2 medium apples, coarsely chopped
- 1 medium sweet potato, peeled and cubed
- 1 medium onion, chopped
- 1 tsp. salt
- ½ tsp. pepper
- 1 can (14½ oz.) reduced-sodium chicken broth
- ½ cup raisins
- 1 Tbsp. minced fresh tarragon or 1 tsp. dried tarragon

1. Place rice in a greased 4- or 5-qt. slow cooker. In a large bowl, combine the squash, apples, sweet potato, onion, salt and pepper; add to slow cooker. Pour chicken broth over the vegetables.
2. Cover and cook on low for 5-6 hours or until vegetables are tender. Stir in raisins and tarragon.
¾ cup: 148 cal., 1g fat (0 sat. fat), 0 chol., 303mg sod., 35g carb. (11g sugars, 5g fiber), 3g pro. **Diabetic exchanges:** 2 starch.

SIMMERED SMOKED LINKS

No one can resist the sweet and spicy glaze on these bite-sized sausages. They're effortless to prepare, and they make the perfect party nibbler. Serve them on frilled toothpicks to make them extra fancy.
—Maxine Cenker, Weirton, WV

Prep: 5 min. • **Cook:** 4 hours
Makes: 80 servings

- 2 pkg. (16 oz. each) miniature smoked sausage links
- 1 cup packed brown sugar
- ½ cup ketchup
- ¼ cup prepared horseradish

Place the sausages in a 3-qt. slow cooker. Combine the brown sugar, ketchup and horseradish; pour over sausages. Cover and cook on low for 4 hours.
1 sausage: 46 cal., 3g fat (1g sat. fat), 7mg chol., 136mg sod., 3g carb. (3g sugars, 0 fiber), 1g pro.

SLOW-COOKED CRAB DIP

Slow-cooked dips are ideal for entertaining since they free up the oven. Plus, leftovers are incredible scooped over a baked potato the next day.
—Susan D'Amore, West Chester, PA

Prep: 20 min. • **Cook:** 1½ hours
Makes: 2⅓ cups

- 1 pkg. (8 oz.) cream cheese, softened
- 2 green onions, chopped
- ¼ cup chopped sweet red pepper
- 2 Tbsp. minced fresh parsley
- 2 Tbsp. mayonnaise
- 1 Tbsp. Dijon mustard
- 1 tsp. Worcestershire sauce
- ¼ tsp. salt
- ¼ tsp. pepper
- 2 cans (6 oz. each) lump crabmeat, drained
- 2 Tbsp. capers, drained
  Dash hot pepper sauce
  Assorted crackers

1. In a 1½-qt. slow cooker, combine the first 9 ingredients; stir in crab.
2. Cover and cook on low for 1-2 hours. Stir in capers and pepper sauce; cook 30 minutes longer to allow the flavors to blend. Serve with crackers.
¼ cup: 153 cal., 12g fat (6g sat. fat), 62mg chol., 387mg sod., 2g carb. (0 sugars, 0 fiber), 10g pro.

SLOW-COOKER CURRIED PUMPKIN SOUP

Looking for something new this holiday? Try my pumpkin soup! A touch of curry powder lends an aromatic spiced appeal, while whipping cream gives the soup its silky texture.
—Debbie Flocco, Norristown, PA

Prep: 20 min. • **Cook:** 6 hours
Makes: 8 servings

- 2½ cups water
- 1 can (15 oz.) solid-pack pumpkin
- 2 medium tomatoes, quartered
- 1 medium potato, peeled and diced
- 1 medium onion, chopped
- 2 to 3 tsp. curry powder
- 2 tsp. chicken bouillon granules
- ½ tsp. salt
- ⅛ tsp. cayenne pepper
- ⅛ tsp. pepper
- 1 cup 2% milk
- ½ cup heavy whipping cream
  Pepitas and crushed red pepper flakes, optional

1. In a 3-qt. slow cooker, combine the first 10 ingredients. Cover and cook on low for 5½-6½ hours or until vegetables are tender.
2. In a blender, process soup in batches until smooth. Return all to slow cooker. Stir in milk and cream. Cook on high for 30 minutes or until heated through. If desired, garnish with additional heavy cream, pepitas and crushed red pepper flakes.
¾ cup: 121 cal., 7g fat (4g sat. fat), 24mg chol., 381mg sod., 13g carb. (6g sugars, 4g fiber), 3g pro. **Diabetic exchanges:** 1 starch, 1 fat.

TEST KITCHEN TIP

Serve soup in "bowls" made from small pumpkins. Wash and dry pumpkins. Cut a wide circle around the stem of each, making a lid. Scrape out seeds and stringy pulp. Place pumpkins and lids in a large shallow roasting pan. Cover with foil and bake at 350° just until tender, 30-50 minutes (do not overbake). Cool pumpkins slightly, then fill.

SLOW-COOKER CURRIED
PUMPKIN SOUP

BUTTER & HERB TURKEY

My kids love turkey for dinner, and this easy recipe lets me make it whenever I want. No special occasion is required, although it is right-sized for small Thanksgiving gatherings. The meat turns out so tender, it almost falls off the bone.

—*Rochelle Popovic, South Bend, IN*

Prep: 10 min. • **Cook:** 5 hours
Makes: 12 servings (3 cups gravy)

- 1 bone-in turkey breast (6 to 7 lbs.)
- 2 Tbsp. butter, softened
- ½ tsp. dried rosemary, crushed
- ½ tsp. dried thyme
- ¼ tsp. garlic powder
- ¼ tsp. pepper
- 1 can (14½ oz.) chicken broth
- 3 Tbsp. cornstarch
- 2 Tbsp. cold water

1. Rub turkey with butter. Combine the rosemary, thyme, garlic powder and pepper; sprinkle over turkey. Place in a 6-qt. slow cooker. Pour broth over top. Cover and cook on low until tender, 5-6 hours.

2. Remove turkey to a serving platter; keep warm. Skim fat from cooking juices; transfer juices to a small saucepan. Bring to a boil. Combine cornstarch and water until smooth. Gradually stir into the pan. Bring to a boil; cook and stir until thickened, about 2 minutes. Serve gravy with turkey.

6 oz. cooked turkey with ¼ cup gravy: 339 cal., 14g fat (5g sat. fat), 128mg chol., 266mg sod., 2g carb. (0 sugars, 0 fiber), 48g pro.

BUTTER & HERB TURKEY

SMASHED SWEET POTATOES & APPLES

I was looking for ways to cut down on the number of dishes that require oven time on Thanksgiving, so I devised a sweet potato dish that can be made ahead in a slow cooker. It's not too sweet, and it makes a perfect side for turkey or ham.
—*Judy Batson, Tampa, FL*

- -

Prep: 20 min. • **Cook:** 5 hours
Makes: 10 servings

- 3 lbs. sweet potatoes, peeled and cubed (about 8 cups)
- 1½ lbs. tart apples, peeled and cubed (about 4 cups)
- 1½ cups unsweetened apple juice
- 1 bottle (12 oz.) light beer or additional unsweetened apple juice
- 1 cup packed brown sugar
- 1 cup sour cream
- 2 Tbsp. butter

1. Place potatoes and apples in a 6-qt. slow cooker. Add apple juice and beer. Cook, covered, on low until potatoes are tender, 5-6 hours.
2. Drain; return to slow cooker. Add brown sugar, sour cream and butter. Mash potato mixture to reach desired consistency.
¾ cup: 338 cal., 7g fat (4g sat. fat), 12mg chol., 48mg sod., 67g carb. (45g sugars, 5g fiber), 3g pro.
Pressure cooker: Place potatoes and apples in a 6-qt. electric pressure cooker; add apple juice and beer. Lock lid; close pressure-release valve. Adjust to pressure-cook on high for 12 minutes. When cooking time ends, let pressure release naturally. Press cancel. Drain; return to pressure cooker. Add brown sugar, sour cream and butter. Mash potato mixture to reach desired consistency.

SLOW-COOKER MUSHROOM POTATOES

I jazzed up sliced potatoes with mushrooms, onions, canned soup and cheese to create this versatile side. With its comforting flavor, it's a accompaniment to a special meal.
—*Linda Bernard, Golden Meadow, LA*

- -

Prep: 25 min. • **Cook:** 6 hours
Makes: 10 servings

- 7 medium potatoes, peeled and thinly sliced
- 1 medium onion, sliced
- 4 garlic cloves, minced
- 2 green onions, chopped
- 1 can (8 oz.) mushroom stems and pieces, drained
- ¼ cup all-purpose flour
- 2 tsp. salt
- ½ tsp. pepper
- ¼ cup butter, cubed
- 1 can (10¾ oz.) condensed cream of mushroom soup, undiluted
- 1 cup shredded Colby-Monterey Jack cheese

In a 3-qt. slow cooker, layer half of the potatoes, onion, garlic, green onions, mushrooms, flour, salt, pepper and butter. Repeat layers. Pour soup over the top. Cover and cook on low for 6-8 hours or until potatoes are tender; sprinkle with cheese during the last 30 minutes of cooking time.
¾ cup: 249 cal., 9g fat (6g sat. fat), 23mg chol., 893mg sod., 35g carb. (4g sugars, 4g fiber), 7g pro.

TEST KITCHEN TIP

The lid on a slow cooker seals in steam that cooks the food. So unless the recipe instructs you to add ingredients or stir contents, do not lift the lid while the slow cooker is cooking. Every time you sneak a peek, the food takes longer to cook. Many slow cookers have clear plastic or glass lids to satisfy curious cooks.

APPLE BETTY WITH
ALMOND CREAM

APPLE BETTY WITH ALMOND CREAM

During the peak of apple season, I make this treat for friends. I plan an easy meal of soup and bread so we can get right to the dessert!
—*Elizabeth Godecke, Chicago, IL*

Prep: 15 min. • **Cook:** 3 hours
Makes: 8 servings

- 3 lbs. tart apples, peeled and sliced
- 10 slices cinnamon-raisin bread, cubed
- ¾ cup packed brown sugar
- ½ cup butter, melted
- 1 tsp. almond extract
- ½ tsp. ground cinnamon
- ¼ tsp. ground cardamom
- ⅛ tsp. salt

WHIPPED CREAM
- 1 cup heavy whipping cream
- 2 Tbsp. sugar
- 1 tsp. grated lemon zest
- ½ tsp. almond extract

1. Place apples in an ungreased 4- or 5-qt. slow cooker. In a large bowl, combine the bread, brown sugar, butter, extract, cinnamon, cardamom and salt; spoon over apples. Cover and cook on low for 3-4 hours or until apples are tender.
2. In a small bowl, beat cream until it begins to thicken. Add the sugar, lemon zest and extract; beat until soft peaks form. Serve with apple mixture.
1 cup with ¼ cup almond cream: 468 cal., 23g fat (14g sat. fat), 71mg chol., 224mg sod., 65g carb. (45g sugars, 5g fiber), 5g pro.

WARM POMEGRANATE PUNCH

If you're looking for something special to serve on a chilly fall evening, try our lightly spiced hot punch. It has a subtle tea flavor, and the juices create just the right balance of sweet and tart.
—*Taste of Home Test Kitchen*

Prep: 10 min. • **Cook:** 2 hours
Makes: 10 servings (2½ qt.)

- 4 cups pomegranate juice
- 4 cups unsweetened apple juice
- 2 cups brewed tea
- ½ cup sugar
- ⅓ cup lemon juice
- 3 cinnamon sticks (3 in.)
- 12 whole cloves

1. In a 4- or 5-qt. slow cooker, combine the first 5 ingredients. Place cinnamon sticks and cloves on a double thickness of cheesecloth; bring up corners of cloth and tie with string to form a bag. Add to slow cooker.
2. Cover and cook on low for 2-3 hours or until heated through. Discard the spice bag. Serve warm.
1 cup: 145 cal., 0 fat (0 sat. fat), 0 chol., 16mg sod., 36g carb. (35g sugars, 0 fiber), 0 pro.

BUTTERSCOTCH PEARS

This grand finale simmers during dinner and impresses as soon as you bring it to the table. Serve as is, or with vanilla ice cream and a slice of pound cake. Leftover pear nectar is heavenly when added to sparkling wine or simply poured over ice.
—*Theresa Kreyche, Tustin, CA*

Prep: 20 min. • **Cook:** 2 hours
Makes: 8 servings

- 4 large firm pears
- 1 Tbsp. lemon juice
- ¼ cup packed brown sugar
- 3 Tbsp. butter, softened
- 2 Tbsp. all-purpose flour
- ½ tsp. ground cinnamon
- ¼ tsp. salt
- ½ cup chopped pecans
- ½ cup pear nectar
- 2 Tbsp. honey

1. Cut pears in half lengthwise; remove cores. Brush pears with lemon juice. In a small bowl, combine the brown sugar, butter, flour, cinnamon and salt; stir in pecans. Spoon into pears; place in a 4-qt. slow cooker.
2. Combine pear nectar and honey; drizzle over pears. Cover and cook on low for 2-3 hours or until pears are tender. Serve warm.
1 stuffed pear half: 209 cal., 10g fat (3g sat. fat), 11mg chol., 109mg sod., 33g carb. (24g sugars, 4g fiber), 1g pro.

A Message for Every Pot

Use chalkboard paint and markers to add a fun message to your slow cooker.

SLOW COOKER
Fine-grit sandpaper
Painter's tape
Spray paint primer
Chalkboard spray paint
Chalk or chalkboard markers

DIRECTIONS
1. Remove the slow-cooker insert, lid and knobs, making note of the settings that the knobs control, as these may need to be re-marked on the painted cooker if desired.

2. Thoroughly wipe clean the outer surface of slow cooker with a damp cloth. Lightly sand the outer surface using sandpaper.

3. Cover the bottom edge, handles, electrical cord and any other areas that should not be painted. Be careful when taping the curved areas, making sure the tape bonds to the surface so the spray paint cannot seep through.

4. In a protected area, evenly spray outer surface with a thin coat of primer. Allow it to dry thoroughly.

5. Evenly spray the outer surface with 2-3 coats of chalkboard paint, allowing the cooker to dry thoroughly between the coats.

6. When the last coat is dry, carefully remove the tape. Reattach knobs; insert liner and lid. If desired, mark knob settings. Write on the outside of the slow cooker using chalk or chalkboard markers.

Note: To avoid drips, keep spray can level and use an even, steady motion.

BAKE IT FORWARD

Bakers, dust off those baking sheets!
The holiday season brings with it a special
opportunity to show the world kindness and compassion.
This year, give some lovin' from the oven by gifting a
homemade treat to a deserving recipient or whipping up
batches of your best baked wonder for a bake sale
fundraiser. Spreading joy never tasted so sweet.

Molasses Cookies with a Kick (p. 99)

CHERRY DANISH

CHERRY DANISH

These ruby-studded pastries will be the first to disappear from your brunch table. You can use apple pie filling with equally good results.
—*Christie Cochran, Canyon, TX*

- -

Prep: 30 min. + rising • **Bake:** 15 min. + cooling
Makes: 40 servings

- 1 pkg. (¼ oz.) active dry yeast
- ¼ cup warm water (110° to 115°)
- 1 cup warm whole milk (110° to 115°)
- ¾ cup shortening, divided
- ⅓ cup sugar
- 3 large eggs, room temperature, divided use
- 1 tsp. salt
- ¼ tsp. each ground mace, lemon extract and vanilla extract
- 4 to 4½ cups all-purpose flour
- 1 can (21 oz.) cherry pie filling

GLAZE

- 1½ cups confectioners' sugar
- ½ tsp. vanilla extract
- 2 to 3 Tbsp. whole milk
- ⅓ cup chopped almonds

1. In a large bowl, dissolve yeast in water. Add the milk, ¼ cup shortening, sugar, 2 eggs, salt, mace, extracts and 2 cups of flour; beat until smooth. Add enough remaining flour to form a soft dough.
2. Turn onto a floured surface; knead until smooth and elastic, 6-8 minutes. Place in a greased bowl, turning once to grease top. Cover and let rise in a warm place until doubled, about 1 hour.
3. Punch dough down. On a large floured surface, roll the dough out to a 24x16-in. rectangle. Dot half of the dough with ¼ cup shortening; fold dough lengthwise. Fold the dough 3 times lengthwise, then 2 times widthwise, each time dotting with some of the remaining shortening. Place dough in a greased bowl; cover and let rise 20 minutes.
4. On a floured surface, roll dough into a 16x15-in. rectangle. Cut into 8x¾-in. strips; coil into spiral shapes, tucking the ends underneath. Place in 2 greased 15x10x1-in. baking pans. Cover and let rise in a warm place until doubled, about 1 hour.
5. Beat remaining egg. Make a depression in the center of each roll; brush with egg. Fill with 1 Tbsp. pie filling. Bake at 375° for 15-18 minutes or until golden brown. Cool on a wire rack. Combine the first 3 glaze ingredients; drizzle over rolls. Sprinkle with chopped almonds.
1 Danish: 137 cal., 5g fat (1g sat. fat), 17mg chol., 70mg sod., 21g carb. (10g sugars, 1g fiber), 2g pro.

MOLASSES COOKIES
WITH A KICK

MOLASSES COOKIES WITH A KICK

Here's my go-to combination of ingredients for the best spice cookies. They're a natural for fall, but I make them all year long. My mom says they're her favorite!
—*Tamara Rau, Medina, ND*

- -

Prep: 40 min. + chilling • **Bake:** 10 min./batch
Makes: 5 dozen

- ¾ cup butter, softened
- ½ cup sugar
- ½ cup packed brown sugar
- ¼ cup molasses
- 1 large egg, room temperature
- 1½ tsp. minced fresh gingerroot
- 2¼ cups all-purpose flour
- 1 tsp. ground cinnamon
- ¾ tsp. baking soda
- ½ tsp. ground cloves
- ¼ to ½ tsp. cayenne pepper
- ¼ tsp. salt
- ¼ tsp. ground nutmeg
- ⅛ tsp. each ground white pepper, cardamom and coriander
- ¾ cup turbinado (washed raw) sugar

1. In a large bowl, cream butter and sugars until light and fluffy. Beat in the molasses, egg and ginger. Combine the flour, cinnamon, baking soda, cloves, cayenne, salt, nutmeg, white pepper, cardamom and coriander; gradually add to creamed mixture and mix well. Cover and refrigerate for 1½ hours or until easy to handle.
2. Roll into 1-in. balls, then roll in turbinado sugar. Place 3 in. apart on lightly greased baking sheets.
3. Bake at 350° for 8-10 minutes or until set. Cool for 2 minutes before removing from pans to wire racks. Store in an airtight container.
1 cookie: 66 cal., 2g fat (2g sat. fat), 9mg chol., 46mg sod., 11g carb. (7g sugars, 0 fiber), 1g pro.

CHAI-CHOCOLATE CHIP BISCOTTI

This crunchy cookie was made to be dunked! Enjoy one or two with a hot cup of coffee or a cold glass of milk.
—*Pat Runtz, Huntley, IL*

Prep: 30 min. + chilling
Bake: 30 min. + cooling
Makes: 2½ dozen

- 2⅓ cups all-purpose flour
- 1 cup sugar
- ¾ tsp. ground cinnamon
- ½ tsp. baking powder
- ½ tsp. baking soda
- ¼ tsp. salt
- ¼ tsp. ground allspice
- ¼ tsp. ground cardamom
- ¼ cup strong brewed chai tea, room temperature
- 1 large egg, room temperature
- 1 large egg white, room temperature
- 1 Tbsp. fat-free milk
- 1 tsp. vanilla extract
- ½ cup chopped walnuts
- ½ cup miniature semisweet chocolate chips

1. In a large bowl, combine first 8 ingredients. In a small bowl, whisk the tea, egg, egg white, milk and vanilla. Stir into dry ingredients just until combined. Stir in walnuts and chocolate chips. Divide dough in half; cover or wrap each portion and refrigerate for 1 hour.
2. On a baking sheet coated with cooking spray, shape each half into a 10x2-in. rectangle. Bake at 350° for 20-25 minutes or until golden brown. Place pans on wire racks. When cool enough to handle, transfer to a cutting board; cut diagonally with a serrated knife into ¾-in. slices. Place cut side down on baking sheets coated with cooking spray.
3. Bake for 6-9 minutes on each side or until firm. Remove to wire racks to cool. Store in an airtight container.

1 cookie: 93 cal., 3g fat (1g sat. fat), 7mg chol., 52mg sod., 16g carb. (9g sugars, 1g fiber), 2g pro. **Diabetic exchanges:** 1 starch, ½ fat.

CHEDDAR CHEESE BATTER BREAD

As a dairy farmer, I like anything that calls for cheese. This golden loaf—a proven winner at our state fair—tastes wonderful either fresh from the oven or cooled and sliced.
—*Jeanne Kemper, Bagdad, KY*

Prep: 30 min. + rising • **Bake:** 25 min. + cooling
Makes: 2 loaves (16 slices each)

- 2 pkg. (¼ oz. each) active dry yeast
- ¾ cup warm water (110° to 115°)
- 3 cups shredded cheddar cheese
- ¾ cup shredded Parmesan cheese
- 2 cups warm 2% milk (110° to 115°)
- 3 Tbsp. sugar
- 1 Tbsp. butter, melted
- 2 tsp. salt
- 6 to 6½ cups all-purpose flour
- 1 large egg white
- 1 Tbsp. water

TOPPING
- ½ cup finely shredded cheddar cheese
- 1 garlic clove, minced
- ½ tsp. sesame seeds
- ½ tsp. poppy seeds
- ½ tsp. paprika
- ¼ tsp. celery seed

1. In a large bowl, dissolve yeast in warm water. Add cheeses, milk, sugar, butter, salt and 3 cups flour. Beat on medium speed for 3 minutes. Stir in enough remaining flour to form a firm dough.
2. Do not knead. Cover and let rise in a warm place until doubled, about 1½ hours.
3. Stir dough down; transfer to 2 greased 9x5-in. loaf pans. Cover and let rise until doubled, about 30 minutes.
4. Preheat oven to 375°. In a small bowl, combine egg white and water. In another bowl, combine topping ingredients. Brush loaves with egg white mixture; sprinkle with topping. Bake 25-30 minutes or until golden brown. Remove from pans to wire racks to cool.

1 slice: 155 cal., 5g fat (3g sat. fat), 17mg chol., 266mg sod., 21g carb. (2g sugars, 1g fiber), 7g pro.

CINNAMON ROLLS

CINNAMON ROLLS

My wife likes to tell people that after I retired, I went from being the breadwinner to being the bread baker! It all started with a bread-making class at a nearby community college. Now my baked goods are favorites of friends and family, including these breakfast rolls.
—*Ben Middleton, Walla Walla, WA*

Prep: 20 min. + rising • **Bake:** 25 min.
Makes: 2 dozen

- 2 pkg. (¼ oz. each) active dry yeast
- ½ cup sugar, divided
- 1 cup warm water (110° to 115°)
- 1 cup whole milk
- 6 Tbsp. butter
- 7 to 7½ cups all-purpose flour
- 3 large eggs, room temperature, beaten
- 1 tsp. salt

FILLING
- ¼ cup butter, softened
- 5 tsp. ground cinnamon
- ¾ cup packed brown sugar
- ¾ cup raisins or dried currants
  Vanilla icing, optional

1. In a large bowl, dissolve yeast and 1 Tbsp. sugar in water. In a saucepan, heat milk and butter to 110°-115°; add to yeast mixture. Stir in 3 cups flour, eggs, salt and the remaining sugar. Stir in enough remaining flour to make a soft dough.

2. Turn out onto a lightly floured surface. Knead until smooth and elastic, 6-8 minutes. Place in a greased bowl, turning once to grease top. Cover and let rise in a warm place until doubled, about 1 hour.

3. Punch dough down and divide in half. Roll each half into a 15x12-in. rectangle. Brush with softened butter. Combine the cinnamon, brown sugar and raisins; sprinkle evenly over rectangle. Roll up tightly, jelly-roll style, starting with a long side. Slice each roll into 12 pieces. Place in 2 greased standard muffin pans or 2 greased 13x9-in. baking pans. Cover and let rise until doubled, about 30 minutes.

4. Bake at 350° until golden brown, 25-30 minutes. Cool in pans for 5 minutes; invert onto a wire rack. Frost with icing if desired. Serve warm.

1 cinnamon roll: 248 cal., 6g fat (3g sat. fat), 41mg chol., 164mg sod., 43g carb. (15g sugars, 1g fiber), 5g pro.

ORANGE-CHIP
CRANBERRY BREAD

ORANGE-CHIP CRANBERRY BREAD

Tart berries, crunchy nuts and sweet chocolate are simply scrumptious when mixed together in this easy quick bread. Sometimes I'll top it off with an orange-flavored glaze.
—*Donna Smith, Fairport, NY*

Prep: 20 min. • **Bake:** 50 min. + cooling
Makes: 2 loaves

- 2½ cups all-purpose flour
- 1 cup sugar
- ½ tsp. baking powder
- ½ tsp. baking soda
- ¼ tsp. salt
- 2 large eggs
- ¾ cup vegetable oil
- 2 tsp. grated orange zest
- 1 cup buttermilk
- 1½ cups chopped fresh or frozen cranberries, thawed
- 1 cup miniature semisweet chocolate chips
- 1 cup chopped walnuts
- ¾ cup confectioners' sugar, optional
- 2 Tbsp. orange juice, optional

1. In a bowl, combine the first 5 ingredients. In another bowl, combine eggs, oil and orange zest; mix well. Add to dry ingredients alternately with buttermilk. Fold in the cranberries, chocolate chips and walnuts.
2. Pour into 2 greased 8x4-in. loaf pans. Bake at 350° for 50-60 minutes or until a toothpick inserted in the center comes out clean. Cool for 10 minutes before removing from pans to wire racks. If glaze is desired, combine confectioners' sugar and orange juice until smooth; spread over cooled loaves.
1 slice: 220 cal., 13g fat (3g sat. fat), 18mg chol., 76mg sod., 25g carb. (14g sugars, 1g fiber), 4g pro.

MINI SWEET POTATO MUFFINS

I'm always looking for ways to make delicious baked goods a little bit healthier. My husband loves the light texture and spicy streusel of these muffins.
—*Meredith Hedeen, New Kensington, PA*

Prep: 35 min. • **Bake:** 10 min./batch
Makes: 4½ dozen

- 1 cup all-purpose flour
- ¾ cup whole wheat flour
- ½ cup sugar
- ½ cup packed brown sugar
- 1 tsp. baking powder
- 1 tsp. ground cinnamon
- 1 tsp. ground allspice
- ½ tsp. salt
- ¼ tsp. baking soda
- 2 large eggs, room temperature, beaten
- 1 cup mashed sweet potatoes
- ½ cup water
- ¼ cup canola oil
- 3 Tbsp. unsweetened applesauce

STREUSEL
- 2 Tbsp. biscuit/baking mix
- 2 Tbsp. quick-cooking oats
- 1 Tbsp. sugar
- 1 Tbsp. brown sugar
- 1½ tsp. cold butter
- 1 Tbsp. finely chopped crystallized ginger

1. In a large bowl, combine first 9 ingredients. In another bowl, combine the eggs, sweet potatoes, water, oil and applesauce. Stir into dry ingredients just until moistened.
2. Coat mini-muffin cups with cooking spray or use paper liners; fill two-thirds full. For streusel, combine the baking mix, oats and sugars; cut in butter until crumbly. Stir in ginger. Sprinkle over batter.
3. Bake at 350° for 10-12 minutes or until a toothpick inserted in the center comes out clean. Cool for 5 minutes before removing from pans to wire racks.
1 muffin: 51 cal., 1g fat (0 sat. fat), 8mg chol., 45mg sod., 9g carb. (5g sugars, 0 fiber), 1g pro.
Diabetic exchanges: ½ starch.

RAISIN PUMPKIN BARS

These moist bars will keep well—if your family doesn't eat them all right away! They're nice to take to a potluck supper or as a snack or dessert anytime.
—*J.B. Hendrix, Ganado, TX*

Prep: 20 min. • **Bake:** 25 min. + cooling
Makes: 2 dozen

- 2 cups sugar
- 1 can (15 oz.) solid-pack pumpkin
- 1 cup canola oil
- 4 large eggs, room temperature
- 2 cups all-purpose flour
- 2 tsp. baking powder
- 1 tsp. baking soda
- 1 tsp. ground cinnamon
- 1 tsp. ground nutmeg
- ½ tsp. salt
- ⅛ tsp. ground cloves
- ½ cup raisins
- ⅓ cup chopped pecans or walnuts

FROSTING
- ⅓ cup butter, softened
- 3 oz. cream cheese, softened
- 1 Tbsp. whole milk
- 1 tsp. vanilla extract
- 2 cups confectioners' sugar

1. In a large bowl, beat the sugar, pumpkin, oil and eggs. Combine the flour, baking powder, baking soda, cinnamon, nutmeg, salt and cloves; gradually add to pumpkin mixture and mix well. Stir in raisins and nuts.
2. Pour into a greased 15x10x1-in. baking pan. Bake at 350° for 25-30 minutes or until a toothpick is inserted in the center comes out clean. Cool on a wire rack.
3. For frosting, combine the butter, cream cheese, milk and vanilla in a bowl; beat until smooth. Gradually beat in confectioners' sugar. Spread over top; cut into bars. Store in the refrigerator.
1 bar: 297 cal., 15g fat (4g sat. fat), 46mg chol., 184mg sod., 39g carb. (28g sugars, 1g fiber), 3g pro.

PECAN APPLE PIE

Apple pie lovers won't be able to resist a fun twist on the classic. My husband often asks me to bake this extra-special crumb-topped delight for dessert.
—*Anne Betts, Kalamazoo, MI*

Prep: 30 min. • **Bake:** 50 min.
Makes: 2 pies (8 servings each)

- Pastry for 2 single-crust pies
- 1 cup sugar
- ⅓ cup all-purpose flour
- 2 tsp. ground cinnamon
- ¼ tsp. salt
- 12 cups thinly sliced peeled tart apples (about 10 apples)

TOPPING
- 1 cup packed brown sugar
- ½ cup all-purpose flour
- ½ cup quick-cooking oats
- ½ cup cold butter, cubed
- ½ to 1 cup chopped pecans
- ½ cup caramel ice cream topping

1. On a lightly floured surface, roll dough to two ⅛-in.-thick circles; transfer to two 9-in. pie plates. Trim and flute edges; set aside. In a large bowl, combine sugar, flour, cinnamon and salt; add apples and toss to coat. Pour into crusts.
2. For the topping, combine brown sugar, flour and oats; cut in butter until crumbly. Sprinkle over apples. Cover edges loosely with foil. Bake at 375° for 25 minutes. Remove foil; bake 25-30 minutes longer or until filling is bubbly. Sprinkle with pecans; drizzle with caramel topping. Cool on wire racks.
1 slice: 392 cal., 14g fat (7g sat. fat), 30mg chol., 231mg sod., 65g carb. (41g sugars, 3g fiber), 4g pro.

ALMOND COCONUT KRINGLES

My mom was famous for her kringle. She made it from memory, and when she passed away, we didn't have a recipe to carry on her tradition. We searched through her recipe box and found what we believe was her starting point. The dough remains the same, but I adjusted the filling ingredients until it was just right. Try this tender, flaky pastry with its almonds and coconut filling, and you'll be hooked the way we are!
—*Deborah Richmond, Trabuco Canyon, CA*

Prep: 1 hour + chilling • **Bake:** 25 min. + cooling
Makes: 4 kringles (9 slices each)

- 2 cups all-purpose flour
- 1 cup cold butter, cubed
- 1 cup sour cream

FILLING

- 1¼ cups butter, softened
- 1 cup packed brown sugar
- 3 cups sliced almonds, toasted
- 1½ cups sweetened shredded coconut, toasted

GLAZE

- 1 cup confectioners' sugar
- 1 Tbsp. butter, softened
- 1 tsp. vanilla extract
- 4 to 6 tsp. 2% milk

1. Place flour in a large bowl; cut in cold butter until crumbly. Stir in sour cream. Wrap and refrigerate overnight.
2. Preheat oven to 375°. In a small bowl, cream softened butter and brown sugar until light and fluffy. Stir in almonds and coconut.
3. Divide dough into 4 portions. On a lightly floured surface, roll 1 portion into a 12x10-in. rectangle. (Keep the remaining dough refrigerated until ready to use.) Spread 1 cup filling lengthwise down the center. Fold in sides of pastry to meet in the center; pinch seam to seal. Repeat with remaining dough and filling. Transfer to 2 ungreased baking sheets. Bake 23-27 minutes or until lightly browned. Remove to wire racks to cool completely.
4. Meanwhile, combine the confectioners' sugar, butter, vanilla and enough milk to achieve desired consistency; drizzle over the pastries.
1 slice: 244 cal., 18g fat (10g sat. fat), 35mg chol., 98mg sod., 18g carb. (11g sugars, 1g fiber), 3g pro.

RUSTIC SQUASH TARTS

RUSTIC SQUASH TARTS

Puff pastry cradles a sweet and spicy pecan layer under tender squash slices. These tarts make a lovely vegetarian side dish. You'll be glad the recipe makes two!
—*Ann Marie Moch, Kintyre, ND*

Prep: 30 min. • **Bake:** 35 min.
Makes: 2 tarts (8 servings each)

- 1 medium butternut squash, peeled, seeded and cut into ⅛-in. slices
- 1 medium acorn squash, peeled, seeded and cut into ⅛-in. slices
- 2 Tbsp. water
- ¼ cup olive oil
- 1 Tbsp. minced fresh thyme
- 1 Tbsp. minced fresh parsley
- ½ tsp. salt
- ¼ tsp. pepper
- ½ cup all-purpose flour
- ½ cup ground pecans
- 6 Tbsp. sugar
- ½ tsp. ground nutmeg
- ½ tsp. ground cinnamon
- 1 pkg. (17.3 oz.) frozen puff pastry, thawed
- 1 large egg, lightly beaten
- 2 Tbsp. butter

1. In a large microwave-safe bowl, combine squash and water. Cover and microwave on high for 5 minutes or until crisp-tender. Drain; return to bowl. In a small bowl, combine oil, thyme, parsley, salt and pepper; drizzle onto squash and toss to coat. In another small bowl, combine the flour, pecans, sugar, nutmeg and cinnamon; set aside.
2. Unfold pastry sheets on a lightly floured surface. Roll each pastry to ⅛-in. thickness; transfer each to an ungreased baking sheet. Sprinkle with pecan mixture. Arrange squash slices to within 1½ in. of edges, alternating slices of butternut and acorn squash.
3. Fold up edges of pastry over filling, leaving centers uncovered. Brush pastry with egg. Dot squash with butter. Bake at 375° for 35-40 minutes or until golden brown.
1 piece: 279 cal., 15g fat (4g sat. fat), 17mg chol., 196mg sod., 34g carb. (7g sugars, 5g fiber), 4g pro.

How to Peel, Chop & Cut Butternut Squash

1. Cut a half-inch off the top and bottom. Cut through the squash right at the spot where it starts to flare out to form the seed bulb.

2. Using a vegetable peeler, remove outer peel from both sections.

3. Cut the bottom portion in half and remove the seeds with a spoon. Cut crosswise into slices and then into cubes of desired size.

4. Cut the top portion into slices and then into cubes.

How to Peel, Chop & Cut Acorn Squash

1. Cut off the top and bottom of the squash. Cut acorn squash in half.

2. Scoop out seeds with a spoon.

3. Cut through each of the deep ridges to form wedges. Using a vegetable peeler, peel each wedge.

4. Cut wedges into cubes of desired size.

HARVEST FAIR

Every year autumn's brilliant color show draws families outdoors to local farms and festivals. Scarecrows, pumpkins and hayrides guarantee memories in the making—and all that cool-weather fun triggers hearty appetites. Bring some classic harvest fair spirit home with from-scratch recipes boasting fall's signature flavors. Caramel apples, cider, soup and rustic bread are just a few of the comforts in store.

Spiced Sweet Potato Doughnuts (p. 115) **Caramel Apples** (p. 116)
Citrus Cider Punch (p. 108)

APPLE, RAISIN & WALNUT BREAD

My rustic bread studded with raisins and walnuts is great for breakfast with a cup of coffee or can even be eaten as a sweet snack. It's divine with melted butter or spread with apple butter or jam.
—*Geneva Garrison, Jacksonville, FL*

Prep: 10 min. + rising • **Bake:** 40 min. + cooling
Makes: 2 loaves (12 slices each)

- 1 cup whole wheat flour
- ½ cup rye flour
- 2 pkg. (¼ oz. each) active dry yeast
- 1 Tbsp. salt
- 3½ to 4 cups bread flour
- 1½ cups unsweetened apple juice
- ¾ cup plain yogurt
- ¼ cup butter, melted
- 1 large egg, room temperature
- 2 cups dried apples, chopped
- 1 cup raisins
- 1 cup chopped walnuts
- 1 large egg, lightly beaten, optional

1. In a large bowl, mix whole wheat flour, rye flour, yeast, salt and 2 cups bread flour. In a small saucepan, heat apple juice, yogurt and butter to 120°-130°. Add liquid mixture to the dry ingredients; beat on medium speed 2 minutes. Add egg; beat on high 2 minutes. Stir in enough remaining bread flour to form a soft dough (dough will be sticky).
2. Turn onto a lightly floured surface; knead in dried apples, raisins and walnuts until dough is smooth and elastic, 6-8 minutes. Place in a greased bowl, turning once to grease the top. Cover and let rise in a warm place until doubled, about 30 minutes.
3. Punch down dough. Turn onto a lightly floured surface; divide in half. Shape into 2 round loaves. Place on greased baking sheets. Cover with kitchen towels; let rise in a warm place until doubled, about 30 minutes.
4. Preheat oven to 350°. Using a sharp knife, make 3 shallow slashes on top of each loaf. If desired, brush loaves with egg. Bake until golden brown, 35-40 minutes. Remove from pans to wire racks to cool.
1 slice: 198 cal., 6g fat (2g sat. fat), 14mg chol., 325mg sod., 32g carb. (10g sugars, 3g fiber), 5g pro.

APPLE STICKY BUNS

We grow wheat, and I bake a lot of bread using our own flour. This is one of my family's favorite recipes. I like it because it's fast and easy to make.
—*Jonita Williams, Stockton, KS*

Prep: 35 min. + rising • **Bake:** 30 min.
Makes: 16 servings

- 3¼ cups all-purpose flour
- 2 pkg. (¼ oz. each) active dry yeast
- ¼ cup sugar
- 1 tsp. salt
- ¾ cup whole milk
- ¼ cup water
- ¼ cup butter, cubed
- 1 large egg, room temperature
- 1½ cups finely chopped peeled apples

TOPPING
- 1 cup packed brown sugar
- ¾ cup butter, cubed
- ¾ cup chopped walnuts or pecans
- 1 Tbsp. water
- 1 Tbsp. corn syrup
- 1 tsp. ground cinnamon

1. In a large bowl, combine 1½ cups flour, yeast, sugar and salt. In a saucepan, heat the milk, water and butter to 120°-130°. Add to the dry ingredients; beat just until moistened. Add egg; beat until smooth. Stir in remaining flour and apples. Do not knead. Cover and let rise in a warm place for 30 minutes.
2. Meanwhile, in a saucepan, combine the topping ingredients. Bring to a boil, stirring until blended. Pour into an ungreased 13x9-in. baking dish. Stir dough down. Spoon dough by tablespoonfuls over the nut mixture. Cover and let rise for 30 minutes.
3. Bake at 375° for 30-35 minutes or until golden brown. Let stand for 1 minute before inverting onto a large serving platter.
1 piece: 315 cal., 16g fat (8g sat. fat), 45mg chol., 280mg sod., 40g carb. (19g sugars, 1g fiber), 5g pro.

CITRUS CIDER PUNCH

I share this refreshing punch recipe with people who visit our apple cider mill. It's the perfect beverage for autumn gatherings.
—*Carolyn Beck, St. Johns, MI*

Takes: 5 min. • **Makes:** 25 servings (4¾ qt.)

- 1 gallon apple cider, chilled
- 1 can (12 oz.) frozen lemonade concentrate, thawed
- 1 medium lemon, sliced
- 4 spiced apple rings

In a large punch bowl, combine cider and lemonade. Add lemon slices and apple rings. If desired, serve with additional lemon slices and apple rings.
1 cup: 138 cal., 0 fat (0 sat. fat), 0 chol., 22mg sod., 35g carb. (30g sugars, 0 fiber), 0 pro.

PUMPKIN SEED TOFFEE

My kids are allergic to nuts, but they can eat pumpkin seeds. Every fall we save the seeds from our pumpkins to add to various recipes, including this one.
—*Suzanne Earl, Spring, TX*

Prep: 30 min. + cooling • **Makes:** 2 lbs.

- 2 tsp. plus 2 cups butter, softened, divided
- 2 cups sugar
- 1 Tbsp. corn syrup
- 1 tsp. pumpkin pie spice
- ¼ tsp. salt
- 1 cup roasted pumpkin seeds or pepitas

1. Grease a 15x10x1-in. pan with 2 tsp. butter; set aside. In a heavy saucepan, melt the remaining butter. Stir in the sugar, corn syrup, pie spice and salt. Cook and stir over medium heat until a candy thermometer reads 300° (hard-crack stage).
2. Remove from the heat; stir in pumpkin seeds. Immediately pour into prepared pan. Let stand at room temperature until cool, about 1 hour. Break into bite-sized pieces. Store the toffee in an airtight container at room temperature.
1 oz.: 176 cal., 14g fat (8g sat. fat), 31mg chol., 122mg sod., 14g carb. (13g sugars, 0 fiber), 1g pro.

CITRUS CIDER
PUNCH

PEAR & ROAST BEEF
SANDWICHES

PEAR & ROAST BEEF SANDWICHES

Here's an easy way to dress up ordinary roast beef sandwiches. A Mediterranean-inspired spread lends tartness while pear slices add fresh flavor and texture.
—*Pat Dazis, Charlotte, NC*

Takes: 20 min. • **Makes:** 6 servings

- ½ cup plain Greek yogurt
- ½ cup mayonnaise
- 1 medium tomato, seeded and chopped
- ¼ cup finely crumbled feta cheese
- 12 slices sourdough bread, toasted
- 1½ lbs. thinly sliced deli roast beef
- 2 medium ripe pears, thinly sliced
- 6 oz. Havarti cheese, thinly sliced
- 12 Bibb lettuce leaves or Boston lettuce leaves

In a small bowl, combine yogurt, mayonnaise, tomato and feta. Spread over one side of toast slices. Top 6 toasts with beef, pears, Havarti cheese and lettuce. Top with remaining toast slices, spread side down.

1 sandwich: 553 cal., 29g fat (11g sat. fat), 99mg chol., 1226mg sod., 36g carb. (10g sugars, 3g fiber), 36g pro.

APPLE SLUSH

I mixed together a few everyday staples that I had in the refrigerator to create this dessertlike beverage. If you like things a little tart, substitute cranberry juice for the apple juice. You also use other flavors of yogurt, too, such as blueberry or cherry.
—*Wendy Ball, Battle Creek, MI*

Takes: 10 min. • **Makes:** 4 servings

- 2 cups sweetened applesauce
- 1 cup (8 oz.) reduced-fat vanilla yogurt
- ¾ cup partially thawed frozen apple juice concentrate
- 8 to 10 ice cubes
  Cinnamon sugar, optional

Place the applesauce, yogurt and apple juice concentrate in a blender; cover and process until blended. While processing, add a few ice cubes at a time until mixture achieves desired thickness. If desired, sprinkle with cinnamon sugar. Serve immediately.

1 cup: 210 cal., 1g fat (1g sat. fat), 4mg chol., 59mg sod., 47g carb. (43g sugars, 1g fiber), 4g pro.

BLACK BEAN PUMPKIN SOUP

I picked up this recipe at my local grocery store during a promotion for creative ways to use pumpkin. Black beans are not usually paired with this hearty fall vegetable, but once I tried this soup, I was a believer! Now it's one of my favorite recipes to make when pumpkin is in season.
—*Lori Karavolis, McMurray, PA*

Prep: 30 min. • **Cook:** 20 min.
Makes: 10 servings (2½ qt.)

- 2 Tbsp. olive oil
- 1 cup chopped sweet onion
- 1 garlic clove, minced
- ½ cup white wine
- 2 cans (15 oz. each) black beans, rinsed and drained
- 1 can (28 oz.) diced tomatoes, undrained
- 2 cups vegetable broth
- 1 can (15 oz.) solid-pack pumpkin
- 4 tsp. ground coriander
- 3 tsp. ground cumin
- ¾ tsp. salt
- ¼ tsp. cayenne pepper
- ¼ tsp. pepper
- 1 cup heavy whipping cream

1. In a Dutch oven, heat oil over medium-high heat. Add onion; cook and stir until tender, 4-5 minutes. Add garlic; cook 1 minute longer. Stir in wine. Bring to a boil; cook until liquid is reduced by half, 3-4 minutes.

2. Add black beans, tomatoes, broth, pumpkin and seasonings. Bring to a boil; reduce heat. Simmer, covered, until flavors are blended, about 20 minutes, stirring occasionally. Add cream; heat through.

Freeze option: Freeze cooled soup in freezer containers. To use, partially thaw soup in the refrigerator overnight. Heat through, stirring occasionally; add broth if necessary.

1 serving: 221 cal., 12g fat (6g sat. fat), 27mg chol., 608mg sod., 23g carb. (6g sugars, 7g fiber), 6g pro.

Garnish this soup with thinly sliced green onions, a dollop of sour cream and a few roasted pumpkin seeds.

SPICED PEAR CHUTNEY

Skip calorie-laden gravy on meat or poultry and try this flavorful chutney instead. With 3 grams of fiber in every serving, and the nutrients from fresh and dried fruit, it's a healthy and tasty option.
—*Ruth Townsend, Salem, OR*

Prep: 20 min. • **Cook:** 45 min.
Makes: 1¾ cups

1	small onion, chopped
1	garlic clove, minced
⅔	cup cider vinegar
¼	cup packed brown sugar
¼	cup chopped dates
1½	tsp. mustard seed
1	tsp. ground ginger
¼	tsp. salt
¼	tsp. ground coriander
3	cups chopped peeled ripe pears

1. In a small saucepan coated with cooking spray, cook and stir the onion and garlic over medium heat for 2 minutes. Stir in the vinegar, brown sugar, dates and seasonings.
2. Bring to a boil. Reduce heat; carefully stir in pears. Cook, uncovered, over low heat for 40-50 minutes or until pears are tender and mixture achieves desired thickness.
¼ cup: 99 cal., 1g fat (0 sat. fat), 0 chol., 88mg sod., 25g carb. (20g sugars, 3g fiber), 1g pro.

DID YOU KNOW?

Chutney has roots in Indian cuisine, where it is often served alongside spicy curry dishes. In North America, it is often served with roasted meats, and various cheeses, including Brie and goat cheese. Chutneys may be savory, sweet, tart, spicy or mild. Most have a chunky consistency similar to fruit preserves.

FROSTED JUMBO PUMPKIN COOKIES

A classic cream cheese frosting tops these spiced pumpkin cookies. Everyone enjoys the chocolate chips inside and the walnuts sprinkled on top.
—*Wendy Altamirano, Fayetteville, NC*

Prep: 40 min. • **Bake:** 15 min./batch + cooling
Makes: about 2 dozen

1	cup butter, softened
1	cup sugar
1	cup packed brown sugar
1	can (15 oz.) solid-pack pumpkin
1	large egg, room temperature
1½	tsp. vanilla extract
2	cups all-purpose flour
1	cup old-fashioned oats
2½	tsp. ground cinnamon
1	tsp. baking soda
½	tsp. salt
½	tsp. baking powder
1	pkg. (11½ oz.) milk chocolate chips
1	cup chopped walnuts

FROSTING

1	pkg. (8 oz.) cream cheese, softened
½	cup butter, softened
3¾	cups confectioners' sugar
1	tsp. vanilla extract
1	to 2 drops orange food coloring, optional
	Additional chopped walnuts, optional

1. In a large bowl, cream butter and sugars until light and fluffy. Add pumpkin; mix well. Beat in egg and vanilla. Combine the flour, oats, cinnamon, baking soda, salt and baking powder; gradually add to pumpkin mixture and mix well. Stir in chocolate chips and chopped walnuts.
2. Drop dough by ¼ cupfuls 2 in. apart onto ungreased baking sheets. Form dough into pumpkin shapes. Bake at 350° until firm, 14-18 minutes. Remove cookies to wire racks to cool.
3. Meanwhile, for frosting, in a small bowl, beat cream cheese and butter until fluffy. Add the confectioners' sugar, vanilla and, if desired, food coloring; beat until smooth. Spread over the cooled cookies. If desired, sprinkle with additional walnuts.
1 cookie: 376 cal., 19g fat (10g sat. fat), 45mg chol., 203mg sod., 49g carb., 2g fiber, 5g pro.

HOMEMADE APPLE CIDER BEEF STEW

We start craving this comforting stew as soon as weather gets crisp and Nebraska's apple orchards start selling fresh cider. Its subtle sweetness is a welcome change from other savory stews. We enjoy it with biscuits, sliced apples and cheddar cheese.
—*Joyce Glaesemann, Lincoln, NE*

Prep: 30 min. • **Cook:** 1¾ hours
Makes: 8 servings

- 2 lbs. beef stew meat, cut into 1-in. cubes
- 2 Tbsp. canola oil
- 3 cups apple cider or juice
- 1 can (14½ oz.) reduced-sodium beef broth
- 2 Tbsp. cider vinegar
- 1½ tsp. salt
- ¼ to ½ tsp. dried thyme
- ¼ tsp. pepper
- 3 medium potatoes, peeled and cubed
- 4 medium carrots, cut into ¾-in. pieces
- 3 celery ribs, cut into ¾-in. pieces
- 2 medium onions, cut into wedges
- ¼ cup all-purpose flour
- ¼ cup water
  Fresh thyme sprigs, optional

1. In a Dutch oven, brown beef on all sides in oil over medium-high heat; drain. Add the cider, broth, vinegar, salt, thyme and pepper; bring to a boil. Reduce heat; cover and simmer for 1¼ hours.
2. Add the potatoes, carrots, celery and onions; return to a boil. Reduce heat; cover and simmer for 30-35 minutes or until beef and vegetables are tender.
3. Combine flour and water until smooth; stir into stew. Bring to a boil; cook and stir for 2 minutes or until thickened. If desired, serve with fresh thyme.

1 cup: 330 cal., 12g fat (3g sat. fat), 72mg chol., 628mg sod., 31g carb. (14g sugars, 2g fiber), 24g pro. **Diabetic exchanges:** 3 lean meat, 1½ starch, 1 vegetable.

HOMEMADE APPLE CIDER BEEF STEW

SPICED SWEET
POTATO DOUGHNUTS

SPICED SWEET POTATO DOUGHNUTS

No one minds eating a nutritious food like sweet potatoes when it's inside doughnuts! These are easy to prepare and make an excellent breakfast or snack.
—*Jan Valdez, Lombard, IL*

Prep: 15 min. • **Cook:** 5 min./batch
Makes: 1 dozen

- 3 Tbsp. butter, softened
- 1 cup sugar
- 3 large eggs, room temperature
- 1 cup mashed sweet potatoes
- ½ cup buttermilk
- 1 tsp. vanilla extract
- 3½ cups self-rising flour
- 2 Tbsp. pumpkin pie spice
- ¾ tsp. salt
-   Oil for deep-fat frying

TOPPING
- 1 cup sugar
- 4 tsp. ground cinnamon

1. In a large bowl, beat butter and sugar until blended. Beat in eggs, sweet potatoes, buttermilk and vanilla. In another bowl, whisk flour, pie spice and salt; gradually beat into creamed mixture.

2. Turn onto a well-floured surface; pat to ½-in. thickness. Cut with a floured 3-in. doughnut cutter. In an electric skillet or deep fryer, heat oil to 375°. Fry doughnuts, a few at a time, 2-3 minutes on each side or until golden brown. Drain on paper towels. In a small bowl, mix sugar and cinnamon; dip warm doughnuts in topping mixture to coat both sides.

1 doughnut: 383 cal., 14g fat (3g sat. fat), 55mg chol., 651mg sod., 59g carb. (27g sugars, 2g fiber), 6g pro.

If you prefer a glazed doughnut, try this easy maple icing. Whisk 2 cups confectioners' sugar, 3 Tbsp. 2% milk, 2 Tbsp. maple syrup and ½ tsp. maple flavoring until smooth. Spread on tops of doughnuts. Makes 1 cup.

Shaping Doughnuts
All you need to flatten this dough is your hands. Pat it down, then cut with a doughnut cutter. To keep the dough from sticking, dip your cutter in a little flour between cuts.

APPLE PIE SNACK MIX

I love homemade apple pie, but I needed a simple sweet treat for my boys that we could take on the go. With real dried apple bits, white chocolate, nuts and fall spices, this crunchy blend is perfect for our busy family.
—*Jennifer Fisher, Austin, TX*

Takes: 15 min. • **Makes:** 2½ qt.

- 3 cups Cinnamon Chex
- 3 cups Rice Chex
- 1 cup chopped walnuts
- ½ cup packed brown sugar
- ¼ cup butter
- 1 tsp. ground cinnamon
- ½ tsp. ground ginger
- ½ tsp. ground nutmeg
- 2 cups coarsely chopped dried apples
- 1 cup white baking chips
- 1 tsp. shortening

1. In a large microwave-safe bowl, combine cereals and walnuts. In a small microwave-safe bowl, combine the brown sugar, butter, cinnamon, ginger and nutmeg. Microwave, uncovered, on high for 2 minutes, stirring after each minute. Pour over cereal mixture and toss to coat.

2. Cook, uncovered, on high for 4 minutes, stirring every 2 minutes. Spread onto waxed paper to cool. Add dried apples. In a small microwave-safe bowl, melt baking chips and shortening; stir until smooth. Pour over mixture. Cool. Break into pieces; store in an airtight container.

¾ cup: 286 cal., 14g fat (5 g sat. fat), 11mg chol., 170mg sod., 39g carb., 2g fiber, 3g pro.

CARAMEL APPLES

Who doesn't love a good, gooey caramel apple? Make a double batch because these treats always go fast!
—*Karen Ann Bland, Gove City, KS*

- -

Prep: 10 min. • **Cook:** 40 min.
Makes: 8 apples

- 1 cup butter
- 2 cups packed brown sugar
- 1 cup light corn syrup
- 1 can (14 oz.) sweetened condensed milk
- 1 tsp. vanilla extract
- 8 wooden sticks
- 8 medium tart apples
   Unsalted peanuts, chopped

In a heavy 3-qt. saucepan, combine butter, brown sugar, corn syrup and milk; bring to a boil over medium-high heat. Cook and stir until mixture reaches 248° (firm-ball stage) on a candy thermometer, 30-40 minutes. Remove from the heat; stir in vanilla. Insert wooden sticks into apples. Dip each apple into hot caramel mixture; turn to coat. Set on parchment or waxed paper to cool. If desired, roll the bottom of the dipped apples into chopped peanuts.

½ apple: 388 cal., 14g fat (9g sat. fat), 39mg chol., 145mg sod., 68g carb. (65g sugars, 2g fiber), 2g pro.

▲

How to Make Caramel Apples

Farm-fresh apples are tempting on their own. But they're impossible to resist when wrapped in sweet caramel. Follow these steps to make your own batch.

1. Start by removing the stems and thoroughly washing the apples. Store-bought apples can have a bit of a waxy coating to keep them fresh, so be sure to scrub them until that finish is gone and they look natural and dull. A dishcloth should do the job just fine. Once they're clean, dry the apples and insert a wooden pop stick into the top of each. Line a baking sheet with a piece of greased parchment or waxed paper. (Greasing the paper is an important step, so the caramel won't stick later.) Set the baking sheet on a counter close to the stovetop.

2. Next, prepare the caramels for all that sticky goodness. Unwrap the candies—this is a great job for little ones—and heat the caramels in a saucepan with the sweetened condensed milk over medium-low heat, stirring frequently. It should take 3-5 minutes for the mix to become smooth. Once the texture is right, remove from the heat and prepare for dipping. To fully coat the apple, tip the saucepan a bit and rotate the apple until the surface is completely covered.

3. Allow the excess caramel to drip off before you place the apple upright onto the paper-lined pan. If you find that the caramel runs off the apples, don't worry! It might just be a touch too warm. Wait a minute and give the apple another dip.

4. Place all the apples on your lined baking sheet. If you're looking to gobble up these sweet treats right away, let the apples stand until the caramel is set, about 10 minutes. Or, you can refrigerate them for a week or so—just be sure to take them out of the fridge 10-15 minutes before eating so the caramel can soften a bit before you take that first bite.

TEST KITCHEN TIP

Make It Your Own

Pick your own apple (variety).
Though we like Gala apples (we love their sweet flavor), feel free to use whatever apple you prefer for eating. Granny Smiths are a traditional option if you want more tartness and a good crunch.

Roll on the toppings.
You don't have to limit yourself to plain caramel! After dipping, while the caramel is still sticky, roll the apples in nuts, sprinkles or candies. You can also drizzle them with melted chocolate. If you like salty with your sweet, sprinkle a little sea salt on top when the caramel is just about set.

CARAMEL
APPLES

EASTER GATHERINGS

As the winter winds and clouds give way to sunshine and a pleasant breeze, find foods to complement the optimism and new life of the spring season. Mix up your traditional Friday fish fry with homemade sides and succulent seafood, and celebrate Easter with an appetizing array of entrees. Finally, host a gorgeous garden party in a whimsical land of flowers and butterflies.

FISH FRY

More of an event than a meal, Friday fish fries
are a culinary tradition, especially during the Lenten
season when many people eat less meat. While fish is the
star of the show, a bounty of sides—rye bread, coleslaw,
applesauce, potato pancakes, tartar sauce—rounds out
the meal. Whether you like your fish battered or baked,
here's the perfect excuse to get your fry on…
any day of the week, any time of the year!

FARMHOUSE
COLESLAW

MOM'S PICKLED BEETS

Zesty and fresh-tasting, these bright, beautiful beet slices add spark to any meal. My mouth still begins to water when I think of how wonderful they tasted when Mother prepared them.
—*Mildred Sherrer, Fort Worth, TX*

- -

Prep: 15 min. + chilling • **Makes:** 8 servings

  ¾ cup sugar
  ¾ cup white vinegar
  ¾ cup water
1½ tsp. salt
  ¾ to 1 tsp. pepper
   1 large onion, thinly sliced
   2 cans (13¼ oz. each) sliced
      beets, undrained
      Sliced green onions, optional

1. In a large saucepan, combine the first 6 ingredients; bring to a boil. Reduce heat; cover and simmer for 5 minutes. Remove from the heat; add beets. Let stand at room temperature for 1 hour. Transfer beets to a large bowl.
2. Cover and chill 6 hours or overnight. Garnish with green onions if desired.
½ cup: 110 cal., 0 fat (0 sat. fat), 0 chol., 626mg sod., 28g carb. (25g sugars, 2g fiber), 1g pro.

FARMHOUSE COLESLAW

A friend from church gave me this recipe that her grandmother handed down to her. The flavors complement each other well, while the fruit creates a refreshing change of pace from the usual coleslaw.
—*Jan Myers, Atlantic, IA*

- -

Prep: 20 min. + chilling • **Makes:** 12 servings

   4 cups shredded cabbage
   1 large apple, chopped
  ¾ cup raisins
  ½ cup chopped celery
  ¼ cup chopped onion
  ¼ cup mayonnaise
   2 Tbsp. lemon juice
   1 Tbsp. sugar
   1 Tbsp. olive oil
  ½ tsp. salt
  ⅛ tsp. pepper

In a serving bowl, combine the cabbage, apple, raisins, celery and onion. In a small bowl, combine the remaining ingredients. Pour over cabbage mixture and toss to coat. Cover and refrigerate for at least 30 minutes.
⅔ cup: 87 cal., 5g fat (1g sat. fat), 0 chol., 131mg sod., 12g carb. (8g sugars, 1g fiber), 1g pro. **Diabetic exchanges:** 1 vegetable, 1 fat, ½ starch.

▲
Cutting Cabbage

Cut the cabbage in half, then cut a "V" to remove the core. Cut the cabbage halves into wedges and chop or shred as finely as you wish. Chopped cabbage holds more water and stays crunchier over time. Shredded gets softer as it sits. The choice is up to you!

OLD-WORLD RYE BREAD

Rye and caraway lend to this bread's flavor, while the surprise ingredient of baking cocoa gives it a rich, dark color. I sometimes stir in a cup each of raisins and walnuts.
—*Perlene Hoekema, Lynden, WA*

Prep: 25 min. + rising
Bake: 35 min.
Makes: 2 loaves (12 slices each)

  2 pkg. (¼ oz. each) active dry yeast
1½ cups warm water (110° to 115°)
  ½ cup molasses
  6 Tbsp. butter, softened
  2 cups rye flour
  ¼ cup baking cocoa
  2 Tbsp. caraway seeds
  2 tsp. salt
3½ to 4 cups all-purpose flour
    Cornmeal

1. In a large bowl, dissolve yeast in warm water. Beat in the molasses, butter, rye flour, cocoa, caraway seeds, salt and 2 cups of the all-purpose flour until smooth. Stir in enough of the remaining all-purpose flour to form a stiff dough.
2. Turn onto a floured surface; knead until smooth and elastic, 6-8 minutes. Place in a greased bowl, turning once to grease top. Cover and let the dough rise in a warm place until doubled, about 1½ hours.
3. Punch dough down. Turn onto a lightly floured surface; divide in half. Shape each piece into a loaf about 10 in. long. Grease 2 baking sheets and sprinkle with cornmeal. Place loaves on prepared pans. Cover and let rise until doubled, about 1 hour.
4. Bake at 350° for 35-40 minutes or until bread sounds hollow when tapped. Remove from pans to wire racks to cool.
1 slice: 146 cal., 3g fat (2g sat. fat), 8mg chol., 229mg sod., 26g carb. (5g sugars, 2g fiber), 3g pro.

OLD-WORLD
RYE BREAD

HUSH PUPPIES

A fish dinner isn't complete without a side of hush puppies, and my mom is well-known for this recipe. It makes the best ones.
—*Mary McGuire, Graham, NC*

- -

Takes: 25 min. • **Makes:** 2 dozen

- 1   cup yellow cornmeal
- ¼   cup all-purpose flour
- 1½ tsp. baking powder
- ½   tsp. salt
- 1   large egg, lightly beaten
- ¾   cup whole milk
- 1   small onion, finely chopped
- Oil for deep-fat frying

1. In a large bowl, combine the cornmeal, flour, baking powder and salt. Whisk the egg, milk and onion; add to dry ingredients just until combined.

2. In a large cast-iron or electric skillet, heat oil to 365°. Drop batter by tablespoonfuls into oil. Fry until golden brown, 2 to 2½ minutes. Drain on paper towels. Serve warm.

1 hush puppy: 55 cal., 3g fat (0 sat. fat), 9mg chol., 86mg sod., 7g carb. (1g sugars, 0 fiber), 1g pro.

DID YOU KNOW?

Hush puppies, deep-fried cornmeal balls typically served alongside fish or seafood, are said to have originated in New Orleans in 1727. Deep frying is a quick process, so make sure you don't overcook or burn your hush puppies by leaving them in the oil for too long.

HUSH PUPPIES

CILANTRO LIME COD

My daughter loves to cook and especially likes dishes with Mexican flair. She bakes these wonderfully seasoned fish fillets in foil to keep them moist and cut down on cleanup.
—*Donna Hackman, Bedford, VA*

Prep: 15 min. • **Bake:** 35 min.
Makes: 8 servings

    4   cod or flounder fillets (2 lbs.)
    ¼   tsp. pepper
    1   Tbsp. dried minced onion
    1   garlic clove, minced
    1   Tbsp. olive oil
    1½ tsp. ground cumin
    ¼   cup minced fresh cilantro
    2   limes, thinly sliced
    2   Tbsp. butter, melted

1. Place each fillet on a 15x12-in. piece of heavy-duty foil. Sprinkle with pepper. In a small saucepan, saute onion and garlic in oil; stir in cumin. Spoon over fillets; sprinkle with cilantro. Place lime slices over each; drizzle with butter. Fold foil around fish and seal seams tightly.
2. Place on a baking sheet. Bake at 375° for 35-40 minutes or until fish just begins to flake easily with a fork.

3 oz. cooked fish: 132 cal., 5g fat (2g sat. fat), 51mg chol., 85mg sod., 3g carb. (1g sugars, 1g fiber), 18g pro. **Diabetic exchanges:** 3 lean meat, 1 fat.

TARTAR SAUCE

You can't have fried fish without tartar sauce! Skip the bottled stuff and opt for this creamy homemade version that takes just minutes to mix together.
—*Alice McGeoghegan, Willows, CA*

Takes: 5 min. • **Makes:** 1 cup

    1   cup mayonnaise
    1   green onion, finely chopped
    2   Tbsp. lemon juice
    1   tsp. dill weed
    1   tsp. ground mustard
    ½   tsp. paprika
    ½   tsp. pepper

In a small bowl, combine all ingredients. Refrigerate until serving.

2 Tbsp.: 184 cal., 20g fat (3g sat. fat), 2mg chol., 141mg sod., 1g carb. (0 sugars, 0 fiber), 0 pro.

NEW ENGLAND APPLESAUCE

We once lived next to an apple orchard and used the fresh fruit to make lots of delicious homemade applesauce. This is my own recipe, and people have been telling me for years that it's so good it should be published.
—*Marilyn Tarr, Palos Heights, IL*

Prep: 30 min. • **Cook:** 20 min. • **Makes:** 6 cups

- 4 lbs. Rome Beauty or McIntosh apples
- 1 cup honey
- 1 cup water
- ½ cup lemon juice
- 1 tsp. grated lemon zest
- ¼ tsp. ground cinnamon
- 2 Tbsp. grenadine syrup, optional

1. Peel, core and cut apples into wedges. In a large kettle, combine all ingredients except grenadine; bring to a boil. Reduce heat and simmer 20-25 minutes or until apples are fork-tender.

2. Mash apples to a chunky texture or process with food mill for smooth sauce. Stir in the grenadine if desired.

½ cup: 161 cal., 0 fat (0 sat. fat), 0 chol., 1mg sod., 43g carb. (39g sugars, 3g fiber), 0 pro.

Freezing Applesauce

Homemade applesauce can be frozen in serving-size portions for future use. Freeze cooled applesauce in freezer containers. To use, thaw in the refrigerator overnight. Serve it cold or heat through in a saucepan, stirring occasionally.

LEMON-BATTER FISH

LEMON-BATTER FISH

Fishing is a popular recreational activity where we live, so folks are always looking for good recipes. My husband ranks this as one of his favorites.
—*Jackie Hannahs, Cedar Springs, MI*

Takes: 25 min. • **Makes:** 6 servings

- 1½ cups all-purpose flour, divided
- 1 tsp. baking powder
- ¾ tsp. salt
- ½ tsp. sugar
- 1 large egg, lightly beaten
- ⅔ cup water
- ⅔ cup lemon juice, divided
- 2 lbs. perch or walleye fillets, cut into serving-size pieces
  Oil for frying
  Lemon wedges, optional

1. Combine 1 cup flour, baking powder, salt and sugar. In another bowl, combine egg, water and ⅓ cup lemon juice; stir into dry ingredients until smooth.

2. Place remaining lemon juice and remaining flour in shallow bowls. Dip fillets in lemon juice, then flour, then coat with egg mixture.

3. In a large skillet, heat 1 in. oil over medium-high heat. Fry fillets until golden brown and fish flakes easily with a fork, 2-3 minutes each side. Drain on paper towels. If desired, serve with lemon wedges.

5 oz. cooked fish: 384 cal., 17g fat (2g sat. fat), 167mg chol., 481mg sod., 22g carb. (1g sugars, 1g fiber), 33g pro.

PERFECT POTATO PANCAKES

Potato pancakes are a staple at any good fish fry. They make a nice alternative to french fries. When my son and his family visited from Winnipeg, one of the first things they asked for were my potato pancakes!
—*Mary Peters, Swift Current, SK*

- -

Prep: 20 min. • **Cook:** 10 min./batch
Makes: 8 servings

4	**large potatoes** (about 3 lbs.)
2	**large eggs,** lightly beaten
½	**cup all-purpose flour**
½	**cup finely diced onion**
1	**tsp. salt**
⅛	**tsp. pepper**
	Oil for frying
	Maple syrup or applesauce, optional

1. Peel and shred potatoes; place in a bowl of cold water. Line a colander with cheesecloth or paper towels. Drain potatoes into cloth and squeeze out as much moisture as possible. In a large bowl, combine the potatoes, eggs, flour, onion, salt and pepper.

2. In an electric skillet, heat ¼ in. of oil over medium heat. Drop batter by ¼ cupfuls into oil, about 3 in. apart. Press lightly to flatten. Fry until golden brown, about 4 minutes on each side. Drain on paper towels. Repeat with remaining batter. If desired top pancakes with maple syrup or applesauce.

2 pancakes: 287 cal., 12g fat (1g sat. fat), 47mg chol., 324mg sod., 39g carb. (2g sugars, 4g fiber), 6g pro.

Potato pancakes are a fantastic canvas for all sorts of toppings. Sour cream and chives are a classic combination, but jelly, butter and maple syrup work nicely, too. For a fruity flavor, we recommend the homemade applesauce on the opposite page.

▲

How to Make Potato Pancakes

Crispy and golden brown, potato pancakes make a perfect side dish. Here's how to get that perfect texture with a bit of crunch.

1. Shred peeled potatoes using the disc attachment on your food processor. If you don't have a food processor, a box grater works, too.

2. Once you've shredded 4 cups' worth, rinse the potatoes in cold water and drain well, squeezing to remove excess water.

3. In a large bowl, mix the beaten eggs, flour, diced onion, salt and pepper. Stir in your drained potatoes well, making sure every shred is coated. You can also incorporate herbs into the batter at this stage if you like a little extra flavor. Try dill, cumin, cayenne and curry powder.

4. Heat ¼ inch of oil in a large nonstick skillet over medium heat. We recommend canola, vegetable or corn oil because of their high smoke points (meaning they won't start to smoke until they hit higher temperatures). Working in batches, drop the potato mixture by ⅓ cupfuls into the oil. Use a spatula to flatten lightly into a pancake shape.

5. The pancakes will need a little room to get nice and crispy, so don't crowd the pan. Use a second spatula to flip the pancakes so you don't contaminate them with raw egg from the first spatula.

6. When golden brown on both sides, drain on paper towels to soak up excess oil. Once drained, they're ready to eat!

COCONUT FRIED SHRIMP

These crisp and crunchy shrimp make a tempting appetizer or a fun change-of-pace main dish. The coconut coating adds a touch of sweetness, and the tangy marmalade and honey sauce is great for dipping.
—*Ann Atchison, O'Fallon, MO*

Takes: 20 min. • **Makes:** 4 servings

- 1¼ cups all-purpose flour
- 1¼ cups cornstarch
- 6½ tsp. baking powder
- ½   tsp. salt
- ¼   tsp. Cajun seasoning
- 1½ cups cold water
- ½   tsp. canola oil
- 2½ cups sweetened shredded coconut
- 1   lb. uncooked shrimp (26-30 per lb.), peeled and deveined
     Additional oil for deep-fat frying
- ½   cup orange marmalade
- 2   Tbsp. honey

1. In a large bowl, combine first 5 ingredients. Stir in the water and oil until smooth. Place coconut in another bowl. Dip shrimp into batter, then coat with coconut.
2. In an electric skillet or deep-fat fryer, heat oil to 375°. Fry shrimp, a few at a time, for 3 minutes or until golden brown. Drain on paper towels.
3. In a small saucepan, heat marmalade and honey; stir until blended. Serve with shrimp.
7 shrimp with about 2 Tbsp. sauce: 906 cal., 40g fat (20g sat. fat), 138mg chol., 1193mg sod., 117g carb. (58g sugars, 4g fiber), 24g pro.

STRAWBERRY SHORTCAKE PIE

(PICTURED ON BACK COVER)
This fresh fruity pie doesn't last long at our house. The crust is a nice variation from traditional pie crust.
—*Jackie Deibert, Klingerstown, PA*

Prep: 20 min. + chilling
Bake: 10 min.
Makes: 8 servings

- 1½ cups biscuit/baking mix
- 6   Tbsp. cold butter, cubed
- 2   to 3 Tbsp. cold water

FILLING
- ⅔   cup sugar
- 2   Tbsp. cornstarch
- 2   cups water, divided
- 1   pkg. (3 oz.) strawberry gelatin
- 2   qt. fresh strawberries, quartered

1. Place dry biscuit mix in a large bowl. Cut in butter until crumbly. Gradually add water, tossing with a fork until dough forms a ball.
2. Press onto the bottom and up the sides of an ungreased 9-in. deep-dish pie plate. Bake at 450° for 10-12 minutes or until golden brown. Cool on a wire rack.
3. Meanwhile, in a small saucepan, sprinkle gelatin over ½ cup cold water; let stand for 1 minute. Heat over low heat, stirring until gelatin is completely dissolved.
4. In a large saucepan, combine sugar and cornstarch. Stir in remaining 1½ cups water until smooth. Bring to a boil. Cook and stir for 2 minutes or until thickened. Remove from the heat; stir in gelatin mixture.
5. Transfer to a large bowl. Cool to room temperature. Add the strawberries; stir gently to coat. Spoon into crust. Refrigerate until set, about 4 hours. Refrigerate leftovers.
1 piece: 319 cal., 11g fat (6g sat. fat), 23mg chol., 327mg sod., 54g carb. (34g sugars, 3g fiber), 4g pro.

Don't be surprised when the biscuit crust puffs up a bit while this pie bakes. That's what gives this dessert a fun shortcake twist.

FROSTED LEMON BARS

FROSTED LEMON BARS

I won the 2010 Scholarship Bake Off contest at Purdue University with this recipe. I think you'll love the dreamy frosting on top.
—*Michael Hunter, Fort Wayne, IN*

- -

Prep: 20 min. • **Bake:** 20 min. + cooling
Makes: 2 dozen

- 1   cup butter, softened
- 2   cups sugar
- 4   large eggs, room temperature
- 2   tsp. lemon extract
- 1¾ cups all-purpose flour
- ½   tsp. salt
- 1   tsp. grated lemon zest

LEMON CREAM CHEESE FROSTING

- 4   oz. cream cheese, softened
- 2   Tbsp. butter, softened
- 2   cups confectioners' sugar
- 2   tsp. lemon juice
- 1½ tsp. grated lemon zest

1. In a large bowl, cream butter and sugar until light and fluffy. Beat in eggs and extract. Combine flour and salt; gradually add to creamed mixture and mix well. Stir in the lemon zest.

2. Spread into a greased 13x9-in. baking pan. Bake at 350° for 18-22 minutes or until center is set and edges are golden brown. Cool the bars completely.

3. For frosting, in a large bowl, beat cream cheese and butter until fluffy. Beat in the confectioners' sugar, lemon juice and zest. Frost bars. Store in the refrigerator.

1 bar: 243 cal., 11g fat (7g sat. fat), 59mg chol., 145mg sod., 34g carb. (27g sugars, 0 fiber), 2g pro.

TEST KITCHEN TIP

When the edges are lightly browned and pull away from the sides of the pan, the bars are ready to come out of the oven. The center will look set.

AN ELEGANT EASTER DINNER

After months of cold weather and cabin fever, the sun is shining, the birds are chirping and spring plans are in the making. Gather the family to feast on the season's favorites with a modern and chic Easter dinner. Be ready for oohs and aahs when you set a succulent apricot-glazed ham or California-inspired roast lamb on the table alongside a fresh, colorful array of accompaniments and desserts. These recipes and entertaining ideas will make it a event to remember.

California Roast Lamb (p. 138)

Easter Day Countdown

This year, make Easter a classy affair. But don't stress over all the fine details. Refer to this handy cooking and party prep timeline to help you create a modern, elegant gathering that's celebratory and delicious!

A FEW WEEKS BEFORE
☐ Prepare two grocery lists—one for nonperishable items to buy now and one for perishable items to buy a few days before Easter.

☐ Bake the Whole Wheat Dinner Rolls, but do not brush with butter. Wrap securely in an airtight container and store in the freezer.

☐ Prepare the dough for the Gouda Puffs, but do not bake. Freeze unbaked puffs on parchment-lined sheets until firm; transfer to freezer bags and return to freezer.

☐ Bake the cake layers for the Pineapple Carrot Cake, but do not assemble. Store in an airtight container.

☐ Make the Poppy Seed Snack Crisps & Vegetable Spread. Store crisps in an airtight container. Place spread in the refrigerator until ready to serve.

☐ Prepare the Rhubarb Relish. Let cool and store in the refrigerator until ready to serve.

EASTER DAY
☐ In the morning, remove the dinner rolls from the freezer to thaw. Assemble and frost the carrot cake; refrigerate until ready to serve.

☐ In the morning, make the Lemon Polenta-Topped Berry Cobbler; cover and set aside until ready to serve. Mix the Raspberry Lemonade ingredients, minus the club soda and ice; refrigerate.

☐ About 4-5 hours before dinner, grill deviled eggs (use prepared hard-boiled eggs or leftover Easter eggs). Pipe filling into eggs and top with paprika and parsley if desired. Cover and refrigerate until ready to serve.

☐ About 4 hours before dinner, bake the California Roast Lamb and/ or the Apricot-Glazed Ham. Keep meats warm until ready to serve.

☐ Prepare Roasted Asparagus immediately after removing the lamb or ham from oven. Roast for 12-15 minutes; keep warm until ready to serve.

☐ About 45 minutes before dinner, assemble the Three-Green Salad and make the Italian dressing. Chill, separately, in the refrigerator for at least 30 minutes.

☐ About 30 minutes before dinner, removed frozen dough for Gouda Puffs from the freezer. Top and bake as directed.

☐ About 30 minutes before dinner, prepare the Creamed Garden Potatoes & Peas.

☐ About 10 minutes before dinner, reheat the rolls in the oven. Brush with melted butter and serve warm.

☐ Just before dinner, remove salad and dressing from the refrigerator. Shake dressing and toss on salad to coat.

☐ Just before dinner, add club soda and ice to the Raspberry Lemonade. Serve immediately.

☐ After dinner, reheat the cobbler in the oven; serve warm. Serve with carrot cake and shortbread cookies.

TWO DAYS BEFORE
☐ Buy remaining grocery items.

☐ Bake the Easy Scottish Shortbread. Store in an airtight container.

☐ Wash the china, stemware and table linens.

THE DAY BEFORE
☐ If you don't have hard-boiled Easter eggs, prepare eggs for Smoked Deviled Eggs. Cover and store in the refrigerator.

How to Cook Peas

Peas are in season April through May, and they are one of spring's most noble vegetables. They should be cooked gently to preserve their fresh, sweet flavor. If you are using frozen peas, there's no need to defrost them before cooking.

1. Steam: Pour about an inch of water into a saucepan. Place basket in the pan and add peas. Bring the water to a boil, then cover the pot. The rising steam will cook the peas. We recommend steaming for 2-4 minutes, testing occasionally along the way. As soon as the peas are tender, they're ready. This is our favorite way to cook fresh peas, which deserve a gentle treatment to preserve their flavor.

2. Saute: This is our favorite method for frozen peas because it's easy to toss in other ingredients. Begin by heating a tablespoon of butter or oil over medium-high heat. For more flavor, add a chopped onion, sliced fresh mushrooms or minced garlic. Let things cook for a couple of minutes until garlic, mushrooms and/or onions are wilted and soft. Add about 2 cups of peas. Stir them around, still over medium-high heat, until they're heated through and tender, 3-5 minutes. Add salt and pepper to taste, and consider sprinkling on a bit of your favorite spice or fresh herbs.

CREAMED GARDEN POTATOES & PEAS

CREAMED GARDEN POTATOES & PEAS

New potatoes and peas are treated to a creamy sauce in this special side.
—*Jane Uphoff, Cunningham, KS*

- -

Takes: 25 min. • **Makes:** 12 servings

- 2   **lbs. small red potatoes, quartered**
- 3   **cups fresh or frozen peas**
- 1   **cup water**
- 2   **Tbsp. chopped onion**
- 2   **Tbsp. butter**
- 3   **Tbsp. plus 1 tsp. all-purpose flour**
- 1½ **tsp. salt**
- ¼   **tsp. pepper**
- 2   **cups 2% milk**
- 1   **cup half-and-half cream**

1. Place the quartered potatoes in a large saucepan and cover with water. Bring to a boil. Reduce heat; cover and simmer until tender, 8-12 minutes. Drain.
2. Meanwhile, place peas and water in a small saucepan. Bring to a boil. Reduce heat; cover and simmer until tender, 3-5 minutes. Drain.
3. In a large saucepan, saute chopped onion in butter until tender. Stir in the flour, salt and pepper until blended; gradually add milk and cream. Bring to a boil; cook and stir until thickened, about 2 minutes. Stir in potatoes and peas; heat through.

⅔ cup: 156 cal., 5g fat (3g sat. fat), 18mg chol., 345mg sod., 22g carb. (6g sugars, 3g fiber), 6g pro. **Diabetic exchanges:** 1½ starch, 1 fat.

GOUDA PUFFS

I brought the recipe for these puffs back from a trip to Nice, France. The original called for Gruyere cheese, but I found that Gouda is a more budget-friendly alternative. These puffs are a wonderful make-ahead bited-size treat. If you have leftovers, float a few of these gems on a bowl of soup in place of croutons.

—*Lily Julow, Lawrenceville, GA*

Prep: 40 min. • **Bake:** 20 min.
Makes: about 3 dozen

- 1 cup water
- 6 Tbsp. unsalted butter, cubed
- ½ tsp. sea salt
- ¼ tsp. pepper
- ¾ cup all-purpose flour
- 4 large eggs, room temperature
- 1 cup (4 oz.) shredded regular or smoked Gouda cheese
- ⅓ cup minced fresh chives
- ⅛ tsp. ground nutmeg

TOPPING

- 1 large egg
- 1 tsp. water
- ⅓ cup shredded regular or smoked Gouda cheese

1. Preheat oven to 425°. In a large heavy saucepan, bring first 4 ingredients to a rolling boil. Remove from heat; add the flour all at once and beat until blended. Cook over medium-low heat, stirring vigorously until mixture pulls away from sides of pan and forms a ball, about 3 minutes.

2. Transfer to a large bowl; beat 1 minute to cool slightly. Add 1 egg at a time, beating well after each addition, until the mixture is smooth. Continue beating until shiny. Beat in cheese, chives and nutmeg. Drop dough by tablespoonfuls 2 in. apart onto parchment-lined baking sheets.

3. For topping, whisk together egg and water; brush lightly over tops. Sprinkle with cheese. Bake until puffed, firm and golden brown, 20-25 minutes. Serve warm.

Freeze option: Freeze unbaked puffs on parchment-lined baking sheets until firm; transfer to resealable freezer bags and return to freezer. To use, place frozen puffs on parchment-lined baking sheets. Top and bake as directed, increasing time by 2-3 minutes.

1 appetizer: 52 cal., 4g fat (2g sat. fat), 36mg chol., 71mg sod., 2g carb. (0 sugars, 0 fiber), 2g pro.

GOUDA PUFFS

POPPY SEED SNACK CRISPS & VEGETABLE SPREAD

I developed these crunchy crisps as a fun and healthy snack for a wedding shower. They're delicious with the homemade vegetable spread, or try them with preserves or jam.
—*Awynne Thurstenson, Siloam Springs, AR*

- -

Prep: 1½ hours + rising • **Bake:** 15 min.
Makes: 34 dozen crisps (1 cup spread)

- 1   pkg. (¼ oz.) active dry yeast
- 1½ cups warm water (110° to 115°)
- ¼   cup canola oil
- 2   Tbsp. sugar
- 2   Tbsp. poppy seeds
- 2   tsp. salt
- 3   to 4 cups bread flour

VEGETABLE SPREAD
- 1   medium cucumber, peeled, seeded and grated
- 1   tsp. salt
- 1   pkg. (8 oz.) cream cheese, softened
- ¼   tsp. garlic powder
- 1   small carrot, grated

1. In a large bowl, dissolve yeast in warm water. Add the oil, sugar, poppy seeds, salt and 2 cups flour. Beat on medium speed for 3 minutes. Stir in enough remaining flour to form a soft dough (dough will be sticky).
2. Turn onto a floured surface; knead until smooth and elastic, 6-8 minutes. Place in a greased bowl, turning once to grease the top. Cover and let rise in a warm place until doubled, about 1 hour.
3. Punch dough down. Divide into fourths. Shape each into a 13-in. long. Place on baking sheets. Cover and let rise in a warm place until doubled, about 30 minutes.
4. Bake at 350° for 15-20 minutes or until golden brown. Cool completely.
5. Cut into ⅛-in. slices; place on ungreased baking sheets. Bake at 350° for 15-20 minutes or until golden brown and crisp.
6. Meanwhile, place cucumber in a colander over a plate; sprinkle with salt and toss. Let stand for 30 minutes. Drain and pat dry. In a small bowl, beat cream cheese and garlic until smooth. Beat in carrot and cucumber. Serve with crisps. Store leftover crisps in an airtight container.
1 cracker with 1 tsp. spread: 24 cal., 2g fat (1g sat. fat), 5mg chol., 76mg sod., 1g carb. (0 sugars, 0 fiber), 1g pro.

SMOKED DEVILED EGGS
(PICTURED ON BACK COVER)

Give all those leftover Easter eggs a flavor upgrade. Grilling gives them a distinctive smoky taste that will have everyone talking.
—*Catherine Woods, Lexington, MO*

- -

Prep: 20 min. • **Grill:** 10 min. + chilling
Makes: 2 dozen

- ½   cup soaked hickory wood chips
- 12 hard-cooked eggs, peeled
- ½   cup Miracle Whip
- 1   tsp. prepared mustard
- ¼   tsp. salt
- ⅛   tsp. pepper
- ⅛   tsp. paprika
      Minced fresh parsley, optional

1. Add wood chips to grill according to the manufacturer's directions. Place eggs on grill rack. Grill, covered, over indirect medium heat for 7-10 minutes or until golden brown. Cool slightly.
2. Cut eggs lengthwise in half. Remove yolks, reserving whites. In a small bowl, mash yolks. Stir Miracle Whip, mustard, salt, pepper, and paprika. Spoon or pipe into egg whites. If desired, top with additional paprika and chopped parsley. Refrigerate, covered, until serving.
1 stuffed egg half: 52 cal., 4g fat (1g sat. fat), 94mg chol., 91mg sod., 1g carb. (1g sugars, 0 fiber), 3g pro.

> **TEST KITCHEN TIP**
>
> Hard-cooked eggs take on a mild smoky flavor from the hickory chips and turn a light amber. The idea isn't to further cook them, just to add flavor. Be sure to place eggs over indirect heat, not over the coals.

▲

How to Carve Perfect Ham Slices

Carving a ham is easy! You're just four steps away from beautiful slices worthy of your best Easter serving platter.

1. Begin by cutting off the cushion (boneless) portion of the meat.

2. Holding the cushion portion steady with a meat fork, cut it into even slices from the top down.

3. Cut the remaining (bone-in) portion of the ham horizontally above the bone.

4. Carve into even vertical slices. Save the remaining bone-in slab for soup.

ROASTED ASPARAGUS

Since asparagus is so abundant here come spring, I like to put it to great use with this recipe. We all look forward to this side dish each year.

—*Vikki Rebholz, West Chester, OH*

Takes: 25 min. • **Makes:** 12 servings

- 4 lbs. fresh asparagus, trimmed
- ¼ cup olive oil
- ½ tsp. salt
- ¼ tsp. pepper
- ¼ cup sesame seeds, toasted

Arrange asparagus spears in a single layer in 2 foil-lined 15x10x1-in. baking pans. Drizzle with oil. Sprinkle with salt and pepper. Bake, uncovered, at 400° for 12-15 minutes or until crisp-tender, turning once. Sprinkle with sesame seeds.

1 serving: 73 cal., 6g fat (1g sat. fat), 0 chol., 122mg sod., 4g carb. (1g sugars, 2g fiber), 2g pro. **Diabetic exchanges:** 1 vegetable, 1 fat.

APRICOT-GLAZED HAM

(PICTURED ON COVER)

I glaze a bone-in ham with apricot jam to give it an attractive look and delicious flavor. It's the star of any special dinner, and yields lots of extra ham for meals you can put together in minutes later in the week.

—*Galelah Dowell, Fairland, OK*

Prep: 15 min. • **Bake:** 1¼ hours
Makes: 20 servings

- 1 fully cooked bone-in ham (6 to 8 lbs.)
- ½ cup packed brown sugar
- 2 to 3 Tbsp. ground mustard
  Whole cloves
- ½ cup apricot preserves

1. Place ham on a rack in a shallow roasting pan. Score the surface of the ham, making diamond shapes ½ in. deep. Combine brown sugar and mustard; rub over surface of ham. Insert a clove in the center of each diamond.
2. Place ham on a rack in a shallow roasting pan. Bake, uncovered, at 325° for 1 hour. Spoon preserves over ham. Bake 15-30 minutes longer or until a thermometer reads 140° and ham is heated through.
3 oz. cooked ham: 233 cal., 13g fat (5g sat. fat), 48mg chol., 926mg sod., 11g carb. (8g sugars, 0 fiber), 17g pro.

THREE-GREEN SALAD

Natural Room Scents

Welcome visitors to your home with simmering spring aromas, or bottle them up as a hostess gift and be the guest that gets invited back. These three scents are so easy to make.

CHOOSE YOUR SCENT

Spring Lemon
- 1 lemon, sliced and seeded
- 2 to 3 stems of dried lavender
- 2 to 3 stems of fresh rosemary

Dreamsicle
- 1 blood orange, halved, seeded and sliced
- 1 vanilla bean, split, or 1 tsp. pure vanilla extract
- 5 to 6 leaves fresh mint

Fresh Cucumber
- ½ medium cucumber, sliced
- 1½-in. piece fresh ginger, peeled and thinly sliced
- 5 leaves fresh basil

WHAT YOU'LL DO:

1. Place citrus or cucumber slices in a small saucepan.

2. Add remaining ingredients and enough water to cover the contents by 1 in.

3. Heat to boiling; reduce heat to low and simmer, adding more water as needed, for 1-2 hours.

THREE-GREEN SALAD

This bright, beautiful vegetable salad is a fine addition to any celebration—and it's good for you, too. The homemade Italian dressing can't be beat.
—*Gina Squires, Salem, OR*

Prep: 15 min. + chilling
Makes: 12 servings (about ¾ cup dressing)

- 4 cups torn iceberg lettuce
- 4 cups torn leaf lettuce
- 4 cups torn fresh spinach
- 1 medium cucumber, sliced
- 2 carrots, sliced
- 2 celery ribs, sliced
- 6 fresh broccoli florets, sliced
- 3 fresh cauliflowerets, sliced
- 6 radishes, sliced
- 4 green onions, sliced
- 5 fresh mushrooms, sliced

ITALIAN DRESSING
- ⅓ cup olive oil
- ¼ cup plus 2 Tbsp. red wine vinegar
- 2 Tbsp. grated Parmesan cheese
- 1 tsp. sugar
- 1 to 2 garlic cloves, minced
- ¼ tsp. dried oregano
- ¼ tsp. dried basil
- Pinch salt and pepper

1. In a large salad bowl, toss the greens and vegetables. Cover and chill. In a blender, combine all dressing ingredients; cover and process until blended. Pour into a jar with tight-fitting lid; chill for at least 30 minutes.
2. Shake dressing before serving; pour desired amount over salad and toss to coat.

1 cup: 136 cal., 12g fat (2g sat. fat), 1mg chol., 51mg sod., 5g carb. (2g sugars, 2g fiber), 2g pro. **Diabetic exchanges:** 2 fat, 1 vegetable.

Lamb 101

Tender and moist, lamb is a delightful change-of-pace entree.

WHEN BUYING LAMB, LOOK FOR:

- A pinkish red color.

- A package with no holes, tears or excessive liquid.

- A sell-by date on the package that is later than the day of your purchase. If it is the same date, then use it that day or freeze it for later.

WHEN ROASTING LAMB, FOLLOW THESE GUIDELINES:

- Place lamb, fat side up, on a rack in a shallow roasting pan. Roast, uncovered, according to your recipe. Roasting is a dry-heat method; no liquid should be added to the pan. Insert an oven-safe thermometer in the thickest part of the roast, not touching bone or fat. Or, test use an instant-read thermometer to test meat for doneness.

- Roasts continue cooking after they are removed from the oven. Remove at 5°-10° below desired doneness. Allow to stand at room temperature, tented with foil, for 10-15 minutes before serving.

WHEN CARVING A LEG OF LAMB, FOLLOW THESE TIPS:

- Cut a few ¼-in. slices on the thin side of the leg and remove to a platter. Turn the roast over so it rests on the cut surface.

- Hold roast steady by using paper towels around bone with one hand. With a carving knife, make a series of ¼-in. slices along leg down to bone. Then cut along the bone to free slices.

RHUBARB RELISH

Use this zippy relish to complement lamb, ham or any meat of your choosing. It's good on cold roast beef, too.
—*Mina Dyck, Boissevain, MB*

- -

Prep: 10 min. • **Cook:** 30 min. • **Makes:** 3 cups

2	cups finely chopped fresh or frozen rhubarb
2	cups finely chopped onion
2½	cups packed brown sugar
1	cup vinegar
1	tsp. salt
½	tsp. ground cinnamon
½	tsp. ground allspice
¼	tsp. ground cloves
¼	tsp. pepper

In a saucepan, combine all ingredients. Cook over medium heat for 30 minutes or until thickened, stirring occasionally. Cool; store in the refrigerator.
¼ cup: 191 cal., 0 fat (0 sat. fat), 0 chol., 212mg sod., 49g carb. (46g sugars, 1g fiber), 1g pro.

WHOLE WHEAT DINNER ROLLS

(PICTURED ON BACK COVER)
It does my heart good to see everyone at our table reach for one of my hearty whole wheat rolls. Rich with old-fashioned goodness, they bake up to a beautiful golden brown.
—*Ruby Williams, Bogalusa, LA*

- -

Prep: 30 min. + rising • **Bake:** 15 min.
Makes: 4 dozen

2	pkg. (¼ oz. each) active dry yeast
2¼	cups warm water (110° to 115°)
½	cup plus 1 Tbsp. sugar
¼	cup shortening
2	tsp. salt
2	large eggs, room temperature
3	cups whole wheat flour
3½	to 4 cups all-purpose flour
¼	cup butter, melted

1. In a large bowl, dissolve yeast in warm water. Add the sugar, shortening, salt, eggs and whole wheat flour. Beat until smooth. Stir in enough all-purpose flour to form a soft dough.
2. Turn onto a floured surface; knead until smooth and elastic, 6-8 minutes. Place in a greased bowl, turning once to grease top. Cover and let rise in a warm place until doubled, about 1 hour.

3. Punch dough down. Turn onto a lightly floured surface; divide into 4 pieces. Shape each into 12 balls. Place 1 in. apart on greased baking sheets. Cover and let rise until doubled, about 25 minutes.
4. Bake at 375° for 11-15 minutes or until browned. Remove from pans to wire racks. Brush with melted butter. Serve warm.
1 roll: 89 cal., 2g fat (1g sat. fat), 11mg chol., 111mg sod., 15g carb. (3g sugars, 1g fiber), 2g pro.

CALIFORNIA ROAST LAMB

Lamb makes any occasion special. This recipe is easy and requires little attention once it's in the oven. Our California artichokes star alongside lemons and fresh herbs, making this entree even more impressive.
—*Ann Eastman, Santa Monica, CA*

- -

Prep: 10 min. • **Bake:** 2½ hours
Makes: 12 servings

1	leg of lamb (4 to 5 lbs.)
2	to 3 garlic cloves, halved
1	tsp. seasoned salt
1	tsp. pepper
1	tsp. dried oregano
2	cans (8 oz. each) tomato sauce
1	cup water
	Juice of 1 lemon
3	to 5 large fresh artichokes, quartered
	Roasted lemon wedges, fresh oregano and fresh thyme sprigs

Cut slits in lamb; insert garlic. Rub meat with salt, pepper and oregano. Roast at 400° for 30 minutes. Reduce heat to 350°; roast 1 hour more. Skim off any fat in pan; pour tomato sauce, water and lemon juice over lamb. Place artichokes around meat. Roast 1 hour longer or until meat reaches desired doneness (for medium-rare, a thermometer should read 135°; medium, 140°; medium-well, 145°). Garnish with lemons and fresh herbs.
3 oz. cooked lamb: 152 cal., 5g fat (2g sat. fat), 68mg chol., 365mg sod., 6g carb. (1g sugars, 3g fiber), 21g pro. **Diabetic exchanges:** 3 lean meat, 1 vegetable.

PINEAPPLE
CARROT CAKE

PINEAPPLE CARROT CAKE

This moist cake with cream cheese frosting is the best I've ever eaten. It's so simple, too, because it uses two jars of baby food instead of fresh carrots that require grating.
—*Jeanette McKenna, Vero Beach, FL*

Prep: 20 min. • **Bake:** 35 min. + cooling
Makes: 12 servings

- 2 cups all-purpose flour
- 2 cups sugar
- 2 tsp. baking soda
- 2 tsp. ground cinnamon
- 1 tsp. salt
- 1½ cups vegetable oil
- 4 large eggs, room temperature
- 2 jars (6 oz. each) carrot baby food
- 1 can (8 oz.) crushed
  pineapple, drained
- ½ cup chopped walnuts
  FROSTING
- 1 pkg. (8 oz.) cream cheese, softened
- ½ cup butter, softened
- 1 tsp. vanilla extract
- 3¾ cups confectioners' sugar
  Additional chopped walnuts and
  edible blossoms, optional

1. In a bowl, combine the dry ingredients. Add the oil, eggs and baby food; mix on low speed until well blended. Stir in pineapple and nuts. Pour into 2 greased and floured 9-in. round baking pans. Bake at 350° for 35-40 minutes or until a toothpick inserted in the center comes out clean. Cool for 10 minutes before removing from pans to wire racks to cool completely.
2. For frosting, in a bowl, beat cream cheese and butter until smooth. Beat in vanilla and confectioners' sugar until mixture reaches spreading consistency. Spread between layers and over top and sides of cake. Garnish with nuts and blossoms if desired. Store in the refrigerator.
1 slice: 798 cal., 46g fat (13g sat. fat), 112mg chol., 569mg sod., 92g carb. (70g sugars, 1g fiber), 7g pro.

RASPBERRY LEMONADE

Sweet and tangy raspberry lemonade makes the perfect spring drink. Pretty enough to serve at a formal dinner and refreshing enough to pour at a picnic, it's a fun change from iced tea or regular lemonade.
—*Dorothy Jennings, Waterloo, IA*

Takes: 15 min. • **Makes:** 3½ qt.

- 2 cans (12 oz. each) frozen
  lemonade concentrate, thawed
- 2 pkg. (10 oz. each) frozen sweetened
  raspberries, partially thawed
- 2 to 4 Tbsp. sugar
- 2 liters club soda, chilled
  Ice cubes

In a blender, combine lemonade concentrate, raspberries and sugar. Cover and process until blended. Strain to remove seeds. In a 4½-qt. container, combine raspberry mixture, club soda and ice cubes. Serve immediately.
1 cup: 144 cal., 0 fat (0 sat. fat), 0 chol., 34mg sod., 37g carb. (32g sugars, 2g fiber), 0 pro.

EASY SCOTTISH SHORTBREAD

These traditional butter cookies require only three ingredients. They're so yummy, you won't be able to stop at just one!
—*Peggy Goodrich, Enid, OK*

Prep: 20 min. • **Bake:** 10 min./batch + cooling
Makes: about 3½ dozen

- ¾ cup plus 2 Tbsp. butter, softened
- ¼ cup sugar
- 2 cups all-purpose flour

1. In a small mixing bowl, cream butter and sugar. Gradually add flour and mix well. (Dough will be crumbly). Shape into a ball.
2. On a lightly floured surface, press dough to ½-in. thickness. Cut out with a floured 1-in. diamond-shaped cookie cutter; place 1 in. apart on ungreased baking sheets. Prick each cookie with a fork. Reroll scraps if desired. Bake at 350° for 12-15 minutes or until firm. Cool for 2 minutes before carefully removing to wire racks to cool completely.
1 cookie: 55 cal., 3g fat (2g sat. fat), 9mg chol., 26mg sod., 6g carb. (1g sugars, 0 fiber), 1g pro.

LEMON POLENTA-TOPPED BERRY COBBLER

I love polenta, so I was excited when I came up with this way to use it in a dessert.
—*Andrea Bollinger, Carmichael, CA*

Prep: 20 min. • **Bake:** 35 min.
Makes: 12 servings

- 3½ cups fresh blueberries
- 3½ cups fresh blackberries
- 3 Tbsp. cornstarch
- 2 Tbsp. plus ⅓ cup sugar, divided
- ½ cup butter, softened
- 2 tsp. grated lemon zest
- ¾ cup all-purpose flour
- ½ cup cornmeal
- 2 tsp. baking powder
- ½ tsp. salt
- ¾ cup reduced-fat sour cream
- 2 Tbsp. coarse sugar
- 2 Tbsp. lemon juice
- 1 Tbsp. honey

1. In a large bowl, combine the blueberries, blackberries, cornstarch and 2 Tbsp. sugar. Transfer to a 13x9-in. baking dish coated with cooking spray.
2. In a large bowl, cream butter and remaining sugar until light and fluffy. Beat in lemon zest. Combine the flour, cornmeal, baking powder and salt; add to creamed mixture alternately with sour cream. Beat just until combined. Drop by tablespoonfuls onto berry mixture.
3. In a small bowl, combine the coarse sugar, lemon juice and honey; brush over dough. Bake at 350° for 35-40 minutes or until filling is bubbly and a toothpick inserted in topping comes out clean. Serve warm.
1 serving: 230 cal., 9g fat (6g sat. fat), 25mg chol., 230mg sod., 35g carb. (19g sugars, 4g fiber), 3g pro.

This rustic cobbler isn't overly sweet, so it allows the flavors of the berries to shine. Consider serving this with a scoop of vanilla bean ice cream or lightly sweetened whipped cream.

SPRING GARDEN PARTY

The return of sunnier, warmer weather provides an excellent opportunity to bring your whole family and your friends' families together for a fanciful backyard gathering. In the kitchen, give the kids a chance to try their hand at easy culinary creations like Dirt Pudding Cups, Mini Dilly Cheese Balls and cutout sugar cookies— then let your own inner sprite come out to play alongside them!

Dirt Pudding Cups (p. 150) **Confetti Macaroni Salad** (p. 149) **Lemon Spiced Tea** (p. 145)

MINI DILLY
CHEESE BALLS

MINI DILLY CHEESE BALLS

These little appetizers are perfect for any gathering, no matter what time of year it is! Kids love the cheesy, salty flavor, and adults appreciate how easy they are to make.
—*Carole Lanthier, Courtice, ON*

- -

Prep: 15 min. + chilling • **Makes:** 2½ dozen

- 1 pkg. (8 oz.) cream cheese, softened
- 1½ cups sharp shredded cheddar cheese
- ½ cup chopped dill pickles
- 2 green onions, finely chopped
- 2 Tbsp. mayonnaise
- 1 tsp. Worcestershire sauce
- 1 cup chopped walnuts
- ¼ cup minced fresh parsley
  Pretzel sticks or assorted crackers

In a small mixing bowl, combine the first 6 ingredients. Shape tablespoonfuls of cheese mixture into balls. Roll in walnuts and parsley. Cover and refrigerate for 20 minutes before serving. Serve with pretzel sticks or crackers.
1 mini cheese ball: 56 cal., 5g fat (2g sat. fat), 10mg chol., 65mg sod., 1g carb. (0 sugars, 0 fiber), 2g pro.

RAISIN FINGER SANDWICHES

As a registered nurse and the mother of four, I keep quite busy. That's why I like these sweet sandwiches—they're simple to assemble, but they look and taste as if you put a lot of effort into them.
—*Jeannie Dobbs, Bartlesville, OK*

- -

Takes: 10 min. • **Makes:** 15 finger sandwiches

- 1 pkg. (8 oz.) cream cheese, softened
- ¼ cup mayonnaise
- ½ cup chopped pecans
- 10 slices raisin bread, crusts removed

In a small bowl, beat the cream cheese and mayonnaise until smooth. Stir in the pecans. Spread over 5 slices of bread; top with the remaining bread. Cut each sandwich into 3 strips. Serve immediately.
1 sandwich strip: 144 cal., 11g fat (4g sat. fat), 16mg chol., 108mg sod., 10g carb. (3g sugars, 2g fiber), 3g pro.

QUICK CRISPY GREEN BEAN SALAD

Younger children might ask if the beans in this flavorful salad came from Jack's magic beanstalk. The dish is an excellent addition to a party spread, whether as a side or an appetizer. Add the hot sauce to give it an extra kick.
—*Lily Julow, Lawrenceville, GA*

- -

Prep: 30 min. • **Cook:** 5 min.
Makes: 10 servings

- 1½ lbs. fresh green beans, trimmed and halved
- ¼ cup red wine vinegar
- 2 tsp. Dijon mustard
- 2 tsp. honey
- 1 garlic clove
- ½ tsp. salt
- ¼ tsp. pepper
- 1 dash Worcestershire sauce
- ¼ tsp. Louisiana-style hot sauce, optional
- 2 Tbsp. olive oil
- ½ cup thinly sliced red onion
- 1 medium sweet red pepper, thinly sliced
- 2 celery rib, thinly sliced
- 1 hard-cooked large egg, chopped

1. In a 6-qt. stockpot, bring 12 cups water to a boil. Add green beans; cook, uncovered, 2-3 minutes or just until beans turn bright green. Remove beans and immediately drop them into ice water. Drain and pat dry.
2. In a large bowl, whisk vinegar, mustard, honey, garlic, salt, pepper, Worcestershire sauce and, if desired, hot sauce. Gradually whisk in oil until blended. Add vegetables and toss to coat; chill until serving. Sprinkle with chopped egg.
¾ cup: 67 cal., 3g fat (1g sat. fat), 19mg chol., 167mg sod., 8g carb. (4g sugars, 3g fiber), 2g pro.

LEMON SPICED TEA

Cinnamon and honey really perk up the flavor of basic lemon tea. Add a splash of lemon extract to take this drink another notch higher.
—*Adeline Russell, Hartford, WI*

- -

Takes: 10 min. • **Makes:** 8 servings

- 8 cups water
- 14 lemon-flavored tea bags
- 6 cinnamon sticks (3 in.)
- ½ cup honey
- ½ to 1 tsp. lemon extract, optional
  Lemon slices and additional cinnamon sticks

1. In a large saucepan, bring water to a boil. Remove from the heat; add tea bags and cinnamon sticks. Cover and steep for 6 minutes.
2. Discard tea bags and cinnamon sticks. Stir in honey and extract if desired. Serve warm in mugs. Garnish with lemon slices and cinnamon sticks.
1 cup: 66 cal., 0 fat (0 sat. fat), 0 chol., 8mg sod., 18g carb. (17g sugars, 0 fiber), 0 pro.
Diabetic exchanges: 1 starch.

Here's a smart way to use cinnamon sticks: When cooking odors linger in your kitchen, boil some Red Hots and a few cinnamon sticks in water for several minutes. Soon a delicious aroma will fill the kitchen and the rest of your home. Even when there are no odors, this is fun at the winter holidays.

CRAB-MELT SANDWICHES

This open-faced classic is irresistible! Melty flavors and the golden appearance make the sandwich a hit at luncheons for all ages, or you could serve it as part of a light dinner.
—*Verla Stapleton, Cibolo, TX*

Takes: 25 min. • **Makes:** 12 servings

- 6 English muffins, split
- 2 Tbsp. butter, melted
- 1 pkg. (8 oz.) cream cheese, softened
- ½ cup mayonnaise
- 2 large egg yolks
- 1 green onion, finely chopped
- ⅛ tsp. salt
- ⅛ tsp. ground mustard
- ⅛ tsp. pepper
  Dash hot pepper sauce
- 1 cup lump crabmeat, drained

1. Brush muffins with butter. Place on an ungreased baking sheet. Broil 3 in. from the heat for 3-5 minutes or until toasted.
2. In a small bowl, combine the cream cheese, mayonnaise, egg yolks, onion and seasonings. Fold in crab. Spread 3 Tbsp. crab mixture over each muffin half.
3. Broil for 2-3 minutes or until tops are golden brown.

Freeze option: Cover and freeze uncooked crab-topped muffins in a single layer for up to 2 months. Place frozen muffins on an ungreased baking sheet. Bake at 350° for 10 minutes, then broil for 5 minutes or until tops are golden brown.

1 English muffin half: 230 cal., 17g fat (7g sat. fat), 73mg chol., 350mg sod., 13g carb. (1g sugars, 1g fiber), 6g pro.

Will you be short on time on the day of your fairy garden party? Not a problem! The crab mixture can be made ahead and chilled until you're ready to assemble and broil the sandwiches.

ITALIAN VEGGIE BITES

These colorful appetizers are not only tasty, but they also pack in a surprising amount of veggies! The addition of mozzarella and Parmesan is the perfect Italian touch.
—*Cathy Horvath, Surrey, BC*

Prep: 35 min. • **Bake:** 5 min. • **Makes:** 4 dozen

- 1 small eggplant, finely chopped
- 1 cup finely chopped onion
- 1 medium sweet red pepper, finely chopped
- 1 medium zucchini, finely chopped
- 2 garlic cloves, minced
- ¼ cup reduced-fat sun-dried tomato salad dressing
- 1 large tomato, finely chopped
- ¼ cup grated Parmesan cheese
- 8 to 10 flavored tortillas of your choice (about 10 in.)
- ¼ cup shredded part-skim mozzarella cheese

1. Preheat oven to 350°. In a large skillet over medium heat, cook and stir the eggplant, onion, red pepper, zucchini and garlic in salad dressing for 3 minutes. Bring to a boil. Reduce heat; cover and simmer for 5-7 minutes or until vegetables are tender. Remove from the heat; stir in tomato and Parmesan cheese.
2. Cut tortillas with a 3-in. biscuit cutter. Cut a slit halfway into each tortilla circle. Shape into a cone; place in a miniature muffin cup. Spoon 4 tsp. vegetable mixture into each cup. Sprinkle with mozzarella cheese.
3. Bake 5-7 minutes or until tortilla cups are crisp and cheese is melted. Serve warm.

1 appetizer: 40 cal., 1g fat (0 sat. fat), 1mg chol., 63mg sod., 7g carb. (1g sugars, 1g fiber), 1g pro. **Diabetic exchanges:** ½ starch.

ITALIAN VEGGIE BITES

ALL-TIME FAVORITE
SUGAR COOKIES

ALL-TIME FAVORITE SUGAR COOKIES

I searched for about 30 years to find the ideal sugar cookie recipe, and this is it! The dough turns out perfectly for cutting the thick cakelike cookies. Buttercream icing takes them over the top. Add sprinkles if you'd like.
—*Diana Krol, Nickerson, KS*

Prep: 30 min. + chilling
Bake: 10 min./batch. + cooling
Makes: about 5½ dozen

- 4 cups all-purpose flour
- 2 Tbsp. baking powder
- ¼ tsp. salt
- 3 large eggs, separated
- 1 cup margarine, melted
- 1 cup sugar
- 2 tsp. vanilla extract

FROSTING

- ½ cup butter, softened
- 4½ cups confectioners' sugar
- 5 to 6 Tbsp. 2% milk
- 1½ tsp. vanilla extract
- Sprinkles, optional

1. Whisk together flour, baking powder and salt. In a small bowl, beat egg whites on high speed until stiff but not dry. In a large bowl, beat the egg yolks on high until thick, about 2 minutes. Fold in whites. Add melted margarine, sugar and vanilla; beat until blended. Stir in flour mixture.

2. Divide dough in half; shape each into a disk. Wrap in plastic; refrigerate until firm enough to roll, 4 hours or overnight.

3. Preheat the oven to 350°. On a lightly floured surface, roll each portion of dough to ¼-in. thickness. Cut with floured 2-in. cookie cutters. Place 2 in. apart on greased baking sheets.

4. Bake until the edges are light brown, 7-9 minutes. Cool completely on wire racks.

5. For frosting, beat butter until creamy; gradually beat in confectioners' sugar until smooth. Beat in 5 Tbsp. milk and vanilla until light and fluffy; thin with additional milk if desired. Spread or pipe onto cookies. If desired, decorate with sprinkles.

1 cookie: 113 cal., 4g fat (2g sat. fat), 12mg chol., 100mg sod., 17g carb. (11g sugars, 0 fiber), 1g pro.

▲

Making Cutout Cookies

1. On a lightly floured surface with a lightly floured rolling pin, roll out chilled dough evenly to the thickness stated in the recipe. Roll from the center to the edges.

2. Dip cookie cutters in flour, then press into dough. With a large metal spatula, move cookies onto the baking sheet.

3. Bake according to the recipe. Remove cookies from baking sheet with a large metal spatula. Cool on wire racks. Cool completely before frosting and/or storing.

CONFETTI
MACARONI SALAD

BLENDED RASPBERRY-ORANGE TWIST

Here's a drink that will get everyone talking. Kids go crazy for the sweet fruity flavor and Pop Rocks, while adults love the refreshing zing from raspberry sorbet and citrus juices.
—*Cathy Justus, Taylor, MI*

Takes: 20 min. • **Makes:** 12 servings

    Strawberry Pop Rocks Candy, finely crushed
    Lime wedges
3 pints raspberry sorbet
6 cups orange juice
¼ cup lime juice
    Sliced fresh pineapple or maraschino cherries, optional

1. Sprinkle candy on a plate. Using lime wedges, moisten the rims of glasses; dip rims in candy.
2. In a blender, cover and process sorbet and juices in batches for 15 seconds or until smooth. Pour into prepared glasses; garnish with pineapple if desired. Serve immediately.
1 cup: 176 cal., 0 fat (0 sat. fat), 0 chol., 0 sod., 43g carb. (37g sugars, 2g fiber), 1g pro.

CONFETTI MACARONI SALAD

The bits of bright red and green in this salad remind me of fun confetti. The inspiration for the dish came from a recipe I found in a church cookbook when I was a young writer responsible for a newspaper's food section.
—*Renee Page, Rochelle, IL*

Prep: 20 min. + chilling • **Makes:** 16 servings

1 pkg. (16 oz.) uncooked elbow macaroni
1½ cups mayonnaise
3 Tbsp. cider vinegar
1 Tbsp. prepared mustard
1½ tsp. salt
¼ tsp. pepper
1 medium sweet red pepper, chopped
1 celery rib, chopped
4 green onions, chopped
1 jar (4 oz.) diced pimientos, drained
¾ tsp. poppy seeds

Cook macaroni according to package directions; drain. Rinse with cold water and drain well. In a large bowl, combine mayonnaise, vinegar, mustard, salt and pepper. Add macaroni and remaining ingredients; toss to coat. Refrigerate, covered, 2 hours or until cold.
¾ cup: 243 cal., 16g fat (2g sat. fat), 2mg chol., 342mg sod., 22g carb. (2g sugars, 1g fiber), 4g pro.

Bright idea!
Create a teacup garden with fresh and silk flowers, succulents and moss.

CINNAMON MINI-MUFFINS

Tuck these miniature beauties inside an empty foil container decorated with pretty paper for a lovely presentation. The muffins are delicious alongside picnic salads or fresh fruit. Add a little cinnamon butter for even more scrumptiousness!
—*Bonnie Larson, New Berlin, WI*

Takes: 25 min. • **Makes:** 2 dozen

1½ cups all-purpose flour
½ cup sugar
2 tsp. baking powder
½ tsp. salt
½ tsp. ground nutmeg
½ tsp. ground allspice
1 large egg, room temperature, lightly beaten
½ cup fat-free milk
⅓ cup butter, melted
TOPPING
2 Tbsp. sugar
½ tsp. ground cinnamon
¼ cup butter, melted

Preheat oven to 400°. In large bowl, combine flour, sugar, baking powder, salt, nutmeg and allspice. Combine egg, milk and butter; mix well. Stir into the dry ingredients just until moistened. Spoon into greased or paper-lined mini muffin cups. Bake until muffins test done, 12-14 minutes. For topping, mix sugar and cinnamon. Brush tops of warm muffins with butter; sprinkle with cinnamon-sugar.
1 muffin: 94 cal., 5g fat (3g sat. fat), 20mg chol., 130mg sod., 12g carb. (6g sugars, 0 fiber), 1g pro.

TEST KITCHEN TIP

Store spices in tightly closed glass or heavy-duty plastic containers in a cool, dry place. Keep them away from direct sunlight or other heat sources. For best flavor, use ground spices within 6 months. They can be used if they are older, but the flavors may not be as intense. Whole spices can be stored for 1-2 years.

MARTIN'S RHUBARB STRUDEL

Although I have always loved strudel, apple strudel was the only kind I ate for many years. But when my Czech husband made his rendition of rhubarb strudel, it became my new favorite. This is a very quick recipe to make, and everyone who's tried it loves it.
—Cyndee Sindelar, Princeton, NJ

- -

Prep: 30 min. • **Bake:** 25 min.
Makes: 16 servings

- 1½ lbs. sliced fresh or frozen rhubarb
- ½ tsp. ground cinnamon
- ¾ cup sugar
- ¼ cup raisins
- ¾ cup chopped walnuts or almonds, divided
- 16 sheets frozen phyllo dough (9x14 in. each), thawed
- ¾ cup butter, melted
- 1 Tbsp. 2% milk
  Confectioners' sugar
  Sweetened whipped cream or vanilla ice cream, optional

1. Preheat oven to 375°. Combine the first 4 ingredients; add ½ cup walnuts. Set aside.
2. Place 1 sheet of phyllo dough on a work surface; lightly brush with butter. (Keep remaining phyllo covered with plastic wrap and a damp towel to prevent it from drying out.) Layer with 7 more sheets of phyllo, brushing each layer with butter.
3. Spoon rhubarb mixture lengthwise over phyllo within 2 in. of a long side; fold in edges to cover filling. Roll up, starting from the long side. Place seam side down in a parchment paper-lined 15x10x1-in. baking pan. Repeat with remaining phyllo, filling and butter, placing second strudel next to first. Brush both with melted butter and milk.
4. Sprinkle with remaining walnuts; bake until golden, 25-30 minutes. Remove from oven; sprinkle with confectioners' sugar and serve warm. If desired, serve with whipped cream or vanilla ice cream.

1 piece: 195 cal., 13g fat (6g sat. fat), 23mg chol., 116mg sod., 20g carb. (12g sugars, 2g fiber), 2g pro.

BLACKBERRY FRITTERS

I based this recipe on my corn fritters, using berries instead of corn, and they turned out beautifully! They have the texture of a funnel cake, with the extra flavor of fresh fruit. I feel as though I'm at a carnival when I eat these little jewels.
—Lisa Renshaw, Kansas City, MO

- -

Prep: 10 min. • **Cook:** 5 min./batch
Makes: 2½ dozen

- 2 cups all-purpose flour
- ½ cup sugar
- 2½ tsp. baking powder
- 1 tsp. salt
- 2 large eggs
- ¾ cup lemon-lime soda
- 1½ cups fresh blackberries
  Oil for deep-fat frying
  Confectioners' sugar

1. In a large bowl, whisk flour, sugar, baking powder and salt. In another bowl, whisk the eggs and soda until blended. Add to dry ingredients, stirring just until moistened. Fold in blackberries.
2. In an electric skillet or deep fryer, heat oil to 375°. Drop batter by tablespoonfuls, a few at a time, into hot oil. Fry 2-3 minutes or until golden brown, turning occasionally. Drain on paper towels. Dust with confectioners' sugar.

3 fritters: 236 cal., 10g fat (1g sat. fat), 42mg chol., 353mg sod., 33g carb. (13g sugars, 2g fiber), 4g pro.

BLUEBERRY ALMOND BISCOTTI

These biscotti are the perfect treats for an indoor tea party or an outdoor garden party! If you're not a fan of almond extract, vanilla works as well.
—Scarlett Elrod, Newnan, GA

- -

Prep: 20 min. • **Bake:** 30 min.
Makes: 2½ dozen

- 2 large eggs, room temperature
- ⅔ cup sugar
- ½ tsp. almond extract
- 1¾ cups all-purpose flour
- ½ tsp. baking soda
- ¼ tsp. salt
- ¾ cup dried blueberries
- ½ cup sweetened shredded coconut
- ½ cup unblanched almonds, coarsely chopped

1. Preheat oven to 350°. In a large bowl, beat the eggs, sugar and extract until thick and lemon-colored. Combine the flour, baking soda and salt; gradually add to egg mixture and mix well. Stir in the blueberries, coconut and almonds.
2. Divide dough in half. Using lightly floured hands, shape each into a 9x2½-in. rectangle on parchment-lined baking sheets. Bake for 20 minutes or until firm and lightly browned.
3. Place pans on wire racks. When cool enough to handle, transfer rectangles to a cutting board; cut diagonally with a serrated knife into ½-in. slices. Place slices cut side down on ungreased baking sheets. Reduce heat to 325°. Bake for 5-7 minutes on each side or until lightly browned. Remove to wire racks. Store in an airtight container.

1 biscotti: 106 cal., 3g fat (1g sat. fat), 18mg chol., 63mg sod., 18g carb. (9g sugars, 1g fiber), 2g pro. **Diabetic exchanges:** 1 starch, ½ fat.

DIRT PUDDING CUPS

These darling little desserts are my daughter Crystal's favorite. At family birthday parties, no matter how fancy the dirt cup looks, each person gets a gummy worm, too.
—Linda Emery, Bearden, AR

- -

Takes: 20 min. • **Makes:** 10 servings

- 2 cups cold 2% milk
- 1 pkg. (3.9 oz.) instant chocolate pudding mix
- 1 carton (8 oz.) frozen whipped topping, thawed
- 1 pkg. (14.3 oz.) Oreo cookies
  Sugar gum succulents, chocolate rocks and edible paper butterflies, optional

In a medium bowl, whisk milk and pudding mix for 2 minutes. Fold in whipped topping. Pulse cookies in a food processor until fine crumbs form or until desired texture is reached. Divide a third of the cookie crumbs and half of the pudding mixture among 10 dessert cups; repeat layers. Top with remaining crumbs. If desired, top with sugar gum succulents, chocolate rocks and edible paper butterflies.

1 pudding cup: 318 cal., 13g fat (7g sat. fat), 4mg chol., 243mg sod., 47g carb. (29g sugars, 2g fiber), 3g pro.

DIRT PUDDING CUPS

SPECIAL CELEBRATIONS

The tantalizing flavors we enjoy during the holidays don't have to stop after Christmas. From an elegant Galentine's Day brunch or pre-prom party to a spooky Halloween cocktail bash—with summer barbecues, breakfast for dinner and taco Tuesdays in between—you'll find all the right ingredients to keep the mouthwatering merriment going all year long.

BREAKFAST FOR DINNER

Everyone loves a hearty homemade breakfast, but morning routines are often so hectic and harried that most of us resort to cereal or frozen waffles. Tonight, shake up the dinner routine by moving your a.m. faves to the evening time slot with a delicious "brinner" (aka breakfast for dinner). Fluffy eggs, fruity French toast, savory strata and other fun twists on rise-and-shine classics easily adapt to a p.m. setting. These breakfast-for-dinner recipes are so good you'll want to eat them morning, noon and night (but let's try them for dinner first).

Potato & Artichoke Frittata (p. 162)

SOUTHERN
SUNSHINE EGGS

SOUTHERN SUNSHINE EGGS

These adorable ramekins are a fresh take on the classic bacon-and-eggs combo. Make sure to use ovenproof bowls when baking.
—*Carol Forcum, Marion, IL*

Prep: 20 min. • **Bake:** 20 min.
Makes: 2 servings

- 4 bacon strips
- 4 large eggs
- ⅓ cup half-and-half cream
- ⅛ tsp. pepper
- ½ cup shredded cheddar cheese
- 2 green onions, chopped

1. In a small skillet, cook bacon over medium heat until cooked but not crisp. Remove to paper towels to drain; keep warm.
2. In a small bowl, whisk 2 eggs, cream and pepper. Wrap 2 bacon strips around the inside edges of each of two 8-oz. ramekins or custard cups coated with cooking spray.
3. Sprinkle each with half of the cheese and onions. Divide the egg mixture between ramekins. Break 1 of the remaining eggs into each ramekin. Sprinkle with remaining cheese and onion. Bake at 350° until the eggs are completely set, 18-22 minutes.
1 serving: 380 cal., 28g fat (14g sat. fat), 486mg chol., 521mg sod., 5g carb. (3g sugars, 0 fiber), 24g pro.

PEAR-MASCARPONE FRENCH TOAST

My twist on French toast features a spiced pear and cheese filling. This dish is great for both Sunday brunch with the family and evening get-togethers with friends.
—*Emily Butler, Canton, OH*

Prep: 30 min. • **Cook:** 10 min.
Makes: 8 servings

- 2 medium pears, peeled and finely chopped
- 4 Tbsp. butter, divided
- 1 carton (8 oz.) Mascarpone cheese
- 2 Tbsp. sugar
- 2 tsp. minced fresh gingerroot
- ⅛ tsp. plus ¼ tsp. ground cinnamon, divided
- 8 slices French bread (1 in. thick)
- 4 large eggs
- ¾ cup whole milk
- ¼ tsp. vanilla extract
  Maple syrup, optional

1. In a small saucepan, cook pears in 1 Tbsp. butter over medium heat for 2-3 minutes or just until pears are tender. Remove from the heat; cool completely.
2. In a small bowl, beat cheese. Stir in the sugar, ginger, ⅛ tsp. cinnamon and pears. Cut a pocket in the side of each slice of bread. Carefully fill each pocket with about ¼ cup of pear mixture.
3. In a shallow bowl, whisk the eggs, milk, vanilla and remaining cinnamon. Carefully dip both sides of bread in egg mixture (be careful to not squeeze out filling).
4. In a large skillet, melt remaining butter over medium heat. Cook stuffed bread on both sides until golden brown. Serve with maple syrup if desired.
1 piece: 321 cal., 23g fat (12g sat. fat), 159mg chol., 238mg sod., 23g carb. (8g sugars, 2g fiber), 8g pro

SWISS QUICHE

I love hosting brunch. This quiche is one of my go-to recipes because it takes minutes to prepare and allows me to enjoy more time with my guests.
—*Terry Frese Masto, Prescott, AZ*

Prep: 20 min. • **Bake:** 20 min. + standing
Makes: 8 servings

- 1 cup crushed butter-flavored crackers
- 2 Tbsp. butter, melted
- 6 bacon strips, diced
- 1 cup chopped onion
- 2 large eggs
- 2 cups shredded Swiss cheese
- ¾ cup sour cream
  Dash pepper
- ½ cup shredded sharp cheddar cheese

1. Combine cracker crumbs and butter; press onto the bottom and up the sides of an ungreased 9-in. pie plate. Set aside.
2. In a large skillet, cook bacon over medium heat until crisp. Using a slotted spoon, remove to paper towels; drain, reserving 2 Tbsp. drippings. Saute onion in drippings until tender. Remove from the heat. In a small bowl, combine the eggs, Swiss cheese, sour cream, pepper, onion and bacon; pour into prepared crust. Sprinkle with cheddar cheese.
3. Bake at 375° for 20-25 minutes or until a knife inserted near the center comes out clean. Let stand for 10 minutes before cutting.
1 piece: 369 cal., 30g fat (15g sat. fat), 105mg chol., 372mg sod., 9g carb. (3g sugars, 1g fiber), 15g pro.

BACON SPINACH STRATA

Full of flavor, fast and filling, this make-ahead dish is versatile enough for both holidays and everyday meals. It disappears in minutes. And preparing it the night before makes handling hectic evenings a snap!
—*Kris Kebisek, Brookfield, WI*

Prep: 30 min. + chilling
Bake: 45 min. + standing
Makes: 12 servings

- 1 pkg. (8 oz.) sliced mushrooms
- 1 bunch green onions, sliced
- 2 tsp. canola oil
- 1 loaf (1 lb.) day old bread, cut into ¾-in. cubes
- 1 cup shredded Swiss cheese
- 1 pkg. (1 lb.) sliced bacon, cooked and crumbled
- 2 cups shredded cheddar cheese
- 1 pkg. (10 oz.) frozen chopped spinach, thawed and squeezed dry
- 9 large eggs
- 3 cups whole milk
- ½ tsp. each onion powder, garlic powder and ground mustard
- ¼ tsp. salt
- ¼ tsp. pepper

1. In a large skillet, saute mushrooms and onions in oil until tender. Place half of the bread cubes and ½ cup Swiss cheese in a greased 13x9-in. baking dish. Layer with the bacon, cheddar cheese, mushroom mixture, spinach and the remaining Swiss cheese and bread cubes.
2. In a large bowl, combine the eggs, milk and seasonings. Pour over casserole. Cover and refrigerate overnight.
3. Remove from the refrigerator 30 minutes before baking. Bake, uncovered, at 375° for 45-55 minutes or until a knife inserted in the center comes out clean (cover loosely with foil if top browns too quickly). Let stand for 10 minutes before cutting.
1 piece: 382 cal., 22g fat (10g sat. fat), 204mg chol., 817mg sod., 25g carb. (6g sugars, 2g fiber), 21g pro.

ASIAN SAUSAGE & EGG NOODLE BOWL

We love the combo of crispy and creamy in this Asian-inspired dish. It fills us up and satisfies without leaving us feeling heavy or overstuffed. It's also a good opportunity to add any leftover veggies you have on hand, such as mushrooms, cauliflower or spinach. You can also use turkey or chicken breakfast sausage instead of pork.
—Lily Julow, Lawrenceville, GA

- -

Takes: 30 min. • **Makes:** 6 servings

- 3 large eggs
- 2 tsp. sesame oil
- ¼ tsp. kosher salt
- ½ lb. bulk pork sausage
- 2 Tbsp. canola oil, divided
- 1 medium sweet onion, halved and thinly sliced
- 4 garlic cloves, thinly sliced
- 2 tsp. minced fresh gingerroot
- 2 cups finely shredded cabbage
- 6 cups cooked egg noodles, cooled
- 3 Tbsp. minced fresh parsley
- 1 Tbsp. soy sauce
- ¾ tsp. sugar
  Optional: Thinly sliced green onions and Sriracha chili sauce

1. Whisk eggs with sesame oil and kosher salt; set aside.
2. In a large nonstick skillet, cook sausage over medium heat, crumbling meat, until no longer pink, 4-6 minutes. Remove with a slotted spoon; keep warm. Discard drippings.
3. In same pan, heat 1 Tbsp. canola oil over medium heat. Add egg mixture and reduce heat to medium-low; cook just until set in the center, about 1-2 minutes (do not scramble). Gently slide egg onto a cutting board; cut into 4x½-in. wide strips.
4. Heat remaining canola oil in same pan over medium heat. Add onion; cook until softened, 3-4 minutes. Add garlic and ginger; cook until fragrant, about 1 minute longer.
5. Add cabbage; cook and stir until tender, 2-3 minutes. Add noodles, parsley, soy sauce and sugar; cook and stir until heated through, about 2 minutes. Transfer to a shallow serving bowl; top with reserved sausage and egg strips. If desired, top with green onions and serve with chili sauce.
1 serving: 359 cal., 19g fat (4g sat. fat), 145mg chol., 517mg sod., 35g carb. (4g sugars, 2g fiber), 14g pro.

ASPARAGUS, GRUYERE & ONION CRISPY WAFFLES

I took one of our family's favorite puff pastry recipes that uses a similar mix of ingredients and translated it to a breakfast waffle. It's a savory change of pace from sweeter fare and, served with a ham steak and fried eggs, this makes a fabulous meal. Feel free to add maple syrup or a spicy glaze.
—Leslie Ponce, Miami, FL

- -

Prep: 35 min. • **Bake:** 25 min.
Makes: 6 servings

- 1 bunch green onions, finely chopped
- 16 fresh asparagus spears, trimmed and cut into ¼-in. pieces
- ¾ tsp. salt, divided
- ¼ tsp. pepper
- 9 large eggs, room temperature, divided use
- 2 cups all-purpose flour
- 1 Tbsp. baking powder
- ¼ tsp. cayenne pepper
- 1½ cups 2% milk
- 6 Tbsp. butter, melted
- 1 cup Gruyere cheese, shredded
- 1 fully cooked boneless ham steak (12 oz.), cubed

1. Preheat oven to 350°. Arrange onions and asparagus on a greased 15x10x1-in. baking pan; toss with ¼ tsp. salt and pepper. Roast until lightly browned, 10-12 minutes. Cool slightly; reserve ¼ cup vegetable mixture for the topping.
2. Preheat a greased waffle maker. Separate 3 eggs. Whisk flour, baking powder, cayenne pepper and remaining salt. Add milk, 3 egg yolks and melted butter; mix gently but thoroughly. Stir in the remaining onion and asparagus mixture and ¾ cup Gruyere cheese
3. In another bowl, beat 3 egg whites on high until soft peaks form. Fold into waffle mixture. Bake waffles according to manufacturer's directions until golden brown.
4. Meanwhile, in a large skillet coated with cooking spray, cook the ham until heated through; keep warm. In same skillet, fry remaining eggs until yolks are set. To serve, top waffle with ham and 1 egg. Sprinkle with the reserved onion, asparagus and remaining Gruyere cheese.
1 serving: 544 cal., 29g fat (15g sat. fat), 364mg chol., 1493mg sod., 38g carb. (4g sugars, 2g fiber), 33g pro.

ASPARAGUS, GRUYERE & ONION CRISPY WAFFLE

Top That!

There's more than one way to dress up a waffle, and the staff at *Taste of Home* doesn't hold back.

PB&J WAFFLES

I like to spread mine with peanut or almond butter for some protein. Then I top them with fresh berries—kind of like a PB&J.
—Shannon Norris, Senior Food Stylist

BANANAS FOSTER WAFFLES

I love waffles topped with bananas Foster or the four B's (sliced bananas, butter, brown sugar and booze). I also like to fold crumbled bacon bits into the batter.
—Rashanda Cobbins, Food Editor

COFFEE BUTTER WAFFLES

The best waffle I've ever had was topped with caramelized bacon, maple syrup and coffee butter.
—Maggie Knoebel, Culinary Assistant

SPICED WAFFLES

I add cinnamon, nutmeg, cardamom, vanilla and almond extract to the batter. For the topping, I make a strawberry, rhubarb and orange sauce every spring and freeze it in small containers.
—Linda Kast, Reminisce Deputy Editor

CHURRO WAFFLES

I make a churro-inspired version: I top waffles with cinnamon whipped cream and dulce de leche sauce.
—Justin Williams, Culinary Assistant

NUTELLA WAFFLES

I top my waffles with peanut butter, Nutella, bananas and a sprinkling of crushed peanuts. Mmm...
—Beth Tomkiw, Chief Content Officer

EGGS FLORENTINE CUPS

I'm always looking for creative ways to use up the baby spinach I have in my fridge. I'm also a fanatic about making sure my children get a nutritious breakfast. So I make these up the night before, bake them in the morning and breakfast is done! If there are any leftover, I reheat them for a quick lunch or dinner.
—Jan Charles, Greeneville, TN

Prep: 20 min. • **Cook:** 15 min.
Makes: 6 servings

- 6 slices deli ham, ⅛-in. thick
- ¼ cup finely chopped onions
- 1 Tbsp. butter
- 6 cups fresh spinach
- 6 Tbsp. half-and-half cream
- 6 tsp. grated Parmesan cheese
- ¾ tsp. salt
- ¾ tsp. pepper
- 6 large eggs

1. Press the ham slices into the bottom and up the sides of 6 greased foil muffin cup liners; set aside.
2. In a large skillet, saute onions in butter until tender. Add spinach; cook 3-4 minutes longer or until wilted. Divide spinach mixture among ham cups. Top each with 1 Tbsp. of cream, 1 tsp. of cheese and a dash of salt and pepper. Break 1 egg into each cup.
3. Bake at 350° for 15-17 minutes or until the eggs are set.

1 muffin cup: 148 cal., 9g fat (4g sat. fat), 209mg chol., 690mg sod., 4g carb. (2g sugars, 1g fiber), 12g pro.

MUSHROOM OAT PANCAKES

Go beyond plain or blueberry-filled pancakes with these light and earthy flapjacks. The mushrooms and oats add a nice texture and the sunflower kernels are a tasty surprise.
—Steven Steuck, St. Louis Park, MN

Prep: 30 min. • **Cook:** 5 min./batch
Makes: 1½ dozen pancakes

- ½ lb. chopped fresh mushrooms
- 1 Tbsp. butter
- 1 cup quick-cooking oats
- 2 cups all-purpose flour
- ⅓ cup sugar
- 4½ tsp. baking powder
- ¼ tsp. salt
- 2 large eggs, room temperature
- 2¼ cups whole milk
- ¼ cup canola oil
- ⅓ cup unsalted sunflower kernels

1. In a large skillet, saute mushrooms in butter until tender. Cool for 15 minutes.
2. Meanwhile, in a small skillet, toast oats over medium heat until lightly browned.
3. In a large bowl, combine the flour, sugar, baking powder, salt and oats. In a small bowl, whisk the eggs, milk and oil. Stir into the dry ingredients just until moistened. Stir in the sunflower kernels and mushrooms.
4. Pour batter by ¼ cupfuls onto a greased hot griddle; turn when bubbles form on top. Cook until the second side is golden brown.

3 pancakes: 493 cal., 23g fat (5g sat. fat), 85mg chol., 475mg sod., 60g carb. (17g sugars, 4g fiber), 14g pro.

ITALIAN GARDEN OMELET

I created this veggie-filled omelet to treat my wife to a meal using some of the fresh herbs from our garden. She loved it. The herbs give the dish a refreshing zing. It's also good with asparagus when it's in season.
—Billy Hensley, Mount Carmel, TN

Takes: 30 min. • **Makes:** 4 servings

- 2 Tbsp. canola oil
- 1 small yellow summer squash, quartered and thinly sliced
- 1 small zucchini, quartered and thinly sliced
- ¼ cup chopped onion
- 2 Tbsp. chopped sweet red pepper
- 1 tsp. Italian seasoning
- ½ tsp. salt
- ¼ tsp. pepper

OMELETS
- 8 large eggs
- ¼ cup heavy whipping cream
- ¾ tsp. minced fresh or ¼ tsp. dried thyme
- ¾ tsp. minced fresh or ¼ tsp. dried basil
- ¼ tsp. salt
- 2 Tbsp. butter, divided
- ½ cup shredded part-skim mozzarella cheese, divided
- 2 Tbsp. shredded Parmesan cheese, divided

1. In a large nonstick skillet, heat canola oil over medium-high heat. Add the vegetables and seasonings; cook and stir until tender. Remove from pan.
2. In a large bowl, whisk eggs, cream and seasonings until blended. In same pan, heat 1 Tbsp. butter over medium-high heat. Add half of the egg mixture (about 1 cup) to skillet. Mixture should set immediately at edges. As eggs set, push cooked portions toward the center, letting uncooked eggs flow underneath.
3. When eggs are thickened and no liquid egg remains, spoon half of the vegetables on 1 side; sprinkle with ¼ cup mozzarella cheese. Fold omelet in half; sprinkle with 1 Tbsp. Parmesan cheese. Cut the omelet in half and slide each half onto a plate. Repeat with the remaining ingredients.

½ omelet: 372 cal., 31g fat (13g sat. fat), 468mg chol., 741mg sod., 6g carb. (3g sugars, 1g fiber), 19g pro.

MEDITERRANEAN HAM PIE

With the exception of the phyllo dough, which I always have on hand, this recipe is made entirely from Easter dinner leftovers. One of my neighbors traded me four freshly caught trout for a slice!
—Teena Petrus, Johnstown, PA

Prep: 30 min. • **Bake:** 45 min. + cooling
Makes: 8 servings

- 3 Tbsp. butter, divided
- 1 medium onion, halved and sliced
- 8 oz. sliced fresh mushrooms
- 1 garlic clove, minced
- 1 pkg. (10 oz.) frozen chopped spinach, thawed and squeezed dry
- 6 sheets phyllo dough (14x9 in.)
- 2 cups finely chopped fully cooked ham
- 1 cup shredded mozzarella cheese
- 3 large eggs, beaten
  Salt and pepper to taste, optional

1. Preheat oven to 350°. In a large skillet, heat 1 Tbsp. butter over medium heat. Add onion; cook and stir until transparent 6-8 minutes. Add mushrooms and garlic; cook and stir until mushrooms are browned, about 6 minutes longer. Add the chopped spinach; cook until heated through.
2. In a microwave, melt remaining butter; stir until smooth. Place 1 sheet of phyllo dough on a work surface; brush with butter. Layer with 3 additional phyllo sheets, brushing each layer. Transfer to a lightly greased 11x7-in. baking dish, letting ends extend up the sides. (Keep remaining phyllo covered with a damp towel to prevent it from drying out.)
3. Layer dish with ham, cheese and spinach mixture; pour eggs over filling. If desired, sprinkle with salt and pepper. Top with remaining phyllo dough. Fold dough ends over filling; pinch edges to seal. Brush with remaining butter. Cut slits in the top. Bake until browned, 40-45 minutes. Cool for 20 minutes before cutting.

1 serving: 195 cal., 11g fat (6g sat. fat), 113mg chol., 633mg sod., 9g carb. (2g sugars, 2g fiber), 16g pro.

MEDITERRANEAN
HAM PIE

POTATO & ARTICHOKE
FRITTATA

▲

How to Make a Frittata

Here are basic steps for making a frittata. Follow as directed or adapt to a specific recipe, such as the one at right.

1. Saute potatoes and onion until tender. Then, in a large bowl, whisk the eggs, parsley, salt and pepper.

2. Top the potato and onion mixture with the egg mixture.

3. Cover and cook over low heat for 8-10 minutes or until eggs are almost set

4. Broil 6 in. from the heat for 2 minutes or until eggs are set.

POTATO & ARTICHOKE FRITTATA

This frittata is a delicious brunch dish, but it's hearty enough for a weeknight dinner, too. If you like Greek or Mediterranean cuisine, you'll want to add this to your keeper files.
—Sarah Newman, Harvest, AL

- -

Prep: 35 min. • **Bake:** 25 min.
Makes: 4 servings

- 3 Tbsp. olive oil, divided
- ½ cup finely chopped red onion
- 1 garlic clove, minced
- 2 medium Yukon Gold potatoes (about 10 oz.), thinly sliced
- 8 large eggs
- ¼ cup 2% milk
- 2 medium tomatoes, chopped
- 1 can (14 oz.) water-packed artichoke hearts, drained and chopped
- ¼ cup crumbled goat cheese, divided
- 2 Tbsp. minced fresh basil or 2 tsp. dried basil, divided
- 1 tsp. salt
- ½ tsp. pepper

1. Preheat oven to 350°. In a 10-in. ovenproof skillet, heat 1 Tbsp. oil over medium heat. Add the onion; cook and stir 3-4 minutes or until tender. Add the garlic; cook 1 minute longer. Remove onion mixture from pan.
2. Add remaining oil to same pan; arrange the potatoes on bottom of pan. Cook over medium-low heat 15-20 minutes or until tender, stirring occasionally.
3. In a large bowl, whisk eggs and milk. Stir in tomatoes, artichokes, onion mixture, 2 Tbsp. goat cheese, 1 Tbsp. fresh basil, salt and pepper. Pour egg mixture over potatoes; sprinkle with remaining cheese. Bake until eggs are completely set, 25-30 minutes.
4. Let stand for 5 minutes. Sprinkle with remaining basil. Cut into wedges.
1 wedge: 420 cal., 22g fat (6g sat. fat), 382mg chol., 1039mg sod., 35g carb. (5g sugars, 3g fiber), 20g pro.

GRILLED BISTRO BREAKFAST SANDWICH

I used to make a classic breakfast sandwich when my kids were still at home. Now that it's just my husband and me, I've jazzed it up with pear, smoked Gouda and spinach.
—Wendy Ball, Battle Creek, MI

Takes: 30 min. • **Makes:** 2 sandwiches

- 2 tsp. butter, divided
- 4 large eggs, beaten
- 4 slices (¾-in. thick) hearty Italian bread
- ⅛ tsp. salt
- ⅛ tsp. pepper
- 4 oz. smoked Gouda or smoked cheddar cheese, cut in 4 slices
- 1 medium pear, thinly sliced
- 4 slices Canadian bacon, cooked
- ½ cup fresh baby spinach

Heat 1 tsp. butter in a small nonstick skillet over medium heat; add the eggs and scramble until set. Divide eggs between 2 slices of bread; sprinkle each with salt and pepper. Layer bread with cheese slices, pear slices, Canadian bacon and spinach. Top with remaining bread.

Note: If using a panini maker, spread butter on both sides of sandwiches. Grill according to manufacturer's directions until golden brown and grill marks show, 6-8 minutes. If using an indoor grill, spread half of remaining butter on 1 side of both sandwiches. Place buttered side down on grill; press down with a heavy skillet or other weight. Grill over medium-high heat until golden brown and grill-marked, 3-5 minutes. Remove weight; spread remaining butter on the other side of sandwiches. Return to grill buttered side down; replace weight. Grill until golden brown, another 3-5 minutes.

1 sandwich: 629 cal., 33g fat (17g sat. fat), 461mg chol., 1510mg sod., 44g carb. (11g sugars, 4g fiber), 38g pro.

GRILLED BISTRO BREAKFAST SANDWICH

BACON APPLE RISOTTO

The beauty of this dish is it can be eaten for breakfast, lunch or dinner. A bit of savory, a touch of sweet and the perfect creaminess of the risotto make it a game-changer. Feel free to replace the consomme with chicken or vegetable broth if desired. You can also use white wine instead of red.
—Evan Young, Studio City, CA

Prep: 15 min. • **Cook:** 40 min.
Makes: 8 servings

- 3 medium Fuji apples, cut into ½-in. dice
- 3 Tbsp. lemon juice, divided
- 2½ cups unsweetened apple juice
- 2 cups condensed beef consomme, undiluted
- 2 Tbsp. butter
- 2 large yellow onions, cut into ½-in. dice
- 2 cups uncooked arborio rice
- ¾ cup dry red wine
- ½ tsp. salt
- ¼ tsp. coarsely ground pepper
- 8 bacon strips, cooked and roughly chopped
  Grated Parmesan cheese

1. Toss apples in 1 Tbsp. lemon juice; set aside. In a large saucepan, heat apple juice and consomme over medium-low heat.
2. In a Dutch oven, melt butter over medium heat. Add onions; saute until softened and translucent, about 10 minutes. Stir in rice. Cook, stirring occasionally, until rice and onions begin to brown, 4-6 minutes.
3. Add wine; cook, stirring, until liquid is almost evaporated, 1-2 minutes. Stir in hot apple juice mixture. Bring to a boil. Reduce heat; simmer, stirring occasionally, until liquid is absorbed, about 20 minutes. Stir in apples, salt, pepper and remaining lemon juice; cook until apples are crisp-tender, about 5 minutes.
4. Sprinkle with bacon and Parmesan cheese.

1¼ cups: 365 cal., 7g fat (3g sat. fat), 19mg chol., 775mg sod., 61g carb. (16g sugars, 3g fiber), 10g pro.

Use Granny Smith or other tart apples in this risotto for a sharper flavor.

GALENTINE'S DAY

What's Galentine's Day? "Oh, it's only the BEST day of the year," according to Leslie Knope, overachieving deputy director of the Pawnee, Indiana, Parks and Recreation Department on TV's *Parks and Recreation*. "Every February 13, my lady friends and I leave our husbands and boyfriends at home and we just come and kick it breakfast-style." Here's how to throw an epic Galentine's Day celebration of your own.

Fresh Strawberry Syrup (p. 167) **Honey Poppy Seed Fruit Salad** (p. 172)
Buttermilk Pecan Waffles (p. 167) **Cotton Candy Champagne Cocktails** (p. 172)

BUTTERMILK
PECAN WAFFLES

BUTTERMILK PECAN WAFFLES

These golden waffles are a favorite for breakfast, so we enjoy them often. They're as easy to prepare as regular waffles, but their unique taste makes them exceptional.
—*Edna Hoffman, Hebron, IN*

Takes: 25 min.
Makes: 7 waffles (about 8 in. each)

- 2 cups all-purpose flour
- 1 Tbsp. baking powder
- 1 tsp. baking soda
- ½ tsp. salt
- 4 large eggs, room temperature
- 2 cups buttermilk
- ½ cup butter, melted
- 3 Tbsp. chopped pecans

1. In a large bowl, combine the flour, baking powder, baking soda and salt; set aside.
2. In a large bowl, beat eggs until light. Add buttermilk; mix well. Add dry ingredients and beat until batter is smooth. Stir in butter.
3. Pour about ¾ cup batter onto a lightly greased preheated waffle iron. Sprinkle with a few pecans. Bake according to manufacturer's directions until golden brown. Repeat with remaining batter and pecans.
1 waffle: 337 cal., 19g fat (10g sat. fat), 159mg chol., 762mg sod., 31g carb. (4g sugars, 1g fiber), 10g pro.

PEANUT BUTTER MALLOW TOPPING

Looking for the perfect topping for ice cream? You've found it! This tasty topper can also be drizzled over sliced apples, bananas or brownies.
—*Sandy DeCosta, Vineland, NJ*

Takes: 10 min. • **Makes:** 2 cups

- 1 jar (7 oz.) marshmallow creme
- ½ cup chunky peanut butter
- ¼ cup hot water
- 1 Tbsp. chocolate syrup

In a mixing bowl, combine all ingredients; beat until blended.
2 Tbsp.: 93 cal., 4g fat (1g sat. fat), 0 chol., 49mg sod., 10g carb. (9g sugars, 1g fiber), 2g pro.

FRESH STRAWBERRY SYRUP

One summer our garden yielded 80 quarts of strawberries! A good portion of that was preserved as strawberry syrup. We treat ourselves to this sweet, warm mixture over waffles or pancakes.
—*Heather Biedler, Martinsburg, WV*

Takes: 15 min. • **Makes:** 2 cups

- ¼ cup sugar
- 2 tsp. cornstarch
  Dash salt
- 2 cups chopped fresh strawberries
- ½ cup water
- ½ tsp. lemon juice

In a small saucepan, combine the sugar, cornstarch and salt. Stir in strawberries, water and lemon juice until blended. Bring to a boil. Reduce heat; simmer, uncovered, for 2-3 minutes or until thickened and the strawberries are tender.
¼ cup: 40 cal., 0 fat (0 sat. fat), 0 chol., 19mg sod., 10g carb. (8g sugars, 1g fiber), 0 pro.

Don't wash strawberries until you're ready to use them. They stay fresh longer if unwashed, with stems on, in a sealed glass jar in the refrigerator. Strawberries soak up moisture from washing, which can make them spoil in a hurry. It's not a long way from wet berries to moldy berries.

Coffee Body Scrub

Looking for a fun party favor for your gal pals? Mix up this invigorating coffee body scrub.

If you're a coffee lover, the idea of using precious coffee beans in a body scrub might shock you, but give this DIY product a shot—you'll be glad you did. Coffee scrubs aren't just for exfoliation and boosting circulation. The caffeine in the beans can also plump and tighten your skin, helping to reduce the appearance of cellulite. Plus, the coconut oil will leave your skin silky smooth.

TO MAKE:
Mix together ½ cup fresh ground coffee and ½ cup brown sugar. Pour ½ cup melted coconut oil into the coffee mixture, then add 1 tsp. vanilla extract. Mix until well combined. Makes 4 applications.

TO USE:
Gently rub the mixture over your body. Leave it on for a few minutes, then rinse thoroughly. (Be careful if using the scrub in the shower, as the oil can make the floor a bit slippery.)

MINI SAUSAGE FRITTATAS

These are perfect for breakfast or brunch. While my gal pals love the spicy kick in hot sausage, I like using sage-flavored sausage and substituting Parmesan for cheddar.
—*Courtney Wright, Birmingham, AL*

- -

Prep: 15 min. • **Bake:** 20 min. • **Makes:** 1 dozen

- 1 lb. bulk pork sausage
- 1 large onion, finely chopped
- 6 large egg whites
- 4 large eggs
- ¼ cup 2% milk
- ¼ tsp. coarsely ground pepper
- ½ cup shredded sharp cheddar cheese

1. Preheat oven to 350°. In a large skillet, cook sausage and onion over medium heat 6-8 minutes or until sausage is no longer pink and onion is tender, breaking up sausage into crumbles; drain.
2. In a large bowl, whisk egg whites, eggs, milk and pepper; stir in sausage mixture and cheese. Fill greased muffin cups almost full; sprinkle with cheese.
3. Bake 20-25 minutes or until a knife inserted near the center comes out clean. Cool for 5 minutes before removing from pans to wire racks.
2 mini frittatas: 302 cal., 23g fat (8g sat. fat), 175mg chol., 629mg sod., 5g carb. (2g sugars, 0 fiber), 19g pro.

BITTERSWEET DOUBLE CHOCOLATE TRUFFLES

Milk chocolate chips enhance the bittersweet flavor in these decadent treats. Tie a few in pretty ribbons for an easy gift.
—*Taste of Home Test Kitchen*

- -

Prep: 30 min. + chilling • **Makes:** 1½ dozen

- 1 cup 60% cacao bittersweet chocolate baking chips
- ¾ cup whipped topping
- ¼ tsp. ground cinnamon
- 1 cup milk chocolate chips
- 1 tsp. shortening
    Optional toppings: Crushed peppermint candies, sprinkles and chopped nuts

1. In a small saucepan, melt bittersweet chips over low heat. Transfer to a bowl; cool to lukewarm, about 7 minutes.
2. Beat in whipped topping and cinnamon. Place in the freezer for 15 minutes or until firm enough to form into balls. Shape mixture into 1-in. balls.
3. In a microwave, melt milk chocolate chips and shortening; stir until smooth. Dip truffles in chocolate and place on waxed paper-lined

baking sheets. Immediately sprinkle with toppings of your choice. Refrigerate until firm. Store the truffles in an airtight container in the refrigerator.
1 truffle: 105 cal., 6g fat (4g sat. fat), 2mg chol., 8mg sod., 12g carb. (10g sugars, 1g fiber), 1g pro.

RASPBERRY MERINGUE HEARTS

Here's a lovely dessert your guests will think is too pretty to eat. I love the way the meringue easily drapes into a heart shape.
—*Mary Lou Wayman, Salt Lake City, UT*

- -

Prep: 30 min. + standing
Bake: 35 min. + cooling • **Makes:** 6 servings

- 3 large egg whites
- ¼ tsp. cream of tartar
    Dash salt
- 1 cup sugar
- ⅓ cup finely chopped almonds, toasted
- 1 tsp. vanilla extract
FILLING
- 3 cups fresh or frozen unsweetened raspberries, thawed
- 1 tsp. cornstarch
- ½ cup seedless raspberry jam
- 3 cups raspberry or lemon sorbet
- ⅓ cup sliced almonds, toasted
    Additional fresh raspberries

1. Place egg whites in a small mixing bowl; let stand at room temperature for 30 minutes. Beat egg whites, cream of tartar and salt on medium speed until soft peaks form. Add sugar, 1 Tbsp. at a time, beating on high until stiff peaks form and sugar is dissolved. Fold in chopped almonds and vanilla.
2. Drop the meringue into 6 mounds on a parchment-lined baking sheet. Shape into 4-in. hearts with back of a spoon, building up the edges slightly. Bake at 300° for 35 minutes. Turn oven off; leave meringue in the oven for 1-1½ hours.
3. For filling, place raspberries in a food processor. Cover and process until blended. Strain and discard seeds. In a small saucepan, combine the cornstarch, pureed raspberries and jam until smooth. Bring to a boil over medium heat, stirring constantly. Cook and stir for 1 minute or until thickened. Cool.
4. To serve, spoon the sauce into meringue hearts. Place scoop of sorbet on top. Sprinkle with sliced almonds. Garnish with raspberries.
1 meringue with ½ cup sorbet and ¼ cup sauce: 423 cal., 7g fat (0 sat. fat), 0 chol., 53mg sod., 89g carb. (78g sugars, 6g fiber), 5g pro.

RASPBERRY
MERINGUE HEARTS

How to Plan a Galentine's Day Party

This Feb. 13, make your girls feel special by throwing a Galentine's Day party that celebrates your cherished friendship.

ASSEMBLE THE SQUAD
Galentine's Day is a day to celebrate the girlfriends who make life wonderful, so be as inclusive as your budget allows. You could even ask each of your friends to invite a friend.

MASTER THE MENU
If you're hosting at home, consider the menu offerings in this chapter or ask each friend to bring a dish to pass. You can even include links to your favorite potluck recipes in the invitation.

SERVE PINK DRINKS
A pink and frothy drink is so befitting of a Galentine's Day bash. You can bet the Cotton Candy Champagne Cocktails on page 172 will be a hit.

TURN ON GREAT MUSIC
Make a playlist that includes classic, upbeat friendship-themed tunes like Cyndi Lauper's "Girls Just Wanna Have Fun," Sister Sledge's "We Are Family" and Queen's "You're My Best Friend."

BREAK OUT THE CHOCOLATE
Girlfriends and chocolate go together like chocolate and, well, everything. Serve chocolate desserts or set out a bowl with Hershey's Hugs and Kisses.

GIVE OUT VALENTINES
Since Valentine's Day is right around the corner, give each of your ladies a handwritten note saying why her friendship is meaningful to you.

PLAY GAL GAMES
Leslie Knope includes storytelling as part of her Galentine's Day tradition. You can do that. Or you can play slumber party-esque games such as "Never Have I Ever." Or organize a game of Pictionary or charades.

INSTAGRAM IT
Come up with an Instagram hashtag and notify your guests about it. Ask them to tag fun photos of themselves with friends, especially mutual friends. During the party, gather everyone around for a group selfie, and upload it to your Insta with the hashtag.

LIME IN THE COCONUT RICKEY

LIME IN THE COCONUT RICKEY

These fruity spritzers are a nice change of pace from lemonade and party punch. The lime, coconut and grape combination is so refreshing. Add a splash of gin if you are feeling bold.
—*Shelly Bevington, Hermiston, OR*

- -

Takes: 5 min. • **Makes:** 6 servings

- 4 cups white grape juice
- 2 tsp. lime juice
  Ice cubes
- 2 cups coconut-flavored sparkling water, chilled
  Lime wedges or slices

In a pitcher, combine grape juice and lime juice. Fill 6 tall glasses with ice. Pour juice mixture evenly into glasses; top off with sparkling water. Stir to combine; garnish with lime wedges, if desired.

1 cup: 94 cal., 0 fat (0 sat. fat), 0 chol., 13mg sod., 24g carb. (21g sugars, 0 fiber), 0 pro.

ZIPPY PRALINE BACON

I'm always looking for recipes to enhance the usual eggs and bacon. My husband came home from a men's brunch raving about this one, and the hostess shared the recipe. Just be sure to make more than you think you might need because everybody will definitely want seconds!
—*Myrt Pfannkuche, Pell City, AL*

- -

Takes: 20 min. • **Makes:** 20 pieces

- 1 lb. bacon strips
- 3 Tbsp. brown sugar
- 1½ tsp. chili powder
- ¼ cup finely chopped pecans

1. Preheat oven to 425°. Arrange bacon in a single layer in 2 foil-lined 15x10x1-in. pans. Bake 10 minutes; carefully pour off drippings.
2. Mix brown sugar and chili powder; sprinkle over bacon. Sprinkle with pecans. Bake until the bacon is crisp, 5-10 minutes. Drain on paper towels.

1 slice: 58 cal., 4g fat (1g sat. fat), 8mg chol., 151mg sod., 2g carb. (2g sugars, 0 fiber), 3g pro.

SUGARED
DOUGHNUT HOLES

SUGARED DOUGHNUT HOLES

These tasty, tender doughnut bites are easy to make. Tuck them in a scalloped box and tie with a bow to give as a party favor.
—*Judy Jungwirth, Athol, SD*

- -

Takes: 20 min. • **Makes:** about 3 dozen

- 1½ cups all-purpose flour
- ⅓ cup sugar
- 2 tsp. baking powder
- ½ tsp. salt
- ½ tsp. ground nutmeg
- 1 large egg, room temperature
- ½ cup whole milk
- 2 Tbsp. butter, melted
  Oil for deep-fat frying
  Confectioners' sugar

1. In a large bowl, combine the flour, sugar, baking powder, salt and nutmeg. In a small bowl, combine the egg, milk and butter. Add to dry ingredients and mix well.
2. In an electric skillet or deep-fat fryer, heat oil to 375°. Drop dough by heaping teaspoonfuls, 5 or 6 at a time, into oil. Fry until browned, about 1-2 minutes, turning once. Drain on paper towels. Roll warm doughnut holes in confectioners' sugar.

1 doughnut hole: 47 cal., 2g fat (1g sat. fat), 7mg chol., 68mg sod., 6g carb. (2g sugars, 0 fiber), 1g pro.

COTTON CANDY CHAMPAGNE COCKTAILS

ICING

¼ cup confectioners' sugar
1½ tsp. 2% milk
¼ tsp. vanilla extract
   Additional raspberries, optional

1. Preheat oven to 350°. In a small bowl, toss raspberries with brown sugar.
2. In a large bowl, whisk flour, sugar, baking powder, baking soda and salt. In another bowl, whisk the egg, sour cream, melted butter and vanilla until blended. Add to flour mixture; stir just until moistened (batter will be thick).
3. Transfer half of the batter to a greased and floured 8-in. round baking pan. Top with the raspberry mixture. Spoon remaining batter over raspberries; sprinkle with almonds.
4. Bake 30-35 minutes or until a toothpick inserted in center comes out clean. Cool in pan 10 minutes before removing to a wire rack to cool.
5. In a small bowl, mix confectioners' sugar, milk and vanilla until smooth; drizzle over top. Serve warm. If desired, serve with additional fresh raspberries.
1 piece: 238 cal., 10g fat (5g sat. fat), 48mg chol., 154mg sod., 32g carb. (19g sugars, 2g fiber), 4g pro.

HONEY POPPY SEED FRUIT SALAD

The subtle honey sauce in this salad steals the show. It pairs well with any morning entree and takes just 10 minutes to assemble.
—*Dorothy Dinnean, Harrison, AR*

- -

Takes: 10 min. • **Makes:** 8 servings

2 medium firm bananas, chopped
2 cups fresh blueberries
2 cups fresh raspberries
2 cups sliced fresh strawberries
5 Tbsp. honey
1 tsp. lemon juice
¾ tsp. poppy seeds

In a large bowl, combine the bananas and berries. In a small bowl, combine the honey, lemon juice and poppy seeds. Pour over fruit and toss to coat.
¾ cup: 117 cal., 1g fat (0 sat. fat), 0 chol., 2mg sod., 30g carb. (23g sugars, 5g fiber), 1g pro.

COTTON CANDY CHAMPAGNE COCKTAILS

You'll love these whimsical champagne cocktails. The cotton candy melts away, leaving behind its pretty pink color.
—*Taste of Home Test Kitchen*

- -

Takes: 5 min. • **Makes:** 6 servings

6 Tbsp. raspberry-flavored vodka
1 bottle (750 ml) champagne, chilled
1½ cups pink cotton candy

Add 1 Tbsp. vodka to each of 6 champagne flutes. Top with champagne; create a cotton candy garnish for each glass. To serve, stir in cotton candy.
1 cocktail: 125 cal., 0 fat (0 sat. fat), 0 chol., 0 sod., 4g carb. (2g sugars, 0 fiber), 0 pro.

RASPBERRY SOUR CREAM COFFEE CAKE

Coffee and cake are like a wink and a smile. You'll take one without the other but given a choice, you want the pair. This fresh and fruity breakfast pastry is perfect for brunch. A drizzle of icing adds a nice finishing touch.
—*Debbie Johnson, Centertown, MO*

- -

Prep: 20 min. • **Bake:** 30 min. + cooling
Makes: 8 servings

1 cup fresh raspberries
3 Tbsp. brown sugar
1 cup all-purpose flour
⅓ cup sugar
½ tsp. baking powder
¼ tsp. baking soda
⅛ tsp. salt
1 large egg, room temperature
⅔ cup sour cream
3 Tbsp. butter, melted
1 tsp. vanilla extract
¼ cup sliced almonds

HONEY POPPY SEED
FRUIT SALAD

MARBLED
MERINGUE
HEARTS

MARBLED MERINGUE HEARTS

Pretty pastel cookies are a fun way to brighten any special occasion. Replace the vanilla with a different extract, such as almond or raspberry, for a change of flavor.
—*Laurie Herr, Westford, VT*

Prep: 25 min. • **Bake:** 20 min. + cooling
Makes: about 2 dozen

3	large egg whites
½	tsp. vanilla extract
¼	tsp. cream of tartar
¾	cup sugar
	Food coloring

1. Place egg whites in a large bowl; let stand at room temperature for 30 minutes. Line baking sheets with parchment.

2. Preheat oven to 200°. Add vanilla extract and cream of tartar to the egg whites; beat on medium speed until soft peaks form. Beat in sugar, a tablespoon at a time, on high until stiff peaks form. Remove ¼ cup and tint pink. Lightly swirl the pink meringue mixture into the remaining meringue.

3. Fill pastry bag with meringue. Pipe 2-in. heart shapes 2 in. apart onto baking sheets.

4. Bake until set and dry, about 20 minutes. Turn oven off; leave meringues in oven until oven has completely cooled.

1 meringue: 27 cal., 0 fat (0 sat. fat), 0 chol., 7mg sod., 6g carb. (6g sugars, 0 fiber), 0 pro.

For the greatest volume, place egg whites in a clean metal or glass mixing bowl. Even a drop of fat from the egg yolk or a film sometimes found on plastic bowls will prevent egg whites from foaming. For this reason, be sure to use clean beaters.

How to Make a Napkin Envelope

Give your table setting some love with this easy envelope napkin fold.

1. Fold a napkin in half diagonally, with the point facing up. Then take the bottom corners and fold to meet in the middle.

2. Fold the outer edges in once again so they meet in the middle.

3. Fold the bottom half up until it meets the base of the triangle.

4. Fold down the triangle flap. Top with a meringue heart.

TACO TUESDAY

It's taco time! Whether it's Tuesday night or you just have a fierce hankering (who doesn't?), turn to this lineup of zesty homemade tacos and other south-of-the-border favorites to breathe a little heat into the ordinary dinner rotation. Filled with fresh ingredients and bold flavor combos, these recipes are guaranteed to make any spicy celebration a hit!

SANTA FE GRILLED
RIBEYE TACOS

SANTA FE GRILLED RIBEYE TACOS

Spicy aioli brings a zesty kick to tacos, and the ribeye steak is a nice upgrade from typical ground beef. Grab one and enjoy the burst of flavor in each bite!
—*Michael Compean, Los Angeles, CA*

Prep: 25 min. • **Grill:** 15 min.
Makes: 4 servings

SPICY AIOLI
- ¼ cup mayonnaise
- 2 tsp. Sriracha chili sauce or 1 tsp. hot pepper sauce
- ⅛ tsp. sesame oil

AVOCADO-CORN SALSA
- 1 medium ripe avocado, peeled and finely chopped
- ½ medium tomato, seeded and chopped
- 3 Tbsp. sliced ripe olives
- 2 Tbsp. canned whole kernel corn
- 2 Tbsp. chopped sweet red pepper
- 2 Tbsp. lime juice
- 4 tsp. minced fresh cilantro
- 1 tsp. kosher salt
- 1 tsp. finely chopped onion
- 1 garlic clove, minced
- ¼ tsp. ground cumin

STEAKS
- 2 tsp. pepper
- 2 tsp. olive oil
- 1 tsp. kosher salt
- 1 tsp. seafood seasoning
- 1 beef ribeye steak (1 lb.), trimmed
- 8 flour tortillas (6 in.)
  Optional toppings: shredded lettuce, cheddar cheese and cotija cheese

1. In a small bowl, combine all of the aioli ingredients. In another bowl, combine the salsa ingredients. Refrigerate until serving.
2. Combine the pepper, oil, salt and seafood seasoning; rub over both sides of steak.
3. Grill, covered, over medium heat until meat reaches desired doneness (for medium-rare, a thermometer should read 135°; medium, 140°; medium-well, 145°), 6-8 minutes on each side. Let stand for 5 minutes.
4. Meanwhile, grill tortillas until warm, about 45 seconds on each side. Thinly slice steak; place on tortillas. Serve with aioli, salsa and toppings of your choice.

2 tacos: 650 cal., 45g fat (10g sat. fat), 72mg chol., 1843mg sod., 35g carb. (2g sugars, 4g fiber), 28g pro.

MINI CHIMIS WITH
JALAPENO CREAM CHEESE

MINI CHIMIS WITH JALAPENO CREAM CHEESE

Oozing with chicken and cheese, these zippy bites bring a little heat to any fiesta. Serve them on their own as appetizers, or with rice and black beans for a satisfying meal.
—*Erika Monroe-Williams, Scottsdale, AZ*

Prep: 35 min. • **Cook:** 10 min. • **Makes:** 1 dozen

- 2 cups shredded cooked chicken breast
- 1 cup shredded Monterey Jack cheese
- ¾ cup refried beans
- ½ cup green enchilada sauce
- 12 egg roll wrappers
- 4 oz. cream cheese, softened
- ¼ cup diced jalapeno peppers
  Oil for deep-fat frying

1. In a large bowl, mix chicken, cheese, beans and enchilada sauce. With a corner of an egg roll wrapper facing you, spoon ¼ cup filling just below center of wrapper. (Cover the remaining wrappers with a damp paper towel until ready to use.) Fold bottom corner over filling; moisten remaining wrapper edges with water. Fold side corners toward center over filling. Roll chimichangas up tightly, pressing at tip to seal. Repeat.
2. In an electric skillet or deep-fat fryer, heat oil to 375°. Fry chimichangas, a few at a time, until golden brown, 2-3 minutes, turning occasionally. Drain on paper towels.
3. In a small bowl, mix cream cheese and jalapeno peppers. Serve chimichangas with jalapeno cream cheese.

1 mini chimichanga with 2 tsp. jalapeno cream cheese: 276 cal., 15g fat (5g sat. fat), 39mg chol., 394mg sod., 22g carb. (1g sugars, 1g fiber), 14g pro.

> **TEST KITCHEN TIP**
>
> Try this easy method for cutting jalapenos. First cut off the tops, then slice them in half the long way. Use the small end of a melon baller to easily scrape out the seeds and membranes. Then cut or dice as the recipe directs. Remember to always wear disposable gloves when handling hot peppers.

Dip those chips!

You can't have taco night without chips. And you can't have chips without dips. Here are two fruity ones to try.

STRAWBERRY SALSA

In a large bowl, combine 1 pint fresh chopped strawberries, 4 seeded and chopped plum tomatoes, 1 finely chopped small red onion and 1 to 2 minced jalapeno peppers. Stir in 2 Tbsp. lime juice, 1 Tbsp. olive oil and 2 minced garlic cloves. Cover and refrigerate 2 hours. Makes 4 cups.

GINGERED MANGO SALSA

Combine 1 cup chopped peeled mango, ¼ cup chopped red onion, ¼ cup minced fresh cilantro, ¼ cup lime juice, 2 Tbsp. minced fresh mint, 1 Tbsp. minced fresh gingerroot, ½ tsp. olive oil and ¼ tsp. salt. Let stand 30 minutes before serving. Makes 1¼ cups.

SIMPLE GUACAMOLE

Because avocados can brown quickly, it's best to make this guacamole just before serving. If you do have to make it a little in advance, place the avocado pit in the guacamole until serving.
—Heidi Main, Anchorage, AK

- -

Takes: 10 min. • **Makes:** 1½ cups

2   medium ripe avocados
1   Tbsp. lemon juice
¼   cup chunky salsa
⅛   to ¼ tsp. salt

Peel and chop avocados; place in a small bowl. Sprinkle with lemon juice. Add chunky salsa and salt; mash coarsely with a fork. Refrigerate until serving.
2 Tbsp.: 53 cal., 5g fat (1g sat. fat), 0 chol., 51mg sod., 3g carb. (0 sugars, 2g fiber), 1g pro. **Diabetic exchanges:** 1 fat.

10-MINUTE ZESTY SALSA

We have a great view of Pikes Peak from our mountain home, so we frequently eat on our wraparound porch in good weather. During family get-togethers, we savor this zippy salsa with chips while enjoying the natural beauty around us.
—Kim Morin, Lake George, CO

- -

Takes: 10 min. • **Makes:** 1½ cups

1   can (10 oz.) diced tomatoes and green chiles, undrained
1   Tbsp. seeded chopped jalapeno pepper
1   Tbsp. chopped red onion
1   Tbsp. minced fresh cilantro
1   garlic clove, minced
1   Tbsp. olive oil
    Dash salt
    Dash pepper
    Tortilla chips

In a small bowl, combine the tomatoes, jalapeno, onion, cilantro, garlic, oil, salt and pepper. Refrigerate until serving. Serve with tortilla chips.
Note: Wear disposable gloves when cutting hot peppers; the oils can burn skin. Avoid touching your face.
¼ cup: 29 cal., 2g fat (0 sat. fat), 0 chol., 214mg sod., 2g carb. (0 sugars, 1g fiber), 0 pro. **Diabetic exchanges:** ½ fat.

SIMPLE GUACAMOLE

10-MINUTE ZESTY SALSA

▲

How to Make Guacamole

Do you put guac on just about everything from burritos to burgers? (We sure do!) To keep up with those cravings, learn how to make this basic guacamole at home— it's super simple and so tasty.

1. Cut avocados into quarters, peel, and place in a bowl. Mash chunks with a fork.

2. Add salt and minced garlic.

3. Stir in onions, tomatoes, lime juice and cilantro. Refrigerate until serving.

PEPPERED
CILANTRO RICE

PEPPERED CILANTRO RICE

This colorful confetti rice is a traditional dish in Puerto Rico. We enjoy it in the summer alongside grilled shrimp kabobs, but it's good with almost any entree.
—*Laura Lunardi, West Chester, PA*

Prep: 10 min. • **Cook:** 25 min.
Makes: 6 servings

- 1 small onion, finely chopped
- 1 small sweet yellow pepper, finely chopped
- 1 small sweet red pepper, finely chopped
- 2 garlic cloves, minced
- 1 Tbsp. olive oil
- 2 cups water
- 1 cup uncooked long grain rice
- ¾ tsp. salt
- ¼ tsp. pepper
- 2 Tbsp. minced fresh cilantro

1. In a large saucepan, saute the onion, peppers and garlic in oil until crisp-tender. Add the water, rice, salt and pepper. Bring to a boil. Reduce heat; cover and simmer for 18-22 minutes or until rice is tender.
2. Remove from the heat; fluff with a fork. Stir in cilantro.
⅔ cup: 156 cal., 3g fat (0 sat. fat), 0 chol., 298mg sod., 30g carb. (1g sugars, 1g fiber), 3g pro. **Diabetic exchanges:** 2 starch, ½ fat.

BLACK BEAN BLUE CORN SPAGHETTI SQUASH TACOS

Who knew that spaghetti squash could be so amazing stuffed inside tacos? This unique recipe is a whole new take on a classic!
—*Kayla Capper, Ojai, CA*

Prep: 35 min. • **Cook:** 10 min.
Makes: 10 servings

- 1 medium spaghetti squash (about 4 lbs.)
- 1 tsp. canola oil
- ½ cup frozen corn
- 1 can (15 oz.) black beans, rinsed and drained
- ½ cup salsa
- 2 green onions, chopped
- ¼ cup chopped fresh cilantro
- ¼ cup salted pumpkin seeds or pepitas
- 2 Tbsp. lime juice
- ½ tsp. garlic salt
- ½ tsp. ground cumin
- ¼ tsp. salt
- 20 corn tortillas (6 in.), warmed Guacamole, optional

1. Cut squash in half lengthwise; discard seeds. Place squash on a microwave-safe plate, cut side down. Microwave, uncovered, on high 18-20 minutes or until tender.
2. In a large skillet, heat oil over medium heat. Add corn; cook and stir 5-7 minutes or until lightly toasted.
3. When squash is cool enough to handle, use a fork to separate strands; stir into skillet. Add black beans, salsa, onions, cilantro, pumpkin seeds, lime juice, garlic salt, cumin and salt; heat through. Serve with tortillas and, if desired, guacamole.
2 tacos: 228 cal., 4g fat (1g sat. fat), 0 chol., 346mg sod., 43g carb. (1g sugars, 8g fiber), 7g pro.

CONFETTI CORN SKILLET

Fresh corn is one of summer's best veggies. After loads have been harvested, we indulge in that sweet taste of boiled corn on the cob. There's so much that we end up freezing a lot, and this southwestern side dish is a tasty way to put it to good use. Store-bought frozen corn yields good results, too.
—*Dana Sheppard, Millen, GA*

Takes: 25 min. • **Makes:** 4 servings

- 5 bacon strips, chopped
- 4 cups frozen corn, thawed
- 1 small onion, chopped
- 1 small green pepper, chopped
- ¼ cup diced pimientos, drained
- ¼ tsp. finely chopped habanero pepper, optional
- ¼ tsp. salt
- ¼ tsp. pepper
   Minced fresh cilantro, optional

1. In a large skillet, cook bacon strips over medium heat until crisp. Remove to paper towels with a slotted spoon; drain, reserving 2 Tbsp. drippings.
2. Saute the corn, onion, green pepper, pimientos and habanero, if desired, in drippings until corn is lightly browned. Stir in salt and pepper. Top with bacon; garnish with cilantro if desired.
Note: Wear disposable gloves when cutting hot peppers; the oils can burn skin. Avoid touching your face.
¾ cup: 259 cal., 11 g fat (4 g sat. fat), 15 mg chol., 348 mg sod., 37 g carb., 5 g fiber, 8g pro.

To cut corn off the cob, stand a cob on end on a cutting board. Starting at the top, run a sharp knife down the cob, cutting deeply to remove whole kernels. One medium cob yields ⅓ to ½ cup kernels.

SALSA PINTO BEANS

Want an alternative to refried beans? Try this side dish. Sometimes I top it off with a sprinkling of shredded cheese or a dollop of sour cream.
—*Lorna Nault, Chesterton, IN*

Takes: 15 min. • **Makes:** 6 servings

- 1 small onion, chopped
- 2 tsp. minced fresh cilantro
- 1 Tbsp. canola oil
- 1 garlic clove, minced
- 2 cans (15 oz. each) pinto beans, rinsed and drained
- ⅔ cup salsa

In a large skillet or saucepan, saute onion and cilantro in oil until tender. Add garlic; cook 1 minute longer. Stir in the beans and salsa; heat through.

½ cup: 159 cal., 3g fat (0 sat. fat), 0 chol., 296mg sod., 26g carb. (4g sugars, 6g fiber), 7g pro. **Diabetic exchanges:** 2 starch, ½ fat.

TEST KITCHEN TIP

Ripen Avocados Quickly

When life hands you hard, less-than-ripe avocados, here's how to ripen them ASAP. Place avocados in a paper bag with an apple or banana. Poke the bag a few times with a toothpick or scissors, and let ripen at room temperature for a day or two. The more fruits (and ethylene gas they give off), the faster the results.

CHICKEN TACOS WITH CORN-JICAMA SALSA

Here's a light, speedy meal you can enjoy anytime. Preparation is so simple—there's nothing to it. The tacos are quite tasty, and adding jicama to the salsa boosts the nutritional value. Win-win!
—*Priscilla Gilbert, Indian Harbour Beach, FL*

Prep: 30 min. • **Cook:** 15 min.
Makes: 4 servings

- 1 cup Mexicorn, drained
- ½ cup canned black beans, rinsed and drained
- ½ cup finely chopped peeled jicama
- 2 Tbsp. minced fresh cilantro
- 1 Tbsp. lime juice
- ¼ tsp. ground cumin
- ¼ tsp. salt

GUACAMOLE
- 1 medium ripe avocado, peeled and pitted
- 1 small tomato, seeded and chopped
- 4½ tsp. lime juice
- ¼ tsp. salt

TACOS
- 2 tsp. chili powder
- 1 tsp. ground cumin
- 1 tsp. dried oregano
- ¼ tsp. salt
- 1 lb. boneless skinless chicken breasts, cut into thin strips
- 8 flour tortillas (6 in.), warmed

1. For salsa, in a small bowl, combine the corn, beans, jicama, cilantro, lime juice, cumin and salt. Cover and refrigerate until serving.
2. For guacamole, in another small bowl, mash avocado. Stir in the tomato, lime juice and salt. Cover and refrigerate until serving.
3. In a large bowl, combine the chili powder, cumin, oregano and salt. Add chicken; toss to coat evenly. In a greased nonstick skillet, saute chicken until no longer pink.
4. Spread each tortilla with 2 Tbsp. guacamole; top with chicken mixture and ¼ cup salsa. Fold tortillas in half.

2 tacos: 465 cal., 16g fat (2g sat. fat), 63mg chol., 1351mg sod., 49g carb. (5g sugars, 8g fiber), 33g pro.

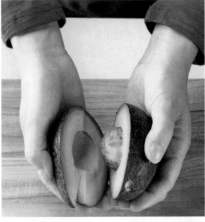

CHICKEN TACOS WITH CORN-JICAMA SALSA

▲

How to Cut an Avocado

1. Wash the avocado. Cut lengthwise around the seed to divide into quarters.

2. Twist halves in opposite directions to separate.

3. Separate the individual quarters; remove seed from final quarter. If necessary, slip a tablespoon under the seed to loosen it from the fruit.

4. Peel skin from wedges. If necessary, slice between the flesh and the skin to loosen it.

WATERMELON SPRITZER

---

2. Roll into walnut-sized balls and roll in sugar; place 3 in. apart on ungreased baking sheets. Bake at 350° for 10-12 minutes (cookies should by soft). Cool 2-3 minutes before removing to wire racks.

1 cookie: 112 cal., 6g fat (2g sat. fat), 7mg chol., 109mg sod., 15g carb. (8g sugars, 0 fiber), 1g pro.

NO-FRY FRIED ICE CREAM

This ice cream has a crispy cinnamon coating just like the fried ice cream served at Mexican restaurants, but minus the oily mess. Make ahead of time and freeze until serving.

—*Tim White, Windsor, ON*

Prep: 15 min. + freezing
Bake: 5 min. + freezing
Makes: 8 servings

- 1 qt. vanilla ice cream
- ¼ cup packed brown sugar
- 1 Tbsp. butter, melted
- 1 tsp. ground cinnamon
- 2 cups crushed cornflakes
  Whipped cream and caramel ice cream topping, optional

1. Preheat oven to 350°. Using a ½-cup ice cream scoop, place 8 scoops of ice cream on a baking sheet. Freeze until firm, about 1 hour. Meanwhile, combine brown sugar, butter and cinnamon. Stir in cornflakes. Transfer to an ungreased 15x10x1-in. baking pan. Bake until lightly browned, 4-6 minutes. Cool completely.
2. Roll ice cream balls in crumb mixture. Cover and freeze until firm, at least 1 hour. If desired, serve with toppings.

½ cup: 216 cal., 8g fat (5g sat. fat), 32mg chol., 168mg sod., 33g carb. (20g sugars, 1g fiber), 3g pro.

> **TEST KITCHEN TIP**
>
> Feel free to use any flavor of ice cream to make this treat—just be sure it complements the cinnamon in the cornflake coating. For a sundae version, make the topping as directed, sprinkle it over ice cream, and top with whipped cream, caramel sauce and a maraschino cherry.

WATERMELON SPRITZER

Watermelon blended with limeade is cool and refreshing. It's a great thirst quencher on a hot summer day.

—*Geraldine Saucier, Albuquerque, NM*

Prep: 5 min. + chilling • **Makes:** 5 servings

- 4 cups cubed seedless watermelon
- ¾ cup frozen limeade concentrate, thawed
- 2½ cups carbonated water
  Lime slices

1. Place watermelon in a blender. Cover and process until blended. Strain and discard pulp; transfer juice to a pitcher. Stir in limeade concentrate. Refrigerate for 6 hours or overnight.
2. Just before serving, stir in carbonated water. Garnish servings with lime slices.

1 cup: 140 cal., 0 fat (0 sat. fat), 0 chol., 4mg sod., 38g carb. (36g sugars, 1g fiber), 0 pro.

MEXICAN CHOCOLATE CRINKLES COOKIES

I love to bake. In fact, my first time baking from scratch is still vivid in my memory. This recipe brings back memories, too—when our girls often took these cinnamon-spiced cookies to their Scout outings.

—*Pat Gregory, Tulsa, OK*

Takes: 30 min. • **Makes:** 2½ dozen

- ¾ cup shortening
- 1 cup sugar
- 1 large egg, room temperature
- ¼ cup light corn syrup
- 1 oz. unsweetened chocolate, melted
- 1¾ cups all-purpose flour
- 2 tsp. baking soda
- ¼ tsp. salt
- 1 tsp. ground cinnamon
  Additional sugar

1. In a large bowl, cream shortening and sugar until light and fluffy. Add the egg, corn syrup and melted chocolate. Combine the flour, baking soda, salt and cinnamon; gradually add to creamed mixture and mix well.

NO-FRY FRIED
ICE CREAM

PRE-PROM PARTY

Prom is the ultimate high school party. Teens wait all year to get dressed up and dance the night away one last time before graduation. A pre-prom gathering is the perfect way to kick off the night! Invite dates, classmates and parents over for snacks, sips and plenty of fun photo ops. Whether your party is a simple get-together with a casual vibe or a glitzy blowout that pulls out all the stops, these recipes and tips will make pre-prom as special as the dance itself!

Easy Citrus Slush (p. 195) **Parmesan-Ranch Snack Mix** (p. 191)
Lemon Cream Cupcakes (p. 195) **Tuxedo Strawberries** (p. 199)

PARMESAN-RANCH
SNACK MIX

PARMESAN-RANCH SNACK MIX

Every party needs a big bowl of snack mix! No one that I've made this for can have just one handful—they always come back again and again!
—*Tammy Landry, Saucier, MS*

Takes: 15 min. • **Makes:** 3 qt.

- 9 cups Corn, Rice or Wheat Chex
- 2 cups miniature pretzels
- 2 cups miniature cheddar cheese fish-shaped crackers
- ½ cup butter, melted
- ½ cup grated Parmesan cheese
- 1 envelope ranch salad dressing mix

1. In a large bowl, combine cereal, pretzels and crackers. Drizzle with butter. Sprinkle with cheese and salad dressing mix; toss to coat.

2. Microwave in batches on high 3 minutes, stirring every minute. Spread onto a baking sheet to cool. Store in an airtight container.

¾ cup: 365 cal., 9g fat (5g sat. fat), 18mg chol., 826mg sod., 67g carb. (7g sugars, 6g fiber), 7g pro.

TEST KITCHEN TIP

Upgrade this snack mix with extra add-ins such as nuts, popcorn or seeds. And don't skimp on the butter, as that's what makes the mix crisp. Be sure to coat the mix evenly.

Made by Hand

Treat the ladies to an afternoon of pampering before the big event. This homemade hand scrub, made from simple pantry ingredients, will leave hands silky and smooth.

Mix 1 Tbsp. each raw honey, ground rolled oats, fresh lemon juice and fine brown sugar until well blended. Over the sink, apply half the mixture to hands and massage it in for 1 minute; leave on for 10 minutes. Wash off with warm water; rinse with cool water. Store remaining mixture in an airtight container in the refrigerator for up to 4 days. Apply twice weekly. Makes 2 applications.

CONTEST-WINNING BEEF STUFFED CRESCENTS

These hand-held bundles are easy to make and require only six ingredients. I've made them for potlucks and family gatherings—and I never have leftovers.
—*Jennifer Bumgarner, Topeka, KS*

Prep: 25 min. • **Bake:** 15 min. • **Makes:** 2 dozen

- 1 lb. ground beef
- 1 can (4 oz.) chopped green chiles
- 1 pkg. (8 oz.) cream cheese, cubed
- ¼ tsp. ground cumin
- ¼ tsp. chili powder
- 3 tubes (8 oz. each) refrigerated crescent rolls

1. In a large skillet, cook beef and chiles over medium heat until meat is no longer pink; drain. Add cream cheese, cumin and chili powder. Cool slightly.

2. Preheat oven to 375°. Separate crescent dough into 24 triangles. Place 1 Tbsp. of beef mixture along the short side of each triangle; carefully roll up.

3. Place point side down 2 in. apart on ungreased baking sheets. Bake 11-14 minutes or until golden brown. Serve warm.

1 crescent: 175 cal., 11g fat (4g sat. fat), 20mg chol., 282mg sod., 12g carb. (2g sugars, 0 fiber), 6g pro.

PARTY NACHOS

Put a new and delicious spin on nachos! Simple to make, these are ideal for most any party or a fun night for teens. Consider a build-your-own nacho bar so guests can choose their toppings.
—*Mike Tchou, Pepper Pike, OH*

Takes: 20 min. • **Makes:** 12 servings

- 1 carton (16 oz.) refrigerated fully cooked barbecued shredded pork
- 1 pkg. (12½ oz.) nacho tortilla chips
- 2 cups shredded Mexican cheese blend
- ½ cup sour cream
- ½ cup salsa
- ½ cup shredded lettuce
- ¼ cup thinly sliced green onions
- ¼ cup sliced ripe olives, optional
- ¼ cup pickled pepper rings, optional

1. Heat pork according to package directions. Place tortilla chips on a large microwave-safe serving plate. Layer with pork and cheese.

2. Microwave, uncovered, on high until cheese is melted, 1-2 minutes. Top with sour cream, salsa, lettuce and onions. Sprinkle with olives and pepper rings if desired.

1 serving: 312 cal., 16g fat (7g sat. fat), 35mg chol., 679mg sod., 28g carb. (10g sugars, 1g fiber), 12g pro.

TOFFEE-PECAN OATMEAL COOKIES

Classic oatmeal cookies get a fun flavor twist when studded with toffee, chocolate mini morsels and pecans. They're outstanding for snacking or for any get-together.
—*Gloria Bradley, Naperville, IL*

- -

Prep: 20 min. • **Bake:** 10 min./batch
Makes: 6 dozen

- 2½ cups old-fashioned oats
- ½ cup butter, softened
- 1 cup sugar
- 1 cup packed brown sugar
- ½ cup egg substitute
  or 2 large eggs, room temperature
- ½ cup buttermilk
- 1 tsp. vanilla extract
- 2 cups all-purpose flour
- 1 tsp. baking powder
- 1 tsp. baking soda
- ½ tsp. salt
- ½ cup miniature semisweet
  chocolate chips
- ½ cup finely chopped pecans, toasted
- ⅓ cup brickle toffee bits
- 2 oz. milk chocolate, grated

1. Place oats in a food processor. Cover and process to a fine powder; set aside. In a large bowl, beat butter and sugars until crumbly. Beat in the egg substitute, buttermilk and vanilla.Combine the flour, baking powder, baking soda, salt and ground oats; gradually add to butter mixture and mix well. Stir in the chocolate chips, pecans, toffee bits and grated chocolate.
2. Drop by rounded tablespoonfuls 2 in. apart onto ungreased baking sheets. Bake at 375° until lightly browned, 10-12 minutes. Remove to wire racks. Store in airtight containers.
1 cookie: 80 cal., 3g fat (1g sat. fat), 4mg chol., 62mg sod., 12g carb. (8g sugars, 1g fiber), 1g pro.

BEE MY HONEY FRUIT DIP

Orange, cinnamon and nutmeg round out this creamy spiced dip. I serve it with apples, pineapple and strawberries when in season.
—*Carol Gillespie, Chambersburg, PA*

- -

Takes: 5 min. • **Makes:** 2 cups

- 1 pkg. (8 oz.) cream cheese, softened
- 1 jar (7 oz.) marshmallow creme
- 1 Tbsp. honey
- 1 tsp. grated orange zest
- ¼ tsp. ground cinnamon
- ⅛ tsp. ground nutmeg
  Assorted fresh fruit

In a small bowl, beat the first 6 ingredients until smooth. Serve with fruit. Refrigerate any leftovers.
2 Tbsp.: 95 cal., 5g fat (3g sat. fat), 16mg chol., 52mg sod., 12g carb. (10g sugars, 0 fiber), 1g pro.

How to Peel a Kiwi

Cut both ends from fruit. Using a spoon, scoop out the flesh. Cut into slices, wedges or chunks with a sharp knife.

BEE MY HONEY
FRUIT DIP

CHOCOLATE CHIP COOKIE BROWNIES

It was so fun to experiment with this brownie recipe. When my daughter tasted the final version, she told me they were the best brownies ever! Now that sure makes a mom feel good.

—*Dion Frischer, Ann Arbor, MI*

- -

Prep: 15 min. • **Bake:** 50 min. + cooling
Makes: 1 dozen

- ¾ cup butter
- 1½ cups sugar
- ½ cup baking cocoa
- 3 large eggs, room temperature
- ¾ cup all-purpose flour
- ½ cup chopped walnuts

CHOCOLATE CHIP LAYER

- ½ cup butter
- 1 cup packed brown sugar
- 1 large egg, room temperature
- 1 cup all-purpose flour
- ½ tsp. baking soda
- 1 cup (6 oz.) semisweet chocolate chips

1. Preheat oven to 350°. Line a 9-in. square baking pan with foil, letting ends extend up sides; grease foil.
2. In a microwave, melt butter in a large microwave-safe bowl. Stir in sugar and cocoa. Add eggs, one at a time, whisking to blend after each addition. Add flour; stir just until combined. Stir in nuts. Spread into prepared pan. Bake 15 minutes.
3. Meanwhile, for chocolate chip layer, melt butter in another microwave-safe bowl. Stir in brown sugar. Whisk in egg. In a small bowl, whisk flour and baking soda; stir into butter mixture just until combined. Stir in chocolate chips. Spoon mixture over hot brownie layer.
4. Bake 35-40 minutes longer or until a toothpick inserted in center comes out with moist crumbs. Cool completely in pan on a wire rack. Lifting foil, remove brownies from pan. Cut into bars.
1 brownie: 536 cal., 29g fat (15g sat. fat), 113mg chol., 236mg sod., 69g carb. (51g sugars, 2g fiber), 6g pro.

EASY CITRUS SLUSH

EASY CITRUS SLUSH

Our church's hostess committee has relied on this refreshing drink for bridal and baby showers and other events. We often use different flavored gelatins to match the decor of the occasion.
—*Joy Bruce, Welch, OK*

- -

Prep: 15 min. + freezing
Makes: about 6 qt. (about 25 servings)

2½ cups sugar
 1 pkg. (3 oz.) lemon gelatin
 1 pkg. (3 oz.) pineapple gelatin
 4 cups boiling water
 1 can (12 oz.) frozen pineapple juice concentrate, thawed
 1 cup lemon juice
 1 envelope (0.23 oz.) unsweetened lemonade Kool-Aid mix
10 cups cold water
 2 liters ginger ale, chilled
    Lime slices, optional

1. In a large container, dissolve sugar and gelatins in boiling water. Stir in the pineapple juice concentrate, lemon juice, drink mix and cold water. If desired, divide among smaller containers. Cover and freeze, stirring several times.
2. Remove from freezer at least 1 hour before serving. Stir until mixture becomes slushy. Just before serving, place 9 cups slush mixture in a punch bowl; stir in 1 liter ginger ale. Repeat with remaining slush and ginger ale. If desired, garnish with lime slices.
1 cup: 157 cal., 0 fat (0 sat. fat), 0 chol., 25mg sod., 40g carb. (39g sugars, 0 fiber), 1g pro.

LEMON CREAM CUPCAKES

LEMON CREAM CUPCAKES

Instead of cake, serve guests these delicate cupcakes tinged with a tangy lemon flavor.
—*Ruth Ann Stelfox, Raymond, AB*

- -

Prep: 20 min. • **Bake:** 25 min. + cooling
Makes: about 2½ dozen

 1 cup butter, softened
 2 cups sugar
 3 large eggs, room temperature
 2 tsp. grated lemon zest
 1 tsp. vanilla extract
3½ cups all-purpose flour
 1 tsp. baking soda
 ½ tsp. baking powder
 ½ tsp. salt
 2 cups sour cream
FROSTING
 3 Tbsp. butter, softened
2¼ cups confectioners' sugar
 2 Tbsp. lemon juice
 ¾ tsp. vanilla extract
 ¼ tsp. grated lemon zest
 1 to 2 Tbsp. whole milk

1. In a large bowl, cream butter and sugar until light and fluffy. Add 1 egg at a time, beating well after each addition. Beat in lemon zest and vanilla. Combine the flour, baking soda, baking powder and salt; add to creamed mixture alternately with sour cream, beating well after each addition (batter will be thick).
2. Fill greased or paper-lined muffin cups with ¼ cup of batter each. Bake at 350° until a toothpick inserted in the center comes out clean, 25-30 minutes. Cool for 10 minutes before removing from pans to wire racks to cool completely.
3. For frosting, cream softened butter and confectioners' sugar in a small bowl until light and fluffy. Add the lemon juice, vanilla, lemon zest and milk; beat until smooth. Frost cupcakes. If desired, sprinkle with additional lemon zest.
1 cupcake: 244 cal., 11g fat (6g sat. fat), 48mg chol., 178mg sod., 34g carb. (22g sugars, 0 fiber), 3g pro.

SUPER ITALIAN SUB

I like recipes that can be made ahead of time, and this sandwich offers that convenience. I just wrap the sub tightly and keep it in the refrigerator. At mealtime, all that's left to do is slice and enjoy.
—Patricia Lomp, Middleboro, MA

Takes: 30 min. • **Makes:** 12 servings

- 1 loaf (1 lb.) unsliced Italian bread
- ⅓ cup olive oil
- ¼ cup cider vinegar
- 8 garlic cloves, minced
- 1 tsp. dried oregano
- ¼ tsp. pepper
- ½ lb. fully cooked ham, thinly sliced
- ½ lb. thinly sliced cooked turkey
- ¼ lb. thinly sliced hard salami
- ¼ lb. sliced provolone cheese
- ¼ lb. sliced mozzarella cheese
- 1 medium green pepper, thinly sliced into rings

1. Cut bread in half lengthwise; hollow out top and bottom, leaving a ½-in. shell (discard removed bread or save for another use).
2. In a small bowl, combine the oil, vinegar, garlic, oregano and pepper; brush on cut sides of bread top and bottom. On the bottom half, layer half of the meats, cheeses and green pepper. Repeat layers. Replace bread top. Wrap tightly; refrigerate for up to 24 hours. Cut into 12 slices to serve.
1 piece: 309 cal., 16g fat (6g sat. fat), 44mg chol., 701mg sod., 22g carb. (1g sugars, 1g fiber), 19g pro.

CHICKEN ENCHILADA CUPS

I took these southwestern cups to an Arizona Cardinals tailgate. I kept them in a thermal wrap to maintain their warmth, but they are also good at room temperature. Mini phyllo shells are one of my favorite go-to ingredients because they're a quick and easy way to make big batches of sweet and savory treats and appetizers.
—Johnna Johnson, Scottsdale, AZ

Prep: 20 min. • **Bake:** 15 min. • **Makes:** 30

- 2 cups shredded rotisserie chicken
- ¾ cup shredded Monterey Jack cheese
- ½ cup sour cream
- ½ tsp. chili powder
- ½ tsp. salt
- ⅛ tsp. ground cumin
- ⅛ tsp. cayenne pepper
- 1 can (10 oz.) enchilada sauce, divided
- 2 pkg. (1.9 oz. each) frozen miniature phyllo tart shells
- 6 oz. Monterey Jack cheese
  Salsa

1. Preheat oven to 350°. Combine the first 7 ingredients with 3 Tbsp. enchilada sauce. Spoon into phyllo shells. Place shells on an ungreased 15x10-in. baking pan. Slice the Monterey Jack cheese into 1½-in. squares about ⅛ in. thick. Top each phyllo shell with cheese.
2. Bake until heated through and cheese is melted, 7-9 minutes. Meanwhile, in a small saucepan, heat remaining enchilada sauce over medium-low heat. Serve chicken cups with salsa and warm enchilada sauce.
1 appetizer: 81 cal., 5g fat (2g sat. fat), 17mg chol., 163mg sod., 3g carb. (0 sugars, 0 fiber), 6g pro.

PIZZA PUFFS

PIZZA PUFFS

What's more fun than pizza puffs? Skip the kind sold in the frozen aisle and try this homemade version. You can substitute any meat or vegetable for the pepperoni and any cheese for the mozzarella.
—*Vivi Taylor, Middleburg, FL*

Takes: 30 min.
Makes: 20 servings

- 1 loaf (1 lb.) frozen pizza dough, thawed
- 20 slices pepperoni
- 8 oz. part-skim mozzarella cheese, cut into 20 cubes
- ¼ cup butter
- 2 small garlic cloves, minced
  Dash salt
  Marinara sauce, warmed
  Crushed red pepper flakes and grated Parmesan cheese, optional

1. Preheat oven to 400°. Shape dough into 1½-in. balls; flatten into ⅛-in. thick circles. Place 1 pepperoni slice and 1 cheese cube in center of each circle; wrap dough around pepperoni and cheese. Pinch edges to seal; shape into a ball. Repeat with the remaining dough, cheese and pepperoni. Place seam side down on greased baking sheets; bake until light golden brown, 10-15 minutes. Cool slightly.
2. Meanwhile, in a small saucepan, melt butter over low heat. Add garlic and salt, taking care not to brown butter or garlic; brush over puffs. Serve with marinara sauce; if desired, sprinkle with red pepper flakes and Parmesan.
Freeze option: Cover and freeze unbaked pizza puffs on waxed paper-lined baking sheets until firm. Transfer to a freezer container; seal and return to freezer. To use, preheat oven to 325°; bake puffs on greased baking sheets as directed, increasing time as necessary to heat through.
1 pizza puff: 120 cal., 6g fat (3g sat. fat), 15mg chol., 189mg sod., 11g carb. (1g sugars, 0 fiber), 5g pro.

TUXEDO
STRAWBERRIES

TUXEDO STRAWBERRIES

These high-fashion treats will be the hit of the party! The strawberries are surprisingly easy to decorate and will elicit oohs and aahs from all the pretty ladies and dapper dudes.
—*Gisella Sellers, Seminole, FL*

- -

Prep: 1 hour + chilling • **Makes:** 1½ dozen

18	medium fresh strawberries with stems
1	cup vanilla or white chips
3½	tsp. shortening, divided
1⅓	cups semisweet chocolate chips

1. Line a tray or baking sheet with waxed paper; set aside. Wash strawberries and pat until completely dry.

2. In a microwave-safe bowl, melt vanilla chips and 1½ tsp. shortening at 70% power; stir until smooth. Dip each strawberry until two-thirds is coated, forming the tuxedo shirt, allowing excess to drip off. Place on prepared tray; chill for 30 minutes or until set.

3. Melt chocolate chips and remaining shortening. To form the tuxedo jacket, dip each side of berry into chocolate from the tip of the strawberry to the top of vanilla coating. Repeat on the other side, leaving a white V-shape in the center. Set the remaining chocolate aside. Chill berries for 30 minutes or until set.

4. Remelt remaining chocolate if necessary. Using melted chocolate and a #2 round pastry tip, pipe a bow tie at the top of the white "V" and 3 buttons down front of shirt. Chill for 30 minutes or until set. Store berries in the refrigerator in a covered plastic container for up to 1 day.

1 strawberry: 121 cal., 8g fat (4g sat. fat), 1mg chol., 10mg sod., 14g carb. (13g sugars, 1g fiber), 1g pro.

3 Easy Ways to Melt Chocolate

Our Test Kitchen uses a handful of different techniques to melt chocolate for recipes. Here are three of our favorite methods.

WATER BATH METHOD

Fill a slow cooker one-third full of hot water. Set the heat to high, leaving the lid off. Place wide-mouth Mason jars filled with chopped chocolate pieces into the water. Take extra care to keep water from getting inside the jars—no seized chocolate, please! Step away for 30 minutes or so, leaving the lid off, and you'll return to beautifully melted chocolate that's ready to drizzle.

MICROWAVE METHOD

Chop chocolate into small pieces and place in a microwave-safe bowl. Microwave at 70% power for 1 minute. Remove from microwave and stir. Continue to microwave in 30-second increments, stirring frequently, until the chocolate has fully melted. Because microwave ovens behave differently, it's easy to overcook chocolate, so keep an eye on it.

DOUBLE BOILER METHOD

Place chopped chocolate in the top of a double boiler over barely simmering water. Stir gently and frequently until the chocolate has completely melted. Use a heat-safe rubber spatula to scrape the sides of the bowl as you stir. If you don't have a double boiler, use a metal bowl over a saucepan; just make sure the bottom of the bowl doesn't touch the water in the pan.

RED, WHITE & BBQ

Summer's here, and that means parades, picnics and fireworks. Hosting the ultimate grillside gathering is as easy as pie when you serve up a lineup of sizzling entrees, sensational sides, cool drinks, pretty desserts and other all-American cookout classics. Pile up a plate and join the party!

Chicken & Bratwurst Kabobs (p. 205) **Feta-Stuffed Cherry Tomatoes** (p. 204)

PICKLED SWEET PEPPERS

I love to can my homegrown produce. In this recipe, which I call Summer in a Jar, the peppers have a nice combination of tart and spicy flavors.
—*Edna Clemens, West Branch, MI*

Prep: 30 min. • **Process:** 15 min.
Makes: 5 pints

- 5 large sweet red peppers
- 8 banana peppers (about 1 lb.)
- 1 medium onion, thinly sliced
- 8 garlic cloves, peeled
- 4 tsp. canola oil
- 2½ cups water
- 2½ cups white vinegar
- 1¼ cups sugar
- 2 tsp. canning salt

1. Cut red and banana peppers into strips, discarding seeds. Pack peppers into 5 hot 1-pint jars to within ½ in. of the top. Divide the onion, garlic and oil among jars.
2. In a large saucepan, bring water, vinegar, sugar and salt to a boil. Carefully ladle hot liquid over pepper mixture, leaving ½-in. headspace. Remove air bubbles and adjust headspace, if necessary, by adding hot liquid. Wipe rims. Center lids on jars; screw on bands until fingertip tight.
3. Place jars into canner with simmering water, ensuring that they are completely covered with water. Bring to a boil; process for 15 minutes. Remove jars and cool.
Note: The processing time listed is for altitudes of 1,000 feet or less. For altitudes up to 3,000 feet, add 5 minutes; 6,000 feet, add 10 minutes; 8,000 feet, add 15 minutes; 10,000 feet, add 20 minutes.
1 oz.: 13 cal., 0 fat (0 sat. fat), 0 chol., 15mg sod., 3g carb. (2g sugars, 1g fiber), 0 pro.

TEST KITCHEN TIP

Be sure to choose the right vinegar when pickling vegetables. Use white vinegar for a little more sharpness. If you're going for a milder flavor, use cider vinegar. For extra crunchy peppers, use 10%-strength vinegar.

GRILLED SUMMER VEGETABLE & COUSCOUS SALAD

GRILLED SUMMER VEGETABLE & COUSCOUS SALAD

This healthy salad features our homegrown eggplant and bell peppers and the fresh herbs we keep in hanging pots in our small condo. It's a welcome partner for any grilled meat or fish. Feel free to add a little crumbled goat cheese or tangy feta.
—*Patricia Levenson, Santa Ana, CA*

Prep: 35 min. • **Grill:** 10 min.
Makes: 10 servings

- ½ cup olive oil
- ⅓ cup balsamic vinegar
- 4 tsp. capers, drained
- 4 tsp. lemon juice
- 2 garlic cloves, minced
- ¾ tsp. Dijon mustard
- 1¼ tsp. minced fresh rosemary or ½ tsp. dried rosemary, crushed
- 1¼ tsp. minced fresh thyme or ½ tsp. dried thyme
- ⅛ tsp. salt
- ⅛ tsp. pepper

SALAD
- 1 pkg. (10 oz.) uncooked couscous
- 2 medium zucchini or yellow summer squash, halved lengthwise
- 2 medium sweet yellow or red peppers, quartered
- 1 Japanese eggplant, halved lengthwise
- 2 Tbsp. olive oil
- ¼ tsp. salt
- ¼ tsp. pepper
- 1 cup grape tomatoes, halved
- ½ cup Greek olives, pitted and sliced
- 1 Tbsp. minced fresh parsley or 1 tsp. dried parsley flakes
- 1 Tbsp. minced fresh basil or 1 tsp. dried basil

1. In a small bowl, whisk together the first 10 ingredients. Refrigerate until serving.
2. Cook couscous according to package directions. Meanwhile, brush the zucchini, yellow peppers and eggplant with oil; sprinkle with salt and pepper. Grill, covered, over medium heat until crisp-tender, 10-12 minutes, turning once.
3. Chop grilled vegetables; place in a large bowl. Add the tomatoes, olives, parsley, basil and couscous. Pour dressing over salad and toss to coat. Serve warm or chilled.
¾ cup: 272 cal., 16g fat (2g sat. fat), 0 chol., 244mg sod., 29g carb. (5g sugars, 3g fiber), 5g pro.

FRUITY WHITE WINE SANGRIA

This light, refreshing beverage goes together in minutes. I like it because it's not overly sugary or bubbly, plus it has a subtle citrus tone from naval oranges.
—*Kathryn Shell, Round Rock, TX*

Takes: 10 min. • **Makes:** 16 servings

- 2 bottles (750 ml each) white wine, chilled
- 2 cups lemon-lime soda, chilled
- 2 cups sliced fresh strawberries
- 2 small navel oranges, halved and thinly sliced
- 2 cups seedless red grapes

In a large pitcher or punch bowl, combine all ingredients. Serve over ice.
¾ cup: 130 cal., 0 fat (0 sat. fat), 0 chol., 13mg sod., 16g carb. (12g sugars, 1g fiber), 0 pro.

PORK & MANGO POPPERS

I'm a big fan of jalapeno poppers and was looking for some interesting flavors to use in them. These have a surprisingly sweet, savory and spicy combination. They are always the talk of the party!
—*Lee Evans, Queen Creek, AZ*

Prep: 30 min. • **Bake:** 15 min.
Makes: 32 appetizers

- 1 lb. ground pork
- 1 medium mango, peeled and chopped
- ½ cup cream cheese, softened
- ½ cup part-skim ricotta cheese
- 1 tsp. ground cinnamon
- ½ tsp. ground cardamom
- 16 large jalapeno peppers
- ¼ tsp. salt
- ¼ tsp. pepper

1. In a small skillet, cook pork over medium heat until no longer pink; drain. Place in a small bowl; stir in the mango, cheeses, cinnamon and cardamom.
2. Cut jalapenos in half lengthwise; remove seeds and membranes. Spoon pork mixture into pepper halves, a scant tablespoonful in each. Place on an ungreased baking sheet. Sprinkle with salt and pepper. Bake at 400° for 15-20 minutes or until heated through.
Note: Wear disposable gloves when cutting hot peppers; the oils can burn skin. Avoid touching your face.
1 popper: 55 cal., 4g fat (2g sat. fat), 15mg chol., 42mg sod., 2g carb. (1g sugars, 0 fiber), 3g pro.

Ban the Buzz
Shoo bugs from the scene with a pretty pot of herbs. Plants like lavender, mint, rue and tansy are a decorative way to repel insects.

RED, WHITE & BLUE CRUNCH MIX

My colorful snack mix makes a festive treat for a large group or potluck or even to bring as a grab-and-go snack for a parade. I took it to my school's faculty lounge once and it was gone before recess! You can use different colored candy disks for various occasions.
—*Bonnie Darr, Flagstaff, AZ*

Prep: 30 min. + standing • **Makes:** 11 cups

- 3 cups Crispix
- 3 cups Rice Krispies
- 2 cups dry roasted peanuts
- 4 cups pretzel sticks, broken
- 1 pkg. (11 oz.) Kraft caramel bits
- 4 cups white candy coating disks
- 1 cup red candy coating disks
- 1 cup blue candy coating disks

1. In a large bowl, combine the cereals, peanuts, pretzels and caramel bits.
2. In a large microwave-safe bowl, microwave the white candy coating at 50% power for 1 minute; stir. Cook at additional 20- to 30-second intervals, stirring until smooth. Drizzle over cereal mixture; toss to coat.
3. Transfer to 2 waxed paper-lined baking sheets. In a microwave, melt red and blue candy coating disks in separate bowls; drizzle over snack mix. Let stand until set. Store in an airtight container.
½ cup: 483 cal., 25g fat (17g sat. fat), 2mg chol., 377mg sod., 64g carb. (48g sugars, 1g fiber), 4g pro.

FETA-STUFFED CHERRY TOMATOES

These tempting beauties are bursting with fresh flavor. Use the small end of a melon scoop to easily remove the pulp.
—*Laura LeRoy, Waxhaw, NC*

Takes: 25 min. • **Makes:** 2 dozen

- 24 firm cherry tomatoes
- 3 oz. cream cheese, softened
- ⅓ cup crumbled feta cheese
- ¼ cup sour cream
- 1 green onion, finely chopped
- ¾ tsp. lemon juice
- ⅛ to ¼ tsp. dried oregano
  Coarsely ground pepper

1. Cut a thin slice off the top of each tomato. Scoop out and discard pulp. Invert tomatoes onto paper towels to drain.
2. In a small mixing bowl, beat the cream cheese, feta cheese, sour cream, onion, lemon juice and oregano until blended. Place mixture in a heavy-duty resealable plastic bag; cut a small hole in a corner of bag. Pipe mixture into tomatoes. If desired, sprinkle with black pepper. Chill until serving.
1 stuffed tomato: 25 cal., 2g fat (1g sat. fat), 6mg chol., 28mg sod., 1g carb. (1g sugars, 0 fiber), 1g pro.

ZESTY GARBANZO GREEN SALAD

I grow an organic vegetable garden, and this salad is a tasty way to make use of my delicious bounty. It's light and refreshing on a hot summer day. I recommend using whatever fresh ingredients you like best. You can also roast the tomatoes whole with the rest of the veggies.
—*Jennifer Huey, Baltimore, MD*

Prep: 15 min. • **Bake:** 20 min.
Makes: 8 servings

- ½ lb. fresh green beans, trimmed
- 1 medium zucchini, cut into ½-in. cubes
- 3 green onions, chopped
- 3 Tbsp. olive oil, divided
- ½ tsp. salt
- ½ tsp. pepper
- ¼ tsp. crushed red pepper flakes
- 3 Tbsp. red wine vinegar
- 2 Tbsp. Dijon mustard
- 1 garlic clove, minced
- 4 cups fresh spinach, torn
- 2 cups cherry tomatoes, halved
- 1 can (15 oz.) garbanzo beans or chickpeas, rinsed and drained
- 2 Tbsp. minced fresh basil

1. In a large bowl, combine the green beans, zucchini and green onions. Add 1 Tbsp. olive oil, salt, pepper and pepper flakes; toss to coat. Transfer to a 15x10x1-in. baking pan coated with cooking spray. Bake at 425° for 20 minutes, stirring once. Cool.
2. Meanwhile, in a large bowl, whisk the vinegar, mustard, garlic and remaining oil. Place the spinach, tomatoes, garbanzo beans, basil and green bean mixture in a large bowl. Drizzle with dressing; toss to coat. Refrigerate until serving.
¾ cup: 124 cal., 6g fat (1g sat. fat), 0 chol., 323mg sod., 15g carb. (4g sugars, 4g fiber), 4g pro. **Diabetic exchanges:** 1 vegetable, 1 fat, ½ starch.

Crushed red pepper flakes add a little heat to this salad. Feel free to omit it if you prefer a milder flavor. If you don't have fresh basil, add ½-1 tsp. dried basil.

CHICKEN & BRATWURST KABOBS

CHICKEN & BRATWURST KABOBS

I made these lively kabobs while visiting my relatives in Norway as a thank-you gift. They loved eating them almost as much as I loved cooking for them! If you prefer less heat in the chutney, you can use honey in place of pepper jelly. Also, any variety of vegetables will work with these.
—*Anna Davis, Springfield, MO*

- -

Prep: 40 min. • **Grill:** 10 min.
Makes: 12 kabobs

- ¼ cup balsamic vinegar
- ¼ cup cider vinegar
- 2 Tbsp. pepper jelly
- 2 Tbsp. stone-ground mustard
- 1 tsp. salt
- ½ tsp. pepper
- ½ cup olive oil, divided
- 1 can (15 oz.) peach halves in light syrup, drained and cut into ½-in. cubes
- ⅔ cup minced onion
- 1 jar (12 oz.) mango chutney
- 6 boneless skinless chicken breasts (6 oz. each)
- 1 pkg. (14 oz.) fully cooked bratwurst links
- 2 each medium green pepper, sweet red pepper and yellow pepper
- 1 large onion
- 3 Tbsp. brown sugar bourbon seasoning

1. Whisk together vinegars, pepper jelly, mustard, salt and pepper. Gradually whisk in ⅓ cup olive oil until blended. Add peaches, minced onion and chutney.
2. Cut chicken into 1-in. cubes and bratwursts into 1-in. slices. Cut peppers into large squares and onion into cubes. Toss with brown sugar bourbon seasoning and remaining oil.
3. On 12 metal or soaked wooden skewers, alternately thread chicken, bratwurst and vegetables. Grill skewers, covered, on a greased grill rack over medium-high direct heat, turning occasionally, until chicken is no longer pink and vegetables are tender, 10-12 minutes. If desired, sprinkle with additional brown sugar bourbon seasoning during grilling. Serve with chutney.
1 kabob: 433 cal., 21g fat (5g sat. fat), 71mg chol., 1249mg sod., 37g carb. (24g sugars, 2g fiber), 23g pro.

SUN-DRIED TOMATO
BISTRO BURGERS

Burgers Deluxe

Is there anything more satisfying than a juicy burger? No matter what type you prefer—cheesy, amped up with condiments, topped with an egg, or with a surprise inside—the perfect burger is yours for the taking when you follow these easy tips.

- Stay loose. The less you handle the patty, the more tender the cooked burger will be.

- Resist the urge to flatten burgers with a spatula as they cook. You'll press out precious juices.

- Allow the cooked burgers to rest for a few minutes before serving.

- Pack a little heat by adding fresh jalapenos and pepper jack cheese.

- Combine sliced ripe tomatoes, fresh mozzarella and a bit of basil for a Caprese burger.

- The classic Greek pairing of spinach and feta creates the ultimate combo in a stuffed burger.

SUN-DRIED TOMATO BISTRO BURGERS

These irresistible burgers bring together many of the flavors my family enjoys, plus there's a delicious filling in the center. You can use almost any cheese—Gorgonzola, feta, smoked Gouda and blue all work!
—*Aaron Shields, Hamburg, NY*

Prep: 40 min. • **Grill:** 10 min.
Makes: 8 servings

- 1   jar (7 oz.) oil-packed sun-dried tomatoes
- 3   medium onions, halved and thinly sliced
- 3   Tbsp. balsamic vinegar
- ½   cup finely chopped red onion
- 2   Tbsp. dried basil
- 2   tsp. ground cumin
- 2   tsp. ground chipotle pepper
- ½   tsp. salt
- ¼   tsp. pepper
- 3   lbs. lean ground beef (90% lean)
- 1   cup crumbled goat cheese
- 8   hamburger buns, split

1. Drain tomatoes, reserving ⅓ cup oil; set aside. In a large skillet, saute sliced onions in 3 Tbsp. reserved oil until softened. Add vinegar. Reduce heat to medium-low; cook, stirring occasionally, until deep golden brown, 30-40 minutes.
2. Meanwhile, chop the sun-dried tomatoes and transfer to a large bowl. Add red onion, seasonings and the remaining oil. Crumble beef over mixture and mix well. Shape into 16 patties. Place 2 Tbsp. goat cheese on the center of 8 patties. Top with remaining patties and press edges firmly to seal.
3. Grill burgers, covered, over medium heat until a thermometer reads 160° and juices run clear, 5-7 minutes on each side.
4. Place buns, cut side down, on grill until toasted, 1-2 minutes. Serve burgers on buns with onions.
1 burger with 2 Tbsp. onions: 596 cal., 32g fat (10g sat. fat), 123mg chol., 588mg sod., 36g carb. (7g sugars, 5g fiber), 42g pro.

CREAMY YELLOW SQUASH CASSEROLE

Here's a simple yet yummy garden recipe my granny used to make. She'd pick her veggies daily, then cook them for dinner. It always tasted so fresh and tender.
—*Mandy Nall, Montgomery, AL*

Prep: 35 min. • **Bake:** 20 min.
Makes: 10 servings

- 1   can (14½ oz.) chicken broth
- 7   cups thinly sliced yellow summer squash (about 5 medium)
- 1   large sweet onion, chopped
- 1   can (10¾ oz.) condensed cream of chicken soup, undiluted
- ½   cup sour cream
- ¼   cup mayonnaise
- 1   tsp. celery salt
- ½   tsp. pepper
- 1   cup (4 oz.) shredded Gouda cheese
- 1   cup (4 oz.) shredded provolone cheese
- 10 bacon strips, cooked and crumbled
- 20 Ritz crackers, crushed
- 1½ cups coarsely crumbled cornbread
- 3   Tbsp. butter, melted

1. Preheat oven to 350°. Place 1½ cups broth in a large skillet; bring to a boil. Add squash and onion; cook, covered, 3-5 minutes or until crisp-tender. Drain well and place in a greased 13x9-in. baking dish.
2. In a small bowl, mix chicken soup, sour cream, mayonnaise, celery salt, pepper and remaining ¼ cup broth. Spread half over top of squash mixture. Sprinkle with cheeses and bacon. Spread remaining chicken soup mixture over top. Sprinkle with the cracker crumbs and cornbread; drizzle with butter.
3. Bake, uncovered, 20-25 minutes or until golden brown and bubbly.
¾ cup: 338 cal., 24g fat (10g sat. fat), 45mg chol., 1068mg sod., 20g carb. (6g sugars, 2g fiber), 12g pro.

CINNAMON-SUGAR
PEACH KUCHEN

BERRY CHEESECAKE PIE

I don't care for traditional pie crust, so I usually eat only the filling. That changed when I discovered this unique dessert. Boasting a luscious cheesecake flavor, the recipe gets creative with phyllo dough.
—Deanne Causey, Midland, TX

- -

Prep: 20 min. • **Bake:** 35 min. + chilling
Makes: 8 servings

- 8   sheets phyllo dough (14x9 in.)
- 6   Tbsp. butter, melted
- 2   pkg. (8 oz. each) cream cheese, softened
- ½   cup sugar
- 1   tsp. vanilla extract
- 2   large eggs, room temperature, lightly beaten
- 2   cups fresh or frozen blueberries
- ½   cup strawberry jelly
- 1   cup whipped topping
     Sliced fresh strawberries and additional blueberries, optional

1. Place 1 phyllo sheet in a greased 9-in. pie plate; brush with butter. Repeat 7 times; trim edges. (Keep remaining phyllo covered with plastic wrap and a damp towel to prevent it from drying out.)
2. Bake at 425° for 6-8 minutes or until edges are lightly browned (center will puff up). Cool on a wire rack.
3. For filling, in a large bowl, beat the cream cheese, sugar and vanilla until smooth. Add eggs; beat on low speed just until combined. Fold in blueberries. Spoon into crust.
4. Bake at 350° for 10 minutes; cover edges with foil to prevent overbrowning. Bake until center is almost set, 23-27 minutes longer. Cool on a wire rack for 1 hour. Refrigerate until chilled.
5. In a small bowl, beat jelly until smooth; spread over filling. Spread with whipped topping. Garnish with strawberries and additional blueberries if desired.
Note: If using frozen blueberries, use without thawing to avoid discoloring the batter.
1 piece: 466 cal., 31g fat (20g sat. fat), 138mg chol., 291mg sod., 41g carb. (30g sugars, 1g fiber), 7g pro.

CINNAMON-SUGAR PEACH KUCHEN

My comforting kuchen showcases fresh summer peaches. You can use other stone fruits, too, such as plums or nectarines. This is one of those homey desserts that begs for a scoop of ice cream on top!
—Mary Bilyeu, Ann Arbor, MI

- -

Prep: 25 min. • **Bake:** 40 min. + cooling
Makes: 15 servings

- 1   cup butter, softened
- 1   cup plus 3 Tbsp. sugar, divided
- 4   large eggs, room temperature
- 2   tsp. vanilla extract
- ½   tsp. almond extract
- 2   cups all-purpose flour
- 2   tsp. baking powder
- 1   tsp. salt
- ¼   cup chopped crystallized ginger
- 4   to 5 medium peaches, sliced
- ½   tsp. ground cinnamon

1. In a large mixing bowl, cream butter and 1 cup sugar until light and fluffy. Add 1 egg at a time, beating well after each addition. Stir in extracts. Combine the flour, baking powder and salt; gradually add to the creamed mixture. Fold in ginger.
2. Transfer to a greased 13x9-in. baking dish. Arrange peaches over batter. Combine the cinnamon and remaining sugar; sprinkle over top of kuchen.
3. Bake at 350° for 40-45 minutes or until a toothpick inserted near the center comes out clean. Cool on a wire rack for 10 minutes before cutting. Serve warm.
1 piece: 273 cal., 14g fat (8g sat. fat), 89mg chol., 318mg sod., 35g carb. (20g sugars, 1g fiber), 4g pro.

The texture of this kuchen is more coarse than cake but is still tender. A hint of ginger complements the cinnamon and peach flavors.

STRAWBERRY MELON FIZZ
Experimenting in the kitchen is so much fun.
I came up with this fizzy drink by combining a
recipe for a melon ball arrangement and one
for a beverage.
—Teresa Messick, Montgomery, AL

- -

Takes: 30 min. • **Makes:** 10 servings

   2   **cups sugar**
   1   **cup water**
   5   **fresh mint sprigs**
   1 **qt. fresh strawberries, halved**
   2   **cups cubed honeydew**
1¾ **cups cubed cantaloupe**
       **Ginger ale or sparkling white grape
       juice**

1. In a large saucepan, combine the sugar,
water and mint; bring to a boil. Reduce heat;
simmer 10 minutes. Remove from the heat;
allow to cool completely. Discard mint.
2. Combine strawberries and melons. Just
before serving, fill tall glasses with fruit and
drizzle each with 1 Tbsp. syrup. Add ginger
ale to each glass.
1 serving: 194 cal., 0 fat (0 sat. fat), 0 chol.,
7mg sod., 49g carb. (46g sugars, 2g fiber),
1g pro.

Pretty Delicious
Infuse your daily dose of H_2O with
refreshing fruit, herbs and/or spices.
Just combine all ingredients with
2 qt. cold water, and refrigerate for
12-24 hours. Strain before serving.

RASPBERRY & LEMON
1 cup fresh raspberries
3 lemon slices

ROSEMARY & GINGER
3 fresh rosemary sprigs
1 Tbsp. minced fresh gingerroot

TANGERINE & THYME
2 tangerines, sliced
3 fresh thyme sprigs

STRAWBERRY
MELON FIZZ

BACKYARD CAMPING

The easiest way to camp? Set up a tent in your own backyard! Not only do you have the comforts of home close by (ahem, a bathroom), you can also enjoy comforts of homemade food. Between hearty grilled campfire dishes, fruity salsa, punch and creamy orange fluff, your next backyard adventure will be unforgettable. Finish the meal with sweet dessert cones or bonfire cookies, or choose from several pudgy pie varieties. Sleeping under the stars has never been so much fun!

Sausage & Potato Campfire Packets (p. 212)
Zucchini & Summer Squash Salad (p. 212) **Bonfire Cookies** (p. 219)

SAUSAGE & POTATO CAMPFIRE PACKETS

My family enjoys camping and cooking over a fire. These hearty packets turn out beautifully over a campfire, on the grill or in the oven at home. We sometimes leave out the sausage and serve the potatoes as a side dish. Either way, it's so easy, and the spuds can be served right from the foil pouch for easy cleanup. The recipe also tastes amazing when cooked in a Dutch oven.
—*Julie Koets, Elkhart, IN*

Prep: 20 min. • **Cook:** 30 min.
Makes: 8 servings

- 3 lbs. red potatoes, cut into ½-in. cubes
- 2 pkg. (12 oz. each) smoked sausage links, cut into ½-in. slices
- 4 bacon strips, cooked and crumbled
- 1 medium onion, chopped
- 2 Tbsp. chopped fresh parsley
- ¼ tsp. salt
- ¼ tsp. garlic salt
- ¼ tsp. pepper
  Additional chopped fresh parsley, optional

1. Prepare campfire or grill for medium heat. In a large bowl, toss potatoes with sausage, bacon, onion, parsley, salts and pepper.
2. Divide mixture among eight 18x12-in. pieces of heavy-duty nonstick foil, placing food on dull side of foil. Fold foil around potato mixture, sealing tightly.
3. Place packets over campfire or grill; cook 15 minutes on each side or until potatoes are tender. Open packets carefully to allow steam to escape. If desired, sprinkle with additional chopped parsley.
1 packet: 414 cal., 25g fat (10g sat. fat), 61mg chol., 1181mg sod., 31g carb. (4g sugars, 3g fiber), 17g pro.

> **TEST KITCHEN TIP**
>
> Change up the flavor with other types of fully cooked sausage, such as spinach and feta chicken sausage. If you don't have heavy-duty foil on hand, use a double thickness of regular foil.

ZUCCHINI & SUMMER SQUASH SALAD

ZUCCHINI & SUMMER SQUASH SALAD

I came up with this colorful and tasty slaw years ago for a recipe contest and was delighted when I won honorable mention! The recipe easily doubles and is the perfect dish to take to potlucks or family gatherings.
—*Paula Wharton, El Paso, TX*

Prep: 25 min. + chilling • **Makes:** 12 servings

- 4 medium zucchini
- 2 yellow summer squash
- 1 medium sweet red pepper
- 1 medium red onion
- 1 cup fresh sugar snap peas, trimmed and halved
- ⅓ cup olive oil
- ¼ cup balsamic vinegar
- 2 Tbsp. reduced-fat mayonnaise
- 4 tsp. fresh sage or 1 tsp. dried sage leaves
- 2 tsp. honey
- 1 tsp. garlic powder
- 1 tsp. celery seed
- 1 tsp. dill weed
- ½ tsp. salt
- ½ tsp. pepper

Thinly slice zucchini, squash, red pepper and onion; place in a large bowl. Add snap peas. In a small bowl, whisk remaining ingredients until blended. Pour over vegetables; toss to coat. Refrigerate, covered, at least 3 hours.
¾ cup: 101 cal., 7g fat (1g sat. fat), 1mg chol., 124mg sod., 8g carb. (6g sugars, 2g fiber), 2g pro. **Diabetic exchanges:** 1½ fat, 1 vegetable.

SAUSAGE & POTATO
CAMPFIRE PACKETS

SOURDOUGH BREAD BOWL SANDWICH

I created this for when my husband and I go to the lake. I don't like to spend a lot of time hovering over a hot pot or grill, especially in the hot Oklahoma summer months, and this filling sandwich is ready in minutes. For extra flavor, brush melted garlic and herb butter over the top prior to cooking.
—Shawna Welsh-Garrison, Owasso, OK

Prep: 15 min. • **Cook:** 30 min. + standing
Makes: 8 servings

- 1 round loaf sourdough bread (1½ lbs.)
- ½ cup honey mustard salad dressing
- 4 slices sharp cheddar cheese
- ⅓ lb. thinly sliced deli ham
- 4 slices smoked provolone cheese
- ⅓ lb. thinly sliced deli smoked turkey
- 1 Tbsp. butter, melted

1. Prepare campfire or grill for low heat. Cut a thin slice off top of bread loaf. Hollow out bottom of loaf, leaving a ½-in.-thick shell (save removed bread for another use). Spread dressing on inside of hollowed loaf and under the top of the bread. Layer with cheddar, ham, provolone and turkey. Replace top. Place on a piece of heavy-duty foil (about 24x18 in.). Brush loaf with butter. Fold foil edges over top, crimping to seal.
2. Cook over campfire or grill until heated through, 25-30 minutes. Let stand 15 minutes before removing foil. Cut into wedges.
1 piece: 346 cal., 17g fat (6g sat. fat), 46mg chol., 865mg sod., 30g carb. (5g sugars, 1g fiber), 19g pro.

This giant sandwich can be tricky to slice. Cut it with a serrated knife using a sawing motion. Consider inserting kabob skewers through each piece prior to cutting to hold layers together.

SOURDOUGH
BREAD BOWL
SANDWICH

LAYERED SUMMERTIME SALAD

Luscious layers of pasta and veggies make up this super summer salad that can be prepared ahead of time for warm-weather picnics and deck parties. It easily feeds a crowd.
—*Betty Fulks, Onia, AR*

- -

Takes: 30 min. • **Makes:** 16 servings

- 2 cups uncooked gemelli or spiral pasta
- 1 cup mayonnaise
- 2 Tbsp. lemon juice
- 1 tsp. sugar
- ½ tsp. garlic powder
- ½ cup sliced green onions
- 4 bacon strips, cooked and crumbled, divided
- 4 cups torn romaine
- 1 cup fresh snow peas, trimmed and halved
- 1 cup fresh cauliflowerets
- 1 cup fresh broccoli florets
- 1 large sweet red pepper, chopped
- ½ cup shredded Swiss cheese

1. Cook pasta according to the package directions. Meanwhile, in a small bowl, combine mayonnaise, lemon juice, sugar and garlic powder; set aside. Drain pasta and rinse in cold water; toss with onions and half of the bacon.
2. In a large salad bowl, layer half the romaine, pasta mixture, peas, cauliflower, broccoli, red pepper, mayonnaise mixture and cheese. Repeat layers. Sprinkle with remaining bacon. Cover and refrigerate until serving.
¾ cup: 186 cal., 13g fat (2g sat. fat), 9mg chol., 115mg sod., 13g carb. (2g sugars, 2g fiber), 4g pro.

Backyard Games & Activities

There's so much adventure to be had outside! From classic backyard games to hikes around the block, here are some fun activities to keep the family entertained all day—and into the night.

NEIGHBORHOOD NATURE HUNT

Make a list of various types of plants and animals to spot in the backyard, around your neighborhood or in a nearby park. Pack a backpack with a camera, a journal and plastic bags, then set out for a neighborhood hike. Point out the objects you find from the list, then take a photo of each object. Record it in the nature journal, and describe how it looks and feels. For small objects, collect them in small plastic bags to inspect later and create your own nature collection.

THROWBACK FUN

Classic games like Simon says, tag, telephone and name that tune are fun for all ages. Plus, they don't require any extra packing!

FLASHLIGHT FORAGING

Someone hides a small trinket or toy anywhere in the backyard, then, when it starts getting dark, everybody goes on a hunt to find the item. The hider may need to give people a hint about where to look, but they'll love the quest to find the treasure!

CAMPFIRE STORIES

What's a campfire without gathering around it for some storytelling? Start with spooky tales regaled while a flashlight eerily illuminates the storyteller's face. Or tell a story in the round, where each person takes turns to build upon the story as it goes. (Get ready for giggles!)

STARGAZING

If it's a clear night, spread out a big blanket, throw down some pillows and cozy up together to look at the stars. You can bring pictures of constellations to search for, or use your imaginations to dream up your own star shapes!

ONION GARLIC DIP

Try this warm creamy dip that can be served with veggies or crackers. It's a delicious snack any time of year, but there's something about grilling it for an outdoor occasion that makes it extra special.

—Zelda DeHoedt, Cedar Rapids, IA

- -

Prep: 20 min. • **Cook:** 25 min. • **Makes:** 5 cups

- 1 medium leek (white portion only), halved and sliced
- 1 small red onion, chopped
- 1 small onion, chopped
- 3 garlic cloves, minced
- 3 pkg. (8 oz. each) cream cheese, softened
- 1¼ cups grated Parmesan cheese
- ¾ cup mayonnaise
- 1 jar (2 oz.) diced pimientos, drained
- ¾ tsp. salt
- ¼ tsp. pepper
- ⅛ tsp. crushed red pepper flakes
  Assorted fresh vegetables, crackers or toasted baguette slices

1. Prepare campfire or grill for medium-low heat. Combine all ingredients in a large bowl. Spread mixture in the bottom of a 8-in. disposable foil square pan. Lightly cover with nonstick foil.
2. Place pan on a grill grate over a campfire or on grill until lightly browned and bubbly, about 25 minutes. Serve with vegetables and crackers.

¼ cup: 201 cal., 19g fat (9g sat. fat), 39mg chol., 329mg sod., 4g carb. (2g sugars, 0 fiber), 4g pro.

FRUIT SALSA WITH CINNAMON CHIPS

I first made this fresh, fruity salsa for a family baby shower. Everyone wanted the recipe. Now, someone makes this juicy snack for just about every family gathering—and I have to keep reminding everyone who introduced it!

—Jessica Robinson, Indian Trail, NC

- -

Takes: 30 min.
Makes: 2½ cups salsa and 80 chips

- 1 cup finely chopped fresh strawberries
- 1 medium navel orange, peeled and finely chopped
- 3 medium kiwifruit, peeled and finely chopped
- 1 can (8 oz.) unsweetened crushed pineapple, drained
- 1 Tbsp. lemon juice
- 1½ tsp. sugar
  CINNAMON CHIPS
- 10 flour tortillas (8 in.)
- ¼ cup butter, melted
- ⅓ cup sugar
- 1 tsp. ground cinnamon

1. In a bowl, combine the first 6 ingredients. Cover and refrigerate until serving.
2. Preheat oven to 350°. For chips, brush tortillas with butter; cut each into 8 wedges. Combine sugar and cinnamon; sprinkle over wedges. Place on ungreased baking sheets.
3. Bake 5-10 minutes or just until crisp. Serve with fruit salsa.

2 Tbsp. salsa with 4 chips: 134 cal., 4g fat (2g sat. fat), 6mg chol., 136mg sod., 22g carb. (7g sugars, 2g fiber), 2g pro.

CAMPFIRE DESSERT CONES

Kids love to make these cute cones. Set out the ingredients so they can mix and match as their hearts desire.

—Bonnie Hawkins, Elkhorn, WI

- -

Takes: 20 min. • **Makes:** 8 servings

- 8 ice cream sugar cones
- ½ cup milk chocolate M&M's
- ½ cup miniature marshmallows
- ½ cup salted peanuts
- ½ cup white baking chips

1. Prepare campfire or grill for medium heat. Fill cones with M&M's, marshmallows, peanuts and white chips. Fully wrap each cone with foil, sealing tightly.
2. Place packets over campfire or grill; cook until heated through, 7-10 minutes. Open foil carefully.

1 cone: 217 cal., 11g fat (5g sat. fat), 4mg chol., 78mg sod., 26g carb. (18g sugars, 1g fiber), 5g pro.

TEST KITCHEN TIP

Whether you spoon out the filling before eating the cone or just dig right in, there's no right or wrong way to eat this fun take on s'mores. Use your favorite candies to fill up the cones—we love the idea of miniature peanut butter cups.

CAMPFIRE
DESSERT CONES

BONFIRE COOKIES

BONFIRE COOKIES

The start of cold weather here in Colorado means bonfire weather. What better way to celebrate than with these cookies!
—*Callie Washer, Conifer, CO*

- -

Prep: 45 min. • **Bake:** 10 min./batch + cooling
Makes: 2 dozen

- 1 cup butter, softened
- 1½ cups sugar
- 2 large eggs, room temperature
- 1 tsp. vanilla extract
- 3 cups all-purpose flour
- 1½ tsp. baking powder
- ¼ tsp. salt
- ¼ tsp. ground nutmeg
- 10 cherry Jolly Rancher hard candies, crushed
- 1 pouch (7 oz.) green decorating icing
- ½ cup chocolate wafer crumbs
- 36 pretzel sticks

1. Preheat oven to 350°. In a large bowl, cream butter and sugar until light and fluffy. Beat in eggs and vanilla. In another bowl, whisk flour, baking powder, salt and nutmeg; gradually beat into creamed mixture.
2. Shape level tablespoons of dough into balls; place 2 in. apart on ungreased baking sheets. Flatten slightly with the bottom of a glass. Bake until edges are light brown, 8-10 minutes. Cool on pans 2 minutes before removing to wire racks to cool completely.
3. Meanwhile, spread crushed candies onto a parchment-lined baking sheet. Bake until candy is melted, 5-7 minutes. Cool completely on pan on a wire rack. Break into pieces.
4. Spread icing over cookies; sprinkle with wafer crumbs. Arrange broken candies to make campfire flames. For logs, break pretzel sticks in half. Place 3 halves, broken edges down, in the wet icing. Hold in place until set.
1 cookie: 238 cal., 10g fat (6g sat. fat), 36mg chol., 166mg sod., 35g carb. (20g sugars, 1g fiber), 2g pro.

If the bottom of the glass sticks to the dough, dip it in flour before flattening the balls into cookie shapes. Cookies can be made ahead and stored in an airtight container overnight until you are ready to decorate.

PINEAPPLE STRAWBERRY PUNCH

For us, this drink has always been a must at holiday gatherings and other special occasions. It's fruity and fun.
—*Heather Dollins, Poplar Bluff, MO*

- -

Takes: 10 min. • **Makes:** 12 servings (3 qt.)

- 2 pkg. (10 oz. each) frozen sweetened sliced strawberries, thawed
- 1 can (46 oz.) pineapple juice, chilled
- 4 cups lemon-lime soda, chilled

In a food processor, puree strawberries. Pour into a large punch bowl. Stir in the pineapple juice and soda. Serve immediately.
1 cup: 109 cal., 0 fat (0 sat. fat), 0 chol., 12mg sod., 28g carb. (23g sugars, 1g fiber), 1g pro.

FRUIT & NUT TRAIL MIX

This mouthwatering mix is filled with nutrition and flavor. Whether you're enjoying the outdoors or heading out the door to work, the munchable medley will hit the spot.
—*Mary Ann Dell, Phoenixville, PA*

- -

Prep: 15 min. • **Bake:** 1 hour + cooling
Makes: 4 cups

- 1 pkg. (6 oz.) dried apricots, quartered
- ¾ cup golden raisins
- ¾ cup walnut halves
- ½ cup salted cashews
- ½ cup sunflower kernels
- ⅓ cup dried cranberries
- ¼ cup sugar
- 1½ tsp. Chinese five-spice powder
- ½ tsp. salt
- ¼ tsp. ground cinnamon
- 1 large egg white
- 1 tsp. water

1. Preheat oven to 250°. Coat a foil-lined 15x10x1-in. baking pan with cooking spray; set aside. In a large bowl, combine the first 10 ingredients. In a small bowl, beat egg white and water on high speed for 1 minute or until frothy; fold into fruit mixture.
2. Spread into prepared pan. Bake for 1 hour, stirring every 15 minutes. Cool completely. Store in an airtight container.
⅓ cup: 203 cal., 10g fat (1g sat. fat), 0 chol., 173mg sod., 28g carb. (21g sugars, 3g fiber), 4g pro.

CREAMY ORANGE FLUFF

I got this recipe from a friend but came up with my own tasty topping. Creamy, fruity and refreshing, this dish is simple to make ahead and cuts nicely into squares for ease in serving. It is perfect for potlucks.
—*Nancy Callis, Woodinville, WA*

Prep: 15 min. + chilling • **Makes:** 15 servings

- 1 pkg. (6 oz.) orange gelatin
- 2½ cups boiling water
- 2 cans (11 oz. each) mandarin oranges, drained
- 1 can (8 oz.) crushed pineapple, undrained
- 1 can (6 oz.) frozen orange juice concentrate, thawed

TOPPING
- 1 pkg. (8 oz.) cream cheese, softened
- 1 cup cold 2% milk
- 1 pkg. (3.4 oz.) instant vanilla pudding mix

1. In a large bowl, dissolve gelatin in boiling water. Stir in oranges, pineapple and orange juice concentrate. Coat a 13x9-in. dish with cooking spray; add gelatin mixture. Chill until firm.

2. In a large bowl, beat cream cheese until smooth. Gradually add milk and pudding mix; beat until smooth. Spread over orange layer. Chill until firm.

1 piece: 181 cal., 6g fat (3g sat. fat), 17mg chol., 125mg sod., 31g carb. (29g sugars, 1g fiber), 3g pro.

TEST KITCHEN TIP

Cook Up Some Camp Chow

One of the best parts about camping? Eating around the fire!

If you have a fire pit in your backyard, it's easy to roast hot dogs, toast marshmallows, and even cook up meats and veggies in foil packets.

If you don't have a fire pit, a small charcoal grill will work. You can make pudgy pies over the coals whenever tummies start to grumble.

Of course, you don't need a campfire to eat like a camper. Pack sandwiches, whole fruit, trail mix, juice boxes and desserts in a cooler to grab at the ready.

PINEAPPLE UPSIDE-DOWN CAMPFIRE CAKE

PINEAPPLE UPSIDE-DOWN CAMPFIRE CAKE

We make this fun recipe while camping or in the backyard around a fire. It's very yummy, but the sandwich iron should be opened only by adults to avoid burns.
—*Cheryl Grimes, Whiteland, IN*

Prep: 10 min. • **Cook:** 5 min./cake
Makes: 6 servings

- 6 tsp. butter
- 6 Tbsp. brown sugar
- 6 canned pineapple slices
- 6 maraschino cherries
- 6 individual round sponge cakes

1. Place 1 tsp. butter in 1 side of sandwich iron. Hold over fire to melt; remove from fire. Carefully sprinkle 1 Tbsp. brown sugar over melted butter. Top with pineapple ring; add cherry to center of pineapple. Top with cake (flat side up); close iron.

2. Cook pineapple side down over a hot campfire until brown sugar is melted and cake is heated through, 5-8 minutes. Invert iron to open, and serve cake on an individual plate.

1 cake: 211 cal., 6g fat (3g sat. fat), 38mg chol., 214mg sod., 39g carb. (32g sugars, 1g fiber), 2g pro.

Milky Way Pudgy Pie
My favorite is made with white bread, chopped Milky Way candy bars, graham cracker crumbs and marshmallows. So irresistible!
—Susan Hein, Burlington, WI

Apple-Cinnamon Pudgy Pie
I remember the first time I tasted a pie-iron pie. My sister buttered two slices of white bread while I peeled a Macintosh apple. She sliced it thin, arranged it on the bread and poured liberal amounts of white sugar and cinnamon over the top. I couldn't believe the sweet magic that came out of that fire!
—Monica Kronemeyer DeRegt, Abbotsford, BC

Reuben Pudgy Pie
Our favorite pudgy pie recipe is the Reuben: Corned beef, sauerkraut and Swiss cheese! We always use buttered bread.
—Kim Goetz, Andover, MN

ROSH HASHANA

To celebrate the Jewish new year, many families prepare festive meals that feature breads, such as round challah, and apples—both of which are traditionally dipped in honey. Other delicacies often eaten during this holiday include carrots, raisins or pomegranate as ingredients. In this chapter, learn about kosher foods, how to braid bread dough and more.

Braided Egg Bread (p. 226)

VEGETABLE SAMOSAS

VEGETABLE SAMOSAS

My family enjoys the wonderful flavors in a traditional samosa. Baked instead of fried, this version has fewer calories but keeps all the classic tastes and textures we love.
—Amy Siegel, Clifton, NJ

- -

Prep: 45 min. • **Bake:** 20 min.
Makes: about 3 dozen

- 2 large potatoes, peeled and cubed
- 1 medium onion, chopped
- 2 Tbsp. olive oil
- 2 garlic cloves, minced
- 1 tsp. salt
- 1 tsp. curry powder
- ½ tsp. ground cumin
- ¼ tsp. pepper
- 1 cup canned garbanzo beans or chickpeas, rinsed, drained and mashed
- 1 cup frozen peas, thawed
- 2 Tbsp. minced fresh cilantro
- 1 pkg. (16 oz., 14x9-in. sheet size) frozen phyllo dough, thawed
  Cooking spray
  Mint chutney, optional

1. Place potatoes in a large saucepan and cover with water. Bring to a boil. Reduce heat; cover and cook for 15-20 minutes or until tender. Drain. Mash potatoes; set aside.
2. In a large skillet, saute onion in oil until tender. Add the garlic, salt, curry powder, cumin and pepper; cook 1 minute longer. Remove from the heat. Stir in the mashed potatoes, garbanzo beans, peas and cilantro.
3. Preheat oven to 375°. Place 1 sheet of phyllo dough on a work surface with a short end facing you. (Keep remaining phyllo covered with plastic wrap and a damp towel to prevent it from drying out.) Spray sheet with cooking spray; repeat with 1 more sheet of phyllo, spraying the sheet with cooking spray. Cut into two 14x4½-in. strips.
4. Place 2 Tbsp. filling on lower corner of each strip. Fold dough over filling, forming a triangle. Fold triangle up, then fold triangle over, forming another triangle. Continue folding, like a flag, to the end of the strip.
5. Spritz end of dough with spray and press onto triangle to seal. Turn triangle and spritz top with spray. Repeat with remaining phyllo and filling.
6. Place triangles on greased baking sheets. Bake 20-25 minutes or until golden brown. If desired, serve with mint chutney.
1 samosa: 79 cal., 2g fat (0 sat. fat), 0 chol., 136mg sod., 13g carb. (1g sugars, 1g fiber), 2g pro.

PARSNIP SWEET POTATO PANCAKES

Golden brown sweet potatoes make these cakes pretty to look at and even better to eat. The green onions and thyme add an extra boost.
—Amy Short, Milton, WV

- -

Prep: 20 min. • **Cook:** 30 min.
Makes: 2 dozen

- 1 cup all-purpose flour
- 3 Tbsp. minced fresh thyme
- 2 tsp. salt
- ¼ tsp. pepper
- 4 large eggs, lightly beaten
- 2 lbs. sweet potatoes, peeled and grated
- 1 lb. parsnips, peeled and grated
- 12 green onions, sliced diagonally
- ½ cup vegetable oil

1. In a large bowl, combine the flour, thyme, salt and pepper. Stir in eggs until blended. Add the sweet potatoes, parsnips and onions; toss to coat.
2. In an electric skillet or deep-fat fryer, heat oil to 375°. Drop batter by ¼ cupfuls, a few at a time, into hot oil; press lightly to flatten. Fry for 3-4 minutes on each side or until golden brown. Drain on paper towels. Serve warm.
2 pancakes: 280 cal., 14g fat (2g sat. fat), 62mg chol., 431mg sod., 34g carb. (10g sugars, 4g fiber), 5g pro.

GARLIC ARTICHOKE DIP

Not only is this chilled dip delicious and lower in fat, but it also offers easy make-ahead convenience.
—Lisa Varner, El Paso, TX

- -

Prep: 25 min. + chilling • **Makes:** 2½ cups

- 1 large onion, chopped
- ½ tsp. dried oregano
- ½ tsp. dried thyme
- 2 Tbsp. olive oil
- 5 garlic cloves, minced
- 1 can (15 oz.) cannellini beans, rinsed and drained
- 1 can (14 oz.) water-packed artichoke hearts, rinsed and drained
- 1 Tbsp. lemon juice
- ½ tsp. salt
- ⅛ tsp. cayenne pepper
  Assorted fresh vegetables and/or baked pita chips

1. In a small nonstick skillet, saute the onion, oregano and thyme in oil until onions are tender. Add garlic; cook 1 minute longer. Remove from the heat; cool slightly.
2. In a food processor, combine the beans, artichokes, lemon juice, salt, cayenne and onion mixture; cover and process until pureed.
3. Transfer to a small bowl. Cover and refrigerate at least 2 hours before serving. Serve with vegetables and/or pita chips.
¼ cup: 81 cal., 3g fat (0 sat. fat), 0 chol., 271mg sod., 11g carb. (1g sugars, 2g fiber), 3g pro. **Diabetic exchanges:** 1 vegetable, ½ starch, ½ fat.

CITRUS SPINACH SALAD

Grapefruit and orange segments add zest to this delightful salad that's tossed with a pleasant honey-lime dressing. It's perfect for a springtime luncheon or shower.
—Pauline Taylor, Spokane, WA

- -

Takes: 15 min. • **Makes:** 12 servings

- 3 Tbsp. honey
- 2 Tbsp. lime juice
- 1 tsp. grated lime zest
- ⅛ to ¼ tsp. ground nutmeg
- ⅓ cup vegetable oil
- 10 cups torn fresh spinach
- 3 medium navel oranges, peeled and sectioned
- 2 medium pink grapefruit, peeled and sectioned
- 1 medium red onion, sliced and separated into rings

1. In a blender, combine the honey, lime juice, lime zest and nutmeg; cover and process until blended. While processing, gradually add oil in a steady stream until dressing is thickened.
2. In a large salad bowl, combine the spinach, oranges and grapefruit. Drizzle with dressing; toss to coat. Top with the onion rings. Serve immediately.
1 serving: 109 cal., 6g fat (1g sat. fat), 0 chol., 21mg sod., 14g carb. (11g sugars, 2g fiber), 1g pro.

TEST KITCHEN TIP

When peeling and sectioning grapefruit, it's sometimes difficult to remove the bitter white pith. An easy solution is to bring water to a boil in a saucepan; place the whole grapefruit in the water. Remove from the heat; let stand for about 5 minutes. With tongs, remove the grapefruit from the water. When it's cool enough to handle, you can easily peel away the skin and pith.

▲

How to Braid Bread Dough

Bake up a gorgeous and golden loaf of braided bread. These instructions are for our favorite way of braiding 6 equal strands of dough; see the Braided Egg Bread recipe at right (photo on opposite page) for instructions for an easy way to braid 6 strands of 2 sizes.

1. On a lightly floured surface, divide dough into 6 even pieces. Roll each piece into a rope. Use even pressure when rolling so the ropes are the same width from end to end, as well as the same length.

2. Arrange the 6 ropes on a greased baking sheet. Pinch ropes together at 1 end and tuck under. Do not remove the ropes from the baking sheet. This way you won't have to transfer the braid just before baking and risk stretching the dough.

3. Starting with the far right rope, weave toward the left in this pattern—over 2 strands, under 1 strand, over 2 strands. Start again at the (new) far right rope and weave toward the left in the same pattern—over 2 strands, under 1 strand, over 2 strands. Repeat this pattern until all the dough is braided.

4. At the end of the braided loaf, pinch the rope ends together and tuck under.

HOLLER FOR CHALLAH!

What is challah bread? Challah is a kosher loaf of braided bread. It has long been a symbolic centerpiece for a Rosh Hashana spread. It's at the heart of many Jewish celebrations, including Shabbat and Purim.

The simple dough is made with eggs, water, flour, yeast and salt. The bread is typically pale yellow in color because so many eggs are used, and it has a rich flavor, too.

Here are more fun tips for making challah bread.

• Add a small handful of raisins to symbolize sweetness and happiness, particularly around joyous holidays.

• Add chocolate chips, cinnamon, orange zest or almonds for a pop of color or flavor.

• Brush loaves with egg whites and honey before baking for a shiny and golden crust.

• Sprinkle poppy or sesame seeds on top of the bread to symbolize the manna that fell from heaven after the Exodus from Egypt.

BRAIDED EGG BREAD

For Rosh Hashana, loaves of braided bread—also commonly called challah—are baked to symbolize continuity. Since I first made this bread some years ago, it has become a much requested recipe.
—Marlene Jeffery, Holland, MB

- -

Prep: 30 min. + rising • **Bake:** 25 min. + cooling
Makes: 1 loaf (16 slices)

    3¼ to 3¾ cups all-purpose flour
    1   Tbsp. sugar
    1   pkg. (¼ oz.) active dry yeast
    ¾   tsp. salt
    ¾   cup water
    3   Tbsp. canola oil
    2   large eggs, room temperature
TOPPING
    1   large egg
    1   tsp. water
    ½   tsp. poppy seeds

1. In a large bowl, combine 2½ cups flour, sugar, yeast and salt. In a small saucepan, heat water and oil to 120°-130°. Add to dry ingredients along with eggs. Beat on medium speed for 3 minutes. Stir in enough remaining flour to form a soft dough.
2. Turn onto a lightly floured surface; knead until smooth and elastic, about 6-8 minutes. Place in a greased bowl, turning once to grease top. Cover and let rise in a warm place until doubled, about 1½ hours.
3. Punch dough down. Turn onto a lightly floured surface. Set a third of the dough aside. Divide remaining dough into 3 pieces. Shape each into a 13-in. rope. Place ropes on a greased baking sheet and braid; pinch ends to seal and tuck under.
4. Divide reserved dough into 3 equal pieces; shape each into a 14-in. rope. Braid ropes. Center 14-in. braid on top of the shorter braid. Pinch ends to seal and tuck under. Cover and let rise until doubled, about 30 minutes.
5. Preheat oven to 375°. In a small bowl, beat egg and water; brush over dough. Sprinkle with poppy seeds. Bake 25-30 minutes or until golden brown. Cover with foil during the last 15 minutes of baking. Remove from pan to a wire rack to cool.
1 slice: 134 cal., 4g fat (1g sat. fat), 40mg chol., 123mg sod., 20g carb. (1g sugars, 1g fiber), 4g pro.

BRAIDED
EGG BREAD

CARROT RAISIN COUSCOUS

Golden raisins add a slightly sweet flavor to this unique side dish featuring couscous and carrots. The recipe will brighten any holiday table.

—*Jordan Sucher, Brooklyn, NY*

Prep: 15 min. • **Cook:** 20 min.
Makes: 10 servings

- ⅓ cup port wine or chicken broth
- ⅓ cup golden raisins
- 1 medium onion, chopped
- 3 Tbsp. olive oil, divided
- 1 pkg. (10 oz.) couscous
- 2 cups chicken broth
- ¼ tsp. salt, divided
- ¼ tsp. pepper, divided
- 4 medium carrots, julienned
- 1 Tbsp. sugar
- 1 tsp. molasses

1. In a small saucepan, heat wine until hot. In a small bowl, soak raisins in wine for 5 minutes. Drain raisins, reserving wine.

2. In a large saucepan, saute onion in 1 Tbsp. oil until tender. Stir in couscous. Cook and stir until lightly browned. Stir in the broth, raisins and half of the salt and pepper. Bring to a boil. Cover and remove from the heat. Let stand for 5 minutes; fluff with a fork.

3. In a small skillet, saute carrots in remaining oil until crisp-tender. Combine sugar, molasses, wine and the remaining salt and pepper. Stir into carrots; heat through.

4. In a large bowl, combine couscous mixture and carrots; toss to combine.

¾ cup: 188 cal., 5g fat (1g sat. fat), 1mg chol., 277mg sod., 32g carb. (8g sugars, 2g fiber), 5g pro. **Diabetic exchanges:** 1½ starch, 1 vegetable, 1 fat.

CARROT RAISIN COUSCOUS

MOM'S CELERY SEED BRISKET

Warning: Keep a close eye on this tangy pot of goodness. Because it's been fine-tuned to perfection, it tends to vanish at gatherings.
—*Aysha Schurman, Ammon, ID*

- -

Prep: 20 min. • **Cook:** 8 hours
Makes: 8 servings

- 1   fresh beef brisket (3 to 4 lbs.)
- 1   can (28 oz.) Italian crushed tomatoes
- 1   large red onion, chopped
- 2   Tbsp. red wine vinegar
- 2   Tbsp. Worcestershire sauce
- 4   garlic cloves, minced
- 1   Tbsp. brown sugar
- 1   tsp. celery seed
- 1   tsp. pepper
- ½   tsp. salt
- ½   tsp. ground cumin
- ½   tsp. liquid smoke
- 4   tsp. cornstarch
- 3   Tbsp. cold water

1. Cut brisket in half; place in a 5-qt. slow cooker. In a large bowl, combine the tomatoes, onion, vinegar, Worcestershire sauce, garlic, brown sugar, celery seed, pepper, salt, cumin and liquid smoke. Pour over beef. Cover and cook on low for 8-10 hours or until meat is tender.
2. Remove meat to a serving platter; keep warm. In a large saucepan, combine the cornstarch and water until smooth. Gradually stir in 4 cups cooking liquid. Bring to a boil; cook and stir for 2 minutes or until thickened. Slice brisket across the grain; serve with gravy.
Note: This is a fresh beef brisket, not corned beef.
5 oz. cooked meat with ½ cup gravy:
262 cal., 7g fat (3g sat. fat), 72mg chol., 425mg sod., 10g carb. (5g sugars, 1g fiber), 36g pro.
Diabetic exchanges: 5 lean meat, 1 vegetable.

Keep It Kosher

"Kosher" is a Hebrew word that means "fit," as in "fit to eat." It sounds simple—but the rules about kosher cooking might surprise you.

The rules that govern kosher cooking and eating are detailed. Truly keeping kosher requires rigorous adherence, and in the case of restaurants and commercial kitchens, the careful watch of a religious supervisor to make sure all rules and spiritual laws are followed.

When it comes to keeping kosher, there are plenty of surprises for the uninitiated. Here are just a few.

WHICH FOODS ARE KOSHER?

You might know that those who keep kosher avoid eating pork, since pigs don't qualify as kosher. But sea creatures without fins and scales are off-limits, too. This means no lobster, crab or beluga caviar (it comes from whales—no scales). Birds of prey also make the nonkosher list, as do any foods derived from animals that aren't considered kosher. Gelatin, for example, is not kosher if derived from pigs or horses.

PREPARATION IS KEY

It's not only about what foods are kosher, but how they're prepared. From the slaughterhouse to the kitchen, strict rules of preparation must be followed to make sure a food remains kosher. For example, meat and dairy must never be combined—or even touched by the same utensil.

Some kosher salt, despite the name, may not be certified kosher at all. Instead, it may have gotten its name from originally being used in the process of koshering meats.

KOSHER FOR PASSOVER

During the eight days of Passover, an additional set of kosher rules apply, which are primarily to avoid any food that contains leavening. Matzah, which can also be spelled matzoh or matzo, is eaten during Passover because it's unleavened bread.

In addition, to be kosher for Passover, food purchased from a store must be certified as "kosher for Passover," and food that is not kosher for Passover must be separated from food that is.

GARLIC CLOVE CHICKEN

My neighbors made this chicken frequently, and I couldn't get enough of it. If you like garlic, you'll love this recipe.
—*Denise Hollebeke, Penhold, AB*

Prep: 10 min. • **Bake:** 2¼ hours + standing
Makes: 6 servings

- 1 roasting chicken (5 to 6 lbs.)
- 1 small onion, quartered
- 40 garlic cloves, peeled
- ¼ cup canola oil
- 1½ tsp. salt
- 1 tsp. dried parsley flakes
- ½ tsp. dried celery flakes
- ½ tsp. each dried tarragon, thyme and rosemary, crushed
- ¼ tsp. pepper

1. Preheat oven to 350°. Place chicken breast side up on a rack in a shallow roasting pan. Stuff onion in chicken; tie drumsticks together. Arrange garlic cloves around chicken. In a small bowl, combine the remaining ingredients. Drizzle over chicken and garlic.

2. Cover and bake for 1¾ hours. Uncover; bake 30-45 minutes longer or until a thermometer reads 170°-175°, basting occasionally with pan drippings. (Cover loosely with foil if chicken browns too quickly.) Cover and let stand for 10 minutes before slicing.

7 oz. cooked chicken: 556 cal., 36g fat (8g sat. fat), 1mg chol., 738mg sod., 8g carb. (1g sugars, 1g fiber), 49g pro.

▲

How to Carve a Chicken

1. Place the chicken on a cutting board with wings facing away from you. Lightly press a carving fork into the breastbone between the 2 breasts to stabilize the chicken. Using a sharp knife, cut the skin between the leg and the body.

2. Pull the leg away from the side of the chicken to expose the hip joint. Pierce the joint with the tip of the knife. (If you have trouble finding the joint, wiggle the leg back and forth, using your fingertip to find the moving joint.) Remove the leg.

3. Placing the carving fork in the thigh meat, cut straight down along the curve of the drumstick until you reach the joint. Gently pierce the joint between the drumstick and the thigh to separate the 2 pieces. Repeat steps 1, 2 and 3 to remove the second thigh and drumstick.

4. Place the cutting fork in the middle of the breastbone. Starting at the base of the left breast, position the knife right above the wing. Make a long, horizontal cut, starting from the top at the wing and continuing until you reach the point where the leg used to meet the breast.

5. With the cutting fork positioned in the right breast, make a deep vertical cut down along the breastbone of the left breast. Then, cut in an angled, downward motion underneath the breast and toward the horizontal cut to remove the breast meat from the rib cage.

6. Pull the wing away from the body of the chicken and cut through the joint. You may remove the wing tip, if desired, by piercing the joint between the wingette and the tip.

GARLIC CLOVE
CHICKEN

MULLED POMEGRANATE SIPPER

This warm and festive drink fills the entire house with the wonderful aroma of spices and simmering fruit juices. Kids and adults both love this spirit-warming sipper.
—*Lisa Renshaw, Kansas City, MO*

Prep: 10 min. • **Cook:** 1 hour
Makes: 16 servings (¾ cup each)

1	bottle (64 oz.) cranberry-apple juice
2	cups unsweetened apple juice
1	cup pomegranate juice
⅔	cup honey
½	cup orange juice
3	cinnamon sticks (3 in.)
10	whole cloves
2	Tbsp. grated orange zest

In a 5-qt. slow cooker, combine the first 5 ingredients. Place cinnamon sticks, cloves and orange zest on a double thickness of cheesecloth. Gather up corners of cloth to enclose seasonings; tie securely with string. Add to slow cooker. Cook, covered, on low 1-2 hours or until heated through. Discard spice bag.

¾ cup: 131 cal., 0 fat (0 sat. fat), 0 chol., 21mg sod., 33g carb. (30g sugars, 0 fiber), 0 pro.

Want to use fresh pomegranate juice? There are 2 ways to juice a pomegranate. One way is to cut the pomegranate in half and juice it like an orange. Or, remove the seeds and mash with a fork or process in a blender; strain, reserving juice.

GINGERED APRICOT-APPLE CRUMBLE

GINGERED APRICOT-APPLE CRUMBLE

Hot or cold, plain or topped with ice cream, this crumble is tasty. For variety, leave out the apricots and make traditional apple crisp if you'd like.
—*Sylvia Rice, Didsbury, AB*

Prep: 15 min. • **Bake:** 50 min.
Makes: 12 servings

- 1 cup apricot nectar
- ¾ cup finely chopped dried apricots
- ⅓ cup honey
- ¼ cup maple syrup
- 2 Tbsp. lemon juice
- 8 cups sliced peeled tart apples (about 8 large)
- 3 Tbsp. all-purpose flour
- 1 tsp. ground cinnamon
- ½ tsp. ground ginger
- ½ tsp. ground cardamom

TOPPING
- ¾ cup all-purpose flour
- ½ cup quick-cooking oats
- ½ cup chopped pecans, optional
- ¼ cup canola oil
- ¼ cup maple syrup

1. Preheat oven to 350°. In a large bowl, combine the first 5 ingredients; set aside. Arrange apples in an ungreased 13x9-in. baking dish.
2. Combine flour, cinnamon, ginger and cardamom; stir into the apricot mixture. Spoon over apples.
3. Combine topping ingredients; sprinkle over fruit. Bake 50-60 minutes or until topping is golden brown and fruit is tender.
1 serving: 228 cal., 5g fat (1g sat. fat), 0 chol., 8mg sod., 46g carb. (32g sugars, 3g fiber), 2g pro.

POACHED ORANGE PEARS

Although these pears are very simple to prepare, they are quite elegant. I especially love to serve them when fresh raspberries are in season. They make a beautiful presentation for special occasions and are always well liked by both young and old.
—*Edna Lee, Greeley, CO*

Takes: 30 min. • **Makes:** 8 servings

- 1½ cups orange juice
- ½ cup packed brown sugar
- 1 cinnamon stick (3 in.)
- 4 large pears, peeled and halved
- ½ cup fresh raspberries

1. In a large saucepan, bring the orange juice, brown sugar and cinnamon stick to a boil. Reduce heat; cook and stir over medium heat until sugar is dissolved. Add pears; cover and simmer until tender but firm, 15-20 minutes.
2. Using a slotted spoon, place each pear half in a dessert dish. Garnish with raspberries. Drizzle with poaching liquid.
1 serving: 138 cal., 0 fat (0 sat. fat), 0 chol., 5mg sod., 35g carb. (29g sugars, 3g fiber), 1g pro.

SIPS & SUSPENSE

This Halloween, leave everyone spooked by just how fantastic your party is. Bewitch the crowd with devilishly delicious drinks, and serve up finger foods that are all treats, no tricks! Whether your guests come in costume or not, no one will be able to disguise their delight with the following dishes.

Witches' Brew (p. 239) **Witches' Brooms** (p. 243) **Witches' Fingers** (p. 237)

WITCHES'
FINGERS

WITCHES' FINGERS

You don't need a cauldron to conjure these frightening fingers. They're a sweet-and-salty treat that's spooky easy to make.
—*Beth Tomkiw, Milwaukee, WI*

Takes: 20 min. • **Makes:** 1 dozen

- 1½ cups vibrant green candy coating disks
- 6 pretzel rods, broken in half
- 6 jelly beans, cut in half lengthwise

In a microwave, melt candy coating; stir until smooth. Dip broken end of pretzel rods in coating; allow excess to drip off. Place on waxed paper; press a jelly bean half onto dipped end of each pretzel to resemble a fingernail. Let stand until almost set. Using a toothpick, make lines on each pretzel to resemble knuckles.

1 pretzel half: 155 cal., 7g fat (7g sat. fat), 1mg chol., 131mg sod., 21g carb. (18g sugars, 0 fiber), 1g pro.

PUMPKIN PIE MARTINIS

My girlfriends start requesting this cocktail in the fall and continue to ask for it through the holidays. Every delectable sip is like a taste of pumpkin pie!
—*Cathleen Bushman, Geneva, IL*

Takes: 5 min. • **Makes:** 2 servings

- 1 vanilla wafer, crushed, optional Ice cubes
- 2 oz. vanilla-flavored vodka
- 2 oz. 2% milk
- 2 oz. heavy whipping cream
- 1 oz. simple syrup
- 1 oz. hazelnut liqueur
- ⅛ tsp. pumpkin pie spice Dash ground cinnamon

1. For a cookie-crumb rim, moisten the rims of 2 chilled cocktail glasses with water. Place cookie crumbs on a plate; dip rims in crumbs. Set aside.
2. Fill a mixing glass three-fourths full with ice. Add the remaining ingredients; stir until condensation forms on outside of glass. Strain into 2 chilled cocktail glasses.

1 martini: 301 cal., 12g fat (7g sat. fat), 44mg chol., 25mg sod., 25g carb. (23g sugars, 0 fiber), 2g pro.

You may substitute 1 oz. pumpkin flavoring syrup for the simple syrup and pie spice. Look for flavoring syrup in the coffee section.

No Tricks
Send friends home with a clever gift bag filled with themed treats, such as black nail polish, herbal lip balm, a witchy pin, temporary tattoos, confetti and even a mood ring.

SAUERKRAUT-SAUSAGE MEATBALLS

I got this recipe in 1979 from another new resident at a Welcome Wagon event when I moved to Ohio. Over the years, I've revised it several times. My youngest daughter began helping me roll and bread these when she was only 9 years old, and she still does today. I'm always asked to bring them to special events, holidays and school functions.
—*Diana Hackenberg, Milford, OH*

Prep: 40 min. + chilling • **Cook:** 5 min./batch
Makes: about 3 dozen

- 1 lb. bulk pork sausage
- 2 cans (16 oz. each) sauerkraut, well drained
- 1 pkg. (8 oz.) cream cheese, softened and cubed
- ¼ cup minced fresh parsley
- 2 tsp. prepared mustard
- ½ tsp. garlic powder
- ½ tsp. pepper
- 2¼ cups dry bread crumbs, divided
- 1 cup all-purpose flour
- 1 Tbsp. ground mustard
- 3 large eggs
- ⅓ cup 2% milk
  Oil for deep-fat frying
  Additional prepared mustard

1. In a large skillet, cook sausage over medium heat until no longer pink; drain.
2. Place sauerkraut in a food processor; cover and process until finely chopped. Add to pan. Stir in the cream cheese, parsley, prepared mustard, garlic powder, pepper and ¼ cup bread crumbs; cook and stir over medium heat until cream cheese is melted. Transfer to a large bowl; cover and refrigerate for at least 2 hours.
3. Shape the meat mixture into 1½-in. balls. Combine the flour and ground mustard in a shallow bowl. In another bowl, whisk eggs and milk. Place remaining bread crumbs in a third shallow bowl. Coat meatballs with flour, then dip in eggs and roll in bread crumbs.
4. In an electric skillet or deep fryer, heat oil to 375°. Fry meatballs, a few at a time, for 2-3 minutes or until golden brown on all sides. Drain on paper towels. Serve with additional prepared mustard.

1 meatball: 131 cal., 10g fat (3g sat. fat), 29mg chol., 282mg sod., 7g carb. (1g sugars, 1g fiber), 3g pro.

DEVIL'S FOOD
WHOOPIE PIES

DEVIL'S FOOD WHOOPIE PIES

These mini cookie cakes were one of my favorite treats while I was growing up in Pennsylvania. We called them Gobs because they are gobs of fun to eat! The recipe can make fewer or more depending on how large or small you make the cookies. Place the finished whoopie pies in large cupcake liners for a professional look.
—Pamela Esposito, Galloway, NJ

- -

Prep: 30 min. • **Bake:** 10 min./batch + cooling
Makes: 2 dozen

- 1 pkg. devil's food cake mix (regular size)
- 1¼ cups all-purpose flour
- 1 cup water
- 3 large eggs, room temperature
- ⅓ cup canola oil
- 2 Tbsp. baking cocoa
- ¼ tsp. baking powder
- ¼ tsp. baking soda

FILLING
- 1 cup 2% milk
- ⅓ cup all-purpose flour
- ¼ cup butter, softened

- ¼ cup shortening
- 3¾ cups confectioners' sugar
- 1 tsp. vanilla extract

1. Preheat oven to 350°. In a large bowl, combine the first 8 ingredients; beat on low speed for 30 seconds. Beat on medium for 2 minutes.
2. Drop batter by tablespoonfuls 2 in. apart onto parchment-lined baking sheets. Bake until firm, 10-12 minutes. Cool on pans for 2 minutes. Remove to wire racks to cool completely.
3. Meanwhile, for filling, in a small saucepan whisk milk and flour until smooth. Bring to a boil, stirring constantly; cook and stir until thickened, 1-2 minutes. Cool completely.
4. In a large bowl, beat butter and shortening until blended. Gradually beat in cooled milk mixture. Beat in confectioners' sugar and vanilla until smooth. Refrigerate until chilled. Spread filling on bottoms of half the cookies. Top with remaining cookies. Refrigerate any leftovers.
1 whoopie pie: 249 cal., 9g fat (3g sat. fat), 29mg chol., 198mg sod., 40g carb. (26g sugars, 1g fiber), 3g pro.

PECANS DIABLO

The spices in this recipe showcase pecans in a new light. They're a zesty snack for any party, but their heat suits the cool and crisp evenings during the Halloween season well.
—Taste of Home *Test Kitchen*

- -

Takes: 25 min. • **Makes:** 5 cups

- ¼ cup butter, melted
- ¾ tsp. dried rosemary, crushed
- ¼ to ½ tsp. cayenne pepper
- ¼ tsp. dried basil
- 5 cups pecan halves
- 2 tsp. kosher salt

1. In a large bowl, combine the butter, rosemary, cayenne and basil. Add pecans and toss to coat. Spread in a single layer in a 15x10x1-in. baking pan. Sprinkle with salt.
2. Bake, uncovered, at 325° until pecans are crisp, stirring occasionally, 17-20 minutes. Cool completely; store in an airtight container.
⅓ cup: 276 cal., 29g fat (4g sat. fat), 8mg chol., 272mg sod., 5g carb. (1g sugars, 3g fiber), 3g pro.

GRILLED TERIYAKI BEEF KABOBS

These kabobs are easy to make and easy to eat—perfect for any party! The horseradish cream sauce pairs well with the flavorful beef.
—*Linda Flaherty, Lake Worth, FL*

Prep: 15 min. + marinating • **Grill:** 10 min.
Makes: 16 kabobs (1 cup sauce)

- 2 cans (8 oz. each) pineapple chunks
- 1 bottle (10 oz.) teriyaki baste and glaze
- 3 Tbsp. minced fresh gingerroot
- 1 lb. beef tenderloin steaks, cut into 1-in. pieces

HORSERADISH CREAM SAUCE
- 1 cup (8 oz.) sour cream
- 1 Tbsp. prepared horseradish

1. Drain pineapple chunks, reserving juice. In a large bowl or shallow dish, combine teriyaki glaze, ginger and pineapple juice. Add beef and turn to coat. Refrigerate for up to 2 hours. Drain beef, discarding marinade.
2. On 16 soaked wooden appetizer skewers, alternately thread beef pieces and pineapple chunks. On a lightly greased grill rack, cook kabobs, covered, over medium heat until beef reaches desired doneness, 6-8 minutes, turning once.
3. In a small bowl, combine sour cream and horseradish; serve with kabobs.

1 kabob with 1 Tbsp. sauce: 96 cal., 4g fat (2g sat. fat), 22mg chol., 233mg sod., 7g carb. (6g sugars, 0 fiber), 7g pro.

WITCHES' BREW

GRILLED TERIYAKI BEEF KABOBS

WITCHES' BREW

Stir up some Halloween beverages that are as bewitching as the rest of your menu. For a nonalcoholic version, just omit the vodka—then the kids can have some, too!
—*Taste of Home Test Kitchen*

Prep: 20 min. + chilling • **Makes:** 6 servings

- 1 cup sugar
- 1 cup water
- 8 medium kiwifruit, peeled and quartered
- ½ cup fresh mint leaves
- 1 cup vodka, optional
- 1 liter ginger ale, chilled
  Ice cubes

1. In a small saucepan, bring sugar and water to a boil. Cook and stir until sugar is dissolved; set aside to cool.
2. Place the kiwi, mint and sugar syrup in a blender; cover and process until blended. Pour into a large pitcher; stir in vodka if desired. Refrigerate until chilled.
3. Just before serving, stir in the ginger ale. Serve over ice.

1 cup: 253 cal., 1g fat (0 sat. fat), 0 chol., 17mg sod., 64g carb. (57g sugars, 4g fiber), 1g pro.

MIDNIGHT
COCKTAILS

MIDNIGHT COCKTAILS

This variation on a mojito uses blackberry spreadable fruit, which gives it a deep purple color and a bit of sweetness in every sip.
—Taste of Home *Test Kitchen*

- -

Prep: 15 min. + chilling • **Makes:** 2 servings

- ⅓ cup seedless blackberry
  spreadable fruit
- 2 Tbsp. water
- ¼ cup fresh mint leaves
- 3 Tbsp. lime juice
- ⅓ cup rum or brandy
- 1 cup club soda
- GARNISH
  Mint sprigs

1. In a small saucepan, combine spreadable fruit and water. Cook and stir over medium heat until smooth; transfer to a small bowl. Refrigerate until chilled.
2. In a small pitcher, muddle mint leaves and lime juice. Add blackberry syrup and rum. Divide between 2 cocktail glasses. Stir in club soda; garnish with mint sprigs.

¾ cup: 203 cal., 0 fat (0 sat. fat), 0 chol., 29mg sod., 30g carb. (22g sugars, 1g fiber), 0 pro.

ROASTED RED PEPPER HUMMUS

My son taught me how to make hummus, which is a tasty and healthy alternative to calorie-filled dips. Fresh roasted red bell peppers make it special.
—Nancy Watson-Pistole, Shawnee, KS

- -

Prep: 30 min. + standing • **Makes:** 3 cups

- 2 large sweet red peppers
- 2 cans (15 oz. each) garbanzo beans
  or chickpeas, rinsed and drained
- ⅓ cup lemon juice
- 3 Tbsp. tahini
- 1 Tbsp. olive oil
- 2 garlic cloves, peeled
- 1¼ tsp. salt
- 1 tsp. curry powder
- ½ tsp. ground coriander
- ½ tsp. ground cumin
- ½ tsp. pepper
  Pita bread, warmed and cut into
  wedges, or assorted crackers
  Additional garbanzo beans or
  chickpeas, optional

1. Broil red peppers 4 in. from the heat until skins blister, about 5 minutes. With tongs, rotate peppers a quarter turn. Broil and rotate until all sides are blistered and blackened. Immediately place peppers in a bowl; cover and let stand for 15-20 minutes.
2. Peel off and discard charred skin. Remove stems and seeds. Place the peppers in a food processor. Add the beans, lemon juice, tahini, oil, garlic and seasonings; cover and process until blended.
3. Transfer to a serving bowl. Serve with pita bread or crackers. Garnish with additional beans if desired.

¼ cup: 113 cal., 5g fat (1g sat. fat), 0 chol., 339mg sod., 14g carb. (3g sugars, 4g fiber), 4g pro. **Diabetic exchanges:** 1 starch, 1 fat.

HOT SPINACH SPREAD WITH PITA CHIPS

This warm, cheesy spread is absolutely scrumptious served on toasted pita wedges. And its colorful appearance makes it stand out on the buffet table.
—Teresa Emanuel, Smithville, MO

- -

Prep: 30 min. • **Bake:** 20 min.
Makes: 16 servings (4 cups spread)

- 2 cups shredded Monterey Jack cheese
- 1 pkg. (10 oz.) frozen chopped
  spinach, thawed and squeezed dry
- 1 pkg. (8 oz.) cream cheese, cubed
- 2 plum tomatoes, seeded and chopped
- ¾ cup chopped onion
- ⅓ cup half-and-half cream
- 1 Tbsp. finely chopped seeded
  jalapeno pepper
- 6 pita breads (6 in.)
- ½ cup butter, melted
- 2 tsp. lemon-pepper seasoning
- 2 tsp. ground cumin
- ¼ tsp. garlic salt

1. Preheat oven to 375°. In a large bowl, combine the first 7 ingredients. Transfer to a greased 1½-qt. baking dish. Bake, uncovered, for 20-25 minutes or until bubbly.
2. Meanwhile, cut each pita bread into 8 wedges. Place in two 15x10x1-in. baking pans. Combine the butter, lemon-pepper, cumin and garlic salt; brush over pita wedges.
3. Bake for 7-9 minutes or until crisp. Serve with spinach spread.

Note: Wear disposable gloves when cutting hot peppers; the oils can burn skin. Avoid touching your face.

¼ cup spread with 3 pita wedges: 231 cal., 16g fat (10g sat. fat), 46mg chol., 381mg sod., 15g carb. (1g sugars, 1g fiber), 8g pro.

HOT SPINACH SPREAD
WITH PITA CHIPS

CARAMEL
HAVARTI

CARAMEL HAVARTI

Havarti is a wonderful dessert cheese made even better by pecans, apples and caramel topping. This recipe is elegant yet simple.
—*Tia Thomas, Mountain City, TN*

- -

Takes: 15 min. • **Makes:** 10 serving s

10 oz. Havarti cheese
¼ cup chopped pecans
1 Tbsp. butter
⅓ to ½ cup caramel ice cream topping, warmed
2 medium tart apples, cut into small wedges

1. Preheat oven to 375°. Place cheese in an ungreased shallow 1-qt. baking dish. Bake for 5-7 minutes or until edges of cheese just begin to melt.
2. Meanwhile, in a small skillet, saute pecans in butter until toasted. Drizzle caramel over cheese; sprinkle with pecans. Serve with apple wedges.
1 serving: 173 cal., 12g fat (6g sat. fat), 30mg chol., 205mg sod., 12g carb. (10g sugars, 1g fiber), 7g pro.

GRAPE PUNCH

With its beautiful purple color, fruity flavor and fun fizz, this punch always prompts requests for refills. I serve it with Mexican and Italian fare, but it's good with anything!
—*Gayle Lewis, Yucaipa, CA*

- -

Takes: 5 min. • **Makes:** 18 servings

2 cups red grape juice, chilled
2 cups white grape juice, chilled
5 cups lemon-lime soda, chilled

In a large punch bowl or pitcher, combine the juices; mix well. Stir in the soda just before serving.
½ cup: 60 cal., 0 fat (0 sat. fat), 0 chol., 11mg sod., 15g carb. (14g sugars, 0 fiber), 0 pro.

To make an ice ring for a punch bowl, fill a ring mold halfway with water; freeze until solid. Top with your choice of fruit; add lemon leaves if desired. Add enough water to almost cover fruit; freeze until solid. Unmold by wrapping the bottom of the mold with a hot, damp dishcloth. Turn out onto a baking sheet; place in punch bowl fruit side up.

WITCHES' BROOMS

Pair these edible mini brooms with Witches' Brew (p. 239) for a spellbinding treat. The only ingredients you need are pretzel rods and licorice.
—Taste of Home *Test Kitchen*

- -

Takes: 30 min. • **Makes:** 6 brooms

6 pieces green shoestring licorice
6 pretzel rods
6 pieces black shoestring licorice

Cut 1 green shoestring licorice into 1-in. lengths. Arrange around end of 1 pretzel rod to form broom bristles; tightly wrap bristles with 1 black shoestring licorice, tucking in end to secure. Repeat with remaining ingredients.
1 broom: 106 cal., 0 fat (0 sat. fat), 0 chol., 142mg sod., 24g carb. (10g sugars, 0 fiber), 1g pro.

HOMEGATING

When it comes to cheering for your favorite team on the day or night of the big game, the celebration is never quite the same without food that's equally deserving of your cheers. From delectable dips and wonderfully tasty wings to perfect pinwheels and touchdown desserts, these recipes for game-day grub will make your team's winning moments even more memorable.

Nacho Wings (p. 249) **Michelada** (p. 247)

MICHELADA

MICHELADA

Like your drinks with a south-of-the-border vibe? Try this kicked-up beer cocktail that's a zesty mix of Mexican lager, lime juice and hot sauce. There are many variations, but this easy recipe is perfect for rookie mixologists.
—*Ian Cliffe, Milwaukee, WI*

Takes: 5 min. • **Makes:** 1 Michelada

>   Coarse salt
>   Lime wedge
>   Ice cubes
> 6   dashes hot sauce, such as
>   Valentina or Tabasco
> 3   dashes Maggi seasoning or soy sauce
> 1   to 3 dashes Worcestershire sauce
> ¼   to ⅓ cup lime juice
> 1   bottle (12 oz.) beer, such as
>   Corona, Modelo or Tecat

Place coarse salt in a shallow dish; run lime wedge around rim of a 1-pint glass. Dip rim of glass into salt, shaking off excess. Fill glass with ice; add hot sauce, Maggi seasoning, Worcestershire sauce and lime juice. Pour beer over the ice. Garnish with lime wedge. Serve immediately.

1 drink: 165 cal., 0 fat (0 sat. fat), 0 chol., 137mg sod., 17g carb. (12g sugars, 0 fiber), 1g pro.

BEER DIP

Shredded cheese is the star in this fast-to-fix mixture that seems made to go with pretzels. Once you start eating it, you can't stop! The dip can be made with any type of beer, including nonalcoholic.
—*Michelle Long, New Castle, CO*

Takes: 5 min. • **Makes:** 3½ cups

> 2   pkg. (8 oz. each) cream cheese,
>   softened
> ⅓   cup beer or nonalcoholic beer
> 1   envelope ranch salad dressing mix
> 2   cups shredded cheddar cheese
>   Pretzels

In a large bowl, beat the cream cheese, beer and dressing mix until smooth. Stir in cheddar cheese. Serve with pretzels.

2 Tbsp.: 89 cal., 8g fat (5g sat. fat), 26mg chol., 177mg sod., 1g carb. (0 sugars, 0 fiber), 3g pro.

MAPLE SAUSAGE SLIDERS WITH SLAW

MAPLE SAUSAGE SLIDERS WITH SLAW

Small in size but big in flavor, these dynamite coleslaw-topped sliders are sure to score a touchdown with hungry fans. They're a welcome change from usual game-day fare.
—*Lisa Huff, Wilton, CT*

Prep: 25 min. • **Cook:** 10 min./batch
Makes: 1½ dozen

> 2   cups coleslaw mix
> 1   cup shredded peeled apple
> 1   cup crumbled blue cheese
> ¼   cup finely chopped red onion
> 3   Tbsp. olive oil
> 2   Tbsp. cider vinegar
> 1½   tsp. maple syrup
> ½   tsp. Dijon mustard
> ⅛   tsp. salt
> ⅛   tsp. pepper
> **SLIDERS**
> 1   cup finely chopped walnuts, toasted
> ½   cup finely chopped red onion
> 2   Tbsp. minced fresh thyme
>   or 2 tsp. dried thyme
> ½   tsp. salt
> ¼   tsp. pepper
> 2   lbs. bulk maple pork sausage
> 18   dinner rolls, split and lightly toasted

1. In a large bowl, combine the coleslaw mix, apple, blue cheese and red onion. In a small bowl, whisk the oil, vinegar, maple syrup, mustard, salt and pepper. Pour over coleslaw mixture; toss to coat. Chill until serving.
2. In a large bowl, combine the walnuts, onion, thyme, salt and pepper. Crumble sausage over mixture and mix well. Shape into 18 patties.
3. In a large skillet, cook patties in batches over medium heat for 3-4 minutes on each side or until a thermometer reads 160°.
4. Top each bottom roll with a burger and 2 Tbsp. coleslaw mixture. Replace roll tops.

1 slider with 2 Tbsp. slaw: 331 cal., 22g fat (6g sat. fat), 50mg chol., 678mg sod., 23g carb. (4g sugars, 2g fiber), 12g pro.

GAME-DAY BOURBON-GLAZED CARAMEL CORN

This is a grown-up version of a favorite kid's treat. The bourbon and ginger combination that is so good in cocktails now finds a home in a munchie that is perfect for snacking.
—*Sally Sibthorpe, Shelby Township, MI*

Prep: 20 min. • **Bake:** 1 hour • **Makes:** 5 qt.

- 6 qt. air-popped popcorn
- 3 cups mixed nuts (pecan halves, unblanched almonds, hazelnuts and unsalted cashews)
- 2 cups packed brown sugar
- 1 cup butter, cubed
- ½ cup dark corn syrup
- ½ cup bourbon
- 1 tsp. salt
- 1 tsp. ground ginger
- 1 tsp. vanilla extract
- ½ tsp. baking soda

1. Preheat oven to 250°. Place popcorn and nuts in a large bowl. In a large heavy saucepan, combine the brown sugar, butter, corn syrup, bourbon, salt and ginger. Bring to a boil over medium heat, stirring occasionally; cook and stir for 6 minutes.

2. Remove from the heat; stir in vanilla and baking soda (mixture will foam). Quickly pour over popcorn and mix well.

3. Transfer to 2 greased 15x10x1-in. baking pans. Bake 1 hour, stirring every 15 minutes. Remove to waxed paper to cool completely. Store in airtight containers.

1 cup: 514 cal., 38g fat (8g sat. fat), 24mg chol., 244mg sod., 43g carb. (30g sugars, 5g fiber), 7g pro.

To pop popcorn on the stove, use a 3- or 4-qt. pan with a loose-fitting lid to allow steam to escape. Add ⅓ cup vegetable oil for every cup of kernels. Heat oil to between 400° and 460° (if oil smokes, it's too hot). Drop in 1 kernel; when it pops, add the rest—just enough to cover bottom of the pan with a single layer. Cover pan and shake to spread oil. When popping begins to slow, remove pan from heat.

ROASTED RED POTATO SALAD WITH CHIPOTLE MAYO

My husband loves potato salad, but I don't enjoy peeling and boiling potatoes. Oven-roasting the potatoes makes it easy and gives them the ideal taste and texture.
—*Karla Sheeley, Worden, IL*

Prep: 30 min. • **Bake:** 25 min.
Makes: 10 servings

- 2½ lbs. red potatoes, cut into 1½-in. cubes
  Olive oil-flavored cooking spray
- 2 tsp. Creole seasoning
- 1 cup mayonnaise
- ¼ cup Dijon mustard
- 1 to 2 chipotle peppers in adobo sauce, seeded
- 2 Tbsp. white wine vinegar
- 1 Tbsp. minced garlic
- 8 hard-cooked large eggs, coarsely chopped
- ⅔ cup chopped sweet onion
- 6 bacon strips, cooked and crumbled

1. Preheat the oven to 425°. Place potatoes in a greased 15x10x1-in. baking pan. Spritz with cooking spray; sprinkle with Creole seasoning. Bake, uncovered, until golden brown and tender, 45-50 minutes, stirring occasionally. Cool.

2. Place mayonnaise, mustard, chipotle peppers, vinegar and garlic in a food processor; cover and process until blended. In a large bowl, combine the eggs, onion, potatoes and dressing; toss to coat. Serve immediately, or chill until serving. Just before serving, sprinkle with bacon.

Note: The following spices may be substituted for 1 tsp. Creole seasoning: ¼ tsp. each salt, garlic powder and paprika; and a pinch each of dried thyme, ground cumin and cayenne pepper.

¾ cup: 338 cal., 24g fat (4g sat. fat), 182mg chol., 551mg sod., 21g carb. (2g sugars, 2g fiber), 9g pro.

NACHO WINGS

I love wings. I love nachos. Together, they're the perfect pairing! This recipe earned an award in a wings and ribs contest we held at our summer cottage.
—*Lori Stefanishion, Drumheller, AB*

- -

Prep: 20 min. • **Cook:** 1 hour • **Makes:** 2 dozen

24 chicken wing sections
½ cup butter, melted
1 pkg. (15½ oz.) nacho-flavored tortilla chips, crushed
2 cups shredded Mexican cheese blend or shredded cheddar cheese
1 can (4 oz.) chopped green chiles
1 cup chopped green onions
  Seeded jalapeno pepper slices, optional
  Optional toppings: salsa, sour cream and guacamole

1. Preheat oven to 350°. Dip wing sections in butter, then roll in crushed nacho chips. Bake wing sections in a greased 15x10x1-in. baking pan until juices run clear, 45-50 minutes. Remove from oven.
2. Top with cheese, chiles, green onions and, if desired, jalapeno slices. Bake until cheese is melted, about 15 minutes. Serve with toppings as desired.
1 piece: 188 cal., 13g fat (5g sat. fat), 45mg chol., 317mg sod., 8g carb. (1g sugars, 1g fiber), 9g pro.

TEST KITCHEN TIP

Disjoint chicken wings to make your own wingettes. Place each chicken wing on a cutting board; with a sharp knife, cut through the joint at the top of the tip end. Take the remaining portion of the wing and cut through center of the joint. Proceed with recipe as directed. (Discard tips or use for making chicken broth.)

NACHO WINGS

EASY TACO CUPS

EASY TACO CUPS

These zesty little cups rank high on my list of favorites because they're fast, easy and delicious! They make a fantastic finger food for parties, and guests have fun selecting their desired toppings.
—*Ashley Jarvies, Manassa, CO*

Prep: 30 min. • **Bake:** 15 min.
Makes: 12 servings

- 1 lb. ground beef
- ½ cup chopped onion
- 1 envelope taco seasoning
- 1 can (16 oz.) refried beans
- 2 tubes (8 oz. each) refrigerated seamless crescent dough sheet
- 1½ cups shredded cheddar cheese
      Optional toppings: Chopped tomatoes, sliced ripe olives, shredded lettuce, sour cream, guacamole and salsa

1. Preheat oven to 375°. In a large skillet, cook beef and onion over medium heat 6-8 minutes or until no longer pink, breaking into crumbles; drain. Stir in taco seasoning and refried beans; heat through.
2. Unroll each tube of dough into a long rectangle. Cut each rectangle into 12 pieces; press lightly onto bottom and up sides of 24 ungreased muffin cups.
3. Fill each muffin cup with a rounded tablespoonful of beef mixture; sprinkle each with 1 Tbsp. cheese. Bake 14-16 minutes or until dough is golden brown. Cool in pans 10 minutes before removing. Serve with toppings as desired.
2 taco cups: 291 cal., 15g fat (7g sat. fat), 37mg chol., 819mg sod., 25g carb. (4g sugars, 2g fiber), 15g pro.

ORANGE CRANBERRY PUNCH

Skip cans of soda and serve this tangy citrus-flavored punch. It has just the right amount of sweetness.
—*Brook Hickle, Enumclaw, WA*

Prep: 10 min. + chilling
Makes: 24 servings (about 4½ qt.)

- 4 qt. cranberry juice
- 2 cups orange juice
- 2 medium oranges, sliced
- 2 medium lemons, sliced
- 2 medium limes, sliced

In a large container, combine juices and fruit; cover and refrigerate overnight. Serve in pitchers or a large punch bowl.
¾ cup: 93 cal., 0 fat (0 sat. fat), 0 chol., 4mg sod., 24g carb. (23g sugars, 0 fiber), 1g pro.

FOOTBALL CAKE POPS

FOOTBALL CAKE POPS

My son loves football! For his eighth birthday, I made cake pops with a rich chocolate cake center and a yummy peanut butter coating. These are sure to be winners at parties, bake sales and sports-watching events.
—*Jenny Dubinsky, Inwood, WV*

Prep: 2 hours + chilling
Bake: 35 min. + cooling
Makes: 4 dozen cake pops

- 1 chocolate cake mix (regular size)
- 1 cup cream cheese frosting
- 1 cup dark chocolate chips
- 1 cup peanut butter chips
- 1 Tbsp. shortening
- 48 4-in. lollipop sticks
- ¼ cup white decorating icing

1. Bake cake according to package directions; cool completely. In a large bowl, break cake into fine crumbles. Add frosting and stir until fully incorporated, adding more frosting if needed, until the mixture maintains its shape when squeezed together with palm of hand.

Shape 1 Tbsp. into a ball, then mold into the shape of a football. Repeat with remaining cake mixture. Place on parchment-lined baking sheets; refrigerate until firm, about 30 minutes.
2. Meanwhile, in a microwave-safe bowl, place the chocolate chips, peanut butter chips and shortening. Microwave 30 seconds and stir; repeat, stirring every 30 seconds until melted and smooth, adding more shortening if needed. Do not overheat.
3. Dip a lollipop stick into chocolate mixture; insert halfway through a football shape, taking care not to break through the other side. Return to baking sheet until set; repeat to form remaining cake pops. Coat each cake pop with the chocolate mixture, allowing excess to drip off, and reheating and stirring chocolate mixture as needed. Return cake pops to baking sheet, ensuring they do not touch one another. Allow chocolate coating to set until firm to the touch. To decorate, use icing to draw laces onto cake pops.
1 cake pop: 132 cal., 7g fat (3g sat. fat), 12mg chol., 96mg sod., 17g carb. (12g sugars, 1g fiber), 2g pro.

TOUCHDOWN COOKIES

With some simple sweet touches, you can transform regular sugar cookies into a special treat for football fans at your party.
—*Sister Judith LaBrozzi, Canton, OH*

Prep: 25 min. + chilling
Bake: 10 min./batch + cooling
Makes: 4½ dozen

- 1   cup butter, softened
- 1   cup sugar
- 2   large eggs, room temperature
- 1   tsp. vanilla extract
- 3   cups all-purpose flour
- 2   tsp. cream of tartar
- 1   tsp. baking soda

GLAZE

- 4   cups confectioners' sugar
- 8   to 10 Tbsp. hot water
    Black paste food coloring
- 6   to 8 tsp. baking cocoa

1. In a large bowl, cream butter and sugar until light and fluffy. Add 1 egg at a time, beating well after each addition. Beat in vanilla. Combine the flour, cream of tartar and baking soda; gradually add to creamed mixture and mix well. Cover and refrigerate for 3 hours or until easy to handle.
2. Preheat oven to 350°. On a lightly floured surface, roll out dough to ⅛-in. thickness. Cut with a football-shaped and a small gingerbread man cookie cutter. Place 2 in. apart on ungreased baking sheets.
3. Bake 8-10 minutes or until lightly browned. Remove to wire racks to cool.
4. In a large bowl, combine confectioners' sugar and enough hot water to achieve spreading consistency; beat until smooth. Divide glaze into thirds. Stir black food coloring into one-third of the glaze; set aside. Add cocoa to another third; stir until smooth. Spread brown glaze over football cookies. Pipe white glaze for the football laces. Spread or pipe remaining white glaze over gingerbread men cookies to make shirts. Pipe black stripes over the white shirts to resemble referee stripes.

1 cookie: 108 cal., 4g fat (2g sat. fat), 16mg chol., 53mg sod., 18g carb. (12g sugars, 0 fiber), 1g pro.

QUICK TORTILLA PINWHEELS

Prepare these easy, cheesy pinwheels several days in advance if desired. Serve with your choice of mild or hot salsa or picante sauce.
—*Barbara Keith, Faucett, MO*

Prep: 15 min. + chilling • **Makes:** about 5 dozen

- 1   cup sour cream
- 1   pkg. (8 oz.) cream cheese, softened
- ¾   cup sliced green onions
- ½   cup finely shredded cheddar cheese
- 1   Tbsp. lime juice
- 1   Tbsp. minced seeded jalapeno pepper
- 8   to 10 flour tortillas (8 in.), room temperature
    Salsa or picante sauce

Combine the first 6 ingredients in a bowl. Spread on 1 side of tortillas and roll up tightly. Wrap and refrigerate for at least 1 hour. Slice into 1-in. pieces. Serve with salsa or picante sauce.

Note: Wear disposable gloves when cutting hot peppers; the oils can burn skin. Avoid touching your face.

1 pinwheel: 47 cal., 3g fat (2g sat. fat), 6mg chol., 51mg sod., 4g carb. (0 sugars, 0 fiber), 1g pro.

SPINACH & TURKEY PINWHEELS

Need an awesome snack for game day? My kids love these easy four-ingredient turkey pinwheels. Go ahead and make them the day before; they won't get soggy!
—*Amy Van Hemert, Ottumwa, IA*

Takes: 15 min. • **Makes:** 8 servings

- 1   carton (8 oz.) spreadable garden vegetable cream cheese
- 8   flour tortillas (8 in.)
- 4   cups fresh baby spinach
- 1   lb. sliced deli turkey

Spread cream cheese over tortillas. Layer with spinach and turkey. Roll up tightly; if not serving immediately, wrap and refrigerate. To serve, cut rolls crosswise into 1-in. slices.

6 pinwheels: 307 cal., 13g fat (6g sat. fat), 52mg chol., 866mg sod., 31g carb. (1g sugars, 2g fiber), 17g pro.

GRIDIRON CAKE

What better way to celebrate a big game than with this easy-to-make snack cake with cream cheese frosting?
—*Sarah Farmer, Waukesha, WI*

Prep: 45 min. • **Bake:** 25 min. + cooling
Makes: 20 servings

CAKE

- ⅔   cup butter, softened
- 1¾   cups sugar
- 1   Tbsp. vanilla extract
- 2   large eggs, room temperature
- 2½   cups all-purpose flour
- 2½   tsp. baking powder
- ½   tsp. salt
- 1¼   cups 2% milk

FROSTING

- 1   pkg. (8 oz.) cream cheese, softened
- ½   cup butter, softened
- 3¾   cups confectioners' sugar
- 1   Tbsp. 2% milk
- 1   tsp. vanilla extract
    Green paste food coloring

DECORATIONS

- 2   goal posts (made from yellow bendable straws)
    Large gumdrops

1. Preheat oven to 350°. Grease a half sheet foil cake pan (17x12x1 in.).
2. In a bowl, cream butter and sugar until light and fluffy. Add vanilla and eggs, 1 at a time, beating well. In another bowl, whisk flour, baking powder and salt; beat into creamed mixture alternately with milk. Transfer to prepared pan.
3. Bake until a toothpick inserted in center comes out clean, 25-30 minutes. Place on a wire rack; cool completely.
4. For frosting, beat cream cheese and butter. Add the confectioners' sugar, milk and vanilla. Reserve ¼ cup of frosting for field markings. Tint remaining frosting green; spread over top of cake. Pipe white yard lines and numbers accordingly. Decorate field with goal posts ; use gumdrops for football players.

1 piece: 365 cal., 16g fat (9g sat. fat), 60mg chol., 255mg sod., 54g carb. (41g sugars, 0 fiber), 4g pro.

Build a Snack Stadium

When it comes to sports and snacks, go big or go home! This stadium is easy to assemble and sure to get people talking. Just fill disposable aluminum pans and trimmed cardboard soda containers wrapped in paper with tasty eats and treats. Here are a few suggestions for a memorable spread.

The Field: A Game-Day Cake
Recipe: Gridiron Cake

Just as in real life, all eyes are on the field. To make this snack stadium pop, you need a centerpiece-style spread in the center. Though we've seen snack stadiums with fields made out of guacamole or green serving trays, we love the idea of the centerpiece being a showstopping cake.

The bright green frosting and clean yard lines—not to mention our gumdrop players (add in the colors of your favorite teams!)—truly make this cake look like the real deal. Pop on a few yellow bendy straws as goalposts and you're ready for kickoff. If you don't have time for an entire snack stadium, this cake is an impressive centerpiece on its own.

The End Zones: Party-Starting Spirals
Recipes: Quick Tortilla Pinwheels and Spinach & Turkey Pinwheels

The snack stadium deserves its fair share of savory treats, too. We loaded the end zones full of spiraled tortilla roll-ups in two flavors. These pack all the flavors of favorite sandwiches but are easier to make for a crowd.

The Skyboxes: Dips and Desserts
Recipes: Beer Dip and Touchdown Cookies

If you ask us, it's not a party without a few good dips. Fill the skyboxes full of Beer Dip (p. 247) and a favorite salsa. There's no need to take sides on which one is yummier. Just don't dribble on the cake—that's the wrong sport!

For those craving more sugar than a cake can offer, a few boxes are filled with candies and decorated football and referee cookies. If you can't manage to finish all these snacky confections, the boxes make adorable to-go gifts. Wrap them up at the end of the game and send your pals home with something sweet.

The Stands: Store-Bought Munchies

To complement those delicious dips, you need lots of nibbles. We're in favor of filling the stands with snack-aisle favorites like pretzels, crackers and chips.

Pro tip: Don't go it alone! Draft friends and family to bring their favorite noshes to help fill the stadium.

The Towers: Healthy Options
Recipe: Veggie Sticks and Veggie Dill Dip

This snack stadium isn't *all* about indulgence (though, we do admit, much of it is!). On the exterior towers, we filled disposable dishes with a creamy dill dip and packed plastic cups full of veggie sticks.

In the end, this snack stadium is such a fun and festive way to celebrate any big game, such as the Super Bowl, the Rose Bowl or even homecoming. Filled with treats and sweets, the stadium is a one-stop destination for game-day snackers.

RECIPE INDEX

CRAFTS, TIMELINES & EXTRAS

SHARE YOUR MOST-LOVED RECIPES

Do you have a special tradition that has become part of your family's holiday tradition? Are homemade gifts and crafts included in your celebrations? We want to hear from you. Visit **tasteofhome.com/submit** to submit a recipe or craft for editorial consideration.

PAGE 189

PAGE 105

PAGE 143

Chelsea

PAGE 22